THE
PLOUGHMAN
AND THE
ASTRONAUT

THE EVOLUTIONARY JOURNEY TO WEALTHNESS

DON NILSON

One Printers Way
Altona, MB R0G 0B0
Canada

www.friesenpress.com

Copyright © 2024 by Don Nilson
First Edition — 2024

All rights reserved.

No part of this publication may be reproduced in any form, or by any means, electronic or mechanical, including photocopying, recording, or any information browsing, storage, or retrieval system, without permission in writing from FriesenPress.

Examples are drawn from real client portfolios for the explicit purpose of educational insights. Rates of return are specific to the time periods involved, as well as to the strategic directives of each client, and should not infer performance at A.F.T. Trivest Management.

Cover design by Ben Reeves

ISBN
978-1-03-918791-7 (Hardcover)
978-1-03-918790-0 (Paperback)
978-1-03-918792-4 (eBook)

1. BUSINESS & ECONOMICS, PERSONAL SUCCESS

Distributed to the trade by The Ingram Book Company

Dear Carolyn,

WEALTHNESS REVEALED:

Enjoy the Journey

Table of Contents

Introduction. 1
Chapter 1: Invocation. 12
    1.1 Key Words and Concepts 26
Chapter 2: Chrematistics 27
    2.1 Money Philosophy. 28
    2.2 Root Attitudes 37
    2.3 Root Purposes 49
    2.4 Root Sources 55
    2.5 Happiness and Meaning. 72
    2.6 Good Decision-Making 81
    2.7 Key Words and Concepts 92
Chapter 3: Families and Finance. 93
    3.1 Couples and Money 94
    3.2 Kids and Money 104
    3.3 Family Confab 118
    3.4 Key Words and Concepts 126
Chapter 4: Financial Planning 127
    4.1 Preparing for the Future. 129
    4.2 Planning for Ages and Stages 135
    4.3 Financial Plans. 146
    4.4 Longevity. 155
    4.5 Key Words and Concepts 167
Chapter 5: Investing. 168
    5.1 Investing Philosophy. 170
    5.2 Investing Strategy 181
    5.3 Safety. 195
    5.4 Rate of Return 201
    5.5 Key Words and Concepts 217
Chapter 6: Legacy. 218
    6.1 Key Words and Concepts 235
Chapter 7: Coda. 236
    7.0 Key Words and Concepts 242
Afterthought 243
Bibliography. 244

Introduction

A Journey to WealthNess

This book is an invitation to a journey…with an end goal of attaining multi-generational, healthy personal finance. This journey will travel along several different roadways, including honest introspection, pragmatic learning, intellectual learning, ignition of change, and the spirituality of personal finances.

Let's start with philosopher Sir Francis Bacon in the sixteenth century: "Nature, to be commanded, must be obeyed."

Let's modernize and amend that a bit: Personal finance, to be commanded, must be obeyed.

A few years ago, I taught a day-long course on personal financial management at a local golf club resort. In mid-morning, I put up a slide screen that asked everybody to spend a few minutes reflecting upon their experiences and lessons with money that had shaped their value systems today. The room was silent for a few minutes whilst I left them to this reflective task. While I waited, I walked over to the eastern wall of the room, which was a long bank of floor-to-ceiling windows looking out onto the golf course. There was the broad, verdant grass of the first fairway, with a small forest of trees on the far edge. At the windowpane, there was one lone bottle fly trying to get out. It was a cold, early spring day, so no windows or doors were open, and the fly was very much trapped. My group finished their soul-searching task, and I continued the class. Later that afternoon, we were wrapping up the day's experiences, and I shared with the attendees about the fly that morning.

I pointed over to the window as I said to them: "Earlier today while you were doing one of McLuhan's probes, I went over to that window. And right there sat a fly. I thought about if he could see through the window to the trees and grass beyond. But even if he could: a) he couldn't get there and b) he didn't know WHY he couldn't, because a fly doesn't understand the concept of a window. I coulda/shoulda opened the door for that fly and let it out. But if you have ever opened a window or door for a fly, you'll know they often don't understand it and don't fly out—they just stay there. It's like they can't smell the fresh air leading them to the opening.

And so maybe it's the same for ***you****…..*

Everything I have shown you today is an **open door** to a world of multi-generational WealthNess that is there for you. I was thinking that fly is perhaps the avatar for your world of financial management. **You** are sitting at that window, but instead of embracing the world of WealthNess we have discussed today, like the fly: a) perhaps you can't get there and b) you don't know why."

How are **your** personal finances? Are you comfortable with where you are and where you are going? Are you financially comfortable and making good financial decisions? Are you confident about your long-term financial health? If not, you too may be one of those folks in that room. You comprehend the value of prudent personal financial management, but you can't seem to get there and, maybe, you also can't see the root causes of the impediments to getting there.

Here are some of the roadblocks to healthy personal finance:

- Knowledge gap and attached fear
- Disinterest
- Time pressures
- Lack of congruence with your partner
- Genomic attitudes to money
- Pressures of today fogging the vision of tomorrow
- Sense of futility
- "Keeping up with Joneses" effect

Unhealthy personal finance is not life-threatening, but it is life**style**-threatening.

> *Scientific research continues to show that simply denying the difficulties of a situation will only lead to worse outcomes.*
> —David Robson, science writer

If so, you are not alone, and this book is for you, your partner, your family around you. This book is also for you who do a pretty good job of personal financial management but would like to raise your game. Lastly, this book is also for those of you who already are aces at this. I aspire to introduce advanced topics and novel insights to you folks that you haven't seen before. I hope to fill you with insights, stories, introspection, inspiration, and core knowledge in personal finance. If we are successful together, you will ascend to a **multi-generational** WealthNess, which I will describe below. Embrace, too, that the job isn't done because you have managed to master yourself. Your bigger job is to instill those healthy values in your **following generations** because even modest wealth is a multi-generational project whose end-game may only expire when the meteorite strikes.

Why I Wrote This Book

While I didn't realize it at the time, perhaps that moment with the fly was the genesis of this book.

With a forty-five-year career in the financial services industry as a tax accountant, financial planner, and wealth manager, I have touched thousands of lives, delving intimately into their finances. I have taught for thirty-seven years on these topics from Asia to the Caribbean and across Canada and into the US. I also have written extensively on numerous financial topics for magazines, newspapers, and the Web. And I have been blessed with various career achievement recognitions, both locally and nationally, from the accounting and financial planning professions and my university alma mater.

I took a half-step into semi-retirement in the fall of 2019, retiring from active duty in the accounting profession and focusing on financial planning and investment management. I decided that writing my first-and-last book would be my semi-retirement project and, aspirationally, my magnum opus.

"So what is with the weird book title?" you may ask.

I am glad you asked. The very month I commenced writing this book, I was reading a book titled *The Angel and the Assassin,* by Donna Jackson Nakazawa. Can you guess what the book was about? How about a fiction piece on international espionage? Wrong! The subtitle was: "The tiny brain cell that changed the course of medicine." The author was a science journalist, not another Robert Ludlum. The entire book was about microglia that inhabit our brains. Both halves of the title referenced microglia as both our friend and our enemy. That night, I was very inspired by this interesting title. I put the book down, turned off my reading light, closed my eyes, and said to my subconscious: "What can you do with this?" In less than five minutes, my free-ranging brain independently submitted to me: "The Ploughman and the Astronaut." No explanation, just there it was!

A significant transition in our genesis as a species was the change from hunter/gatherer to "farmer" approximately 10,000 to 12,000 years ago. This brought us together in larger communities, changed how we obtained the sustenance needed to stay alive, and eventually brought us to where we are now. (Forgive the very condensed course on evolution.) As nascent farmers, we learned that the land needed to be tilled, which we did with painstaking manual labour. At some point, we invented an assistant, a tool, called a plough to help with the tilling. Ironically, it has been suggested that the invention and evolution of the plough gave birth to the gender divisions of labour. Gathering was a gender-neutral task, and modern-day archeological findings suggest that hunting, too, was gender neutral. But then enter the "ploughman," as males had substantially more upper-body strength to push the technologically advanced and heavier plow. This job was very important to make the land fertile to sustain life. But it was a head-down, repetitive task. Occasionally, objects (rocks) might impede the ploughman's pathway, but largely the job was up-and-down, up-and-down.

Meanwhile, for thousands of years, we have stood on Earth and gazed up into the stars. It was only in the 1950s that we summoned the intelligence to be able to project ourselves up into those heavens, and we called ourselves "astronauts."

"Astronaut" comes from the Greek astro, meaning space, or star, and naut meaning sailor. According to the Canadian Space Agency, "Astronauts are modern-day explorers. They courageously travel beyond the Earth to help discover new (scientific) knowledge. Being an astronaut is both exciting and incredibly demanding. It requires exceptional commitment…astronauts embark upon a thrilling adventure." In the early days of space travel in the 1950s, the prime criterion for selection as an astronaut was simply "individuals who could endure flights." Over time, advanced and diverse education became the focus, along with high-stress skills and the ability to work with others.

I ran the title by some friends and family and got a variety of responses:

- From my Danish farming cousin: "Astronaut because he is looking with a great overview in time and space. Ploughman because he is a primary producer. Could be standing for a simple economy based upon supply and demand, when you ignore speculation, trading futures, etc."
- From my professional colleague and fellow educator: "Two ways of creating wealth: ploughing steadily versus big risky adventure? Or the merits of both feet on the ground vs. head in space thinking? Am I even close?"
- From my client and PhD friend: "How about Plough*woman*?"

I think there is no correct interpretation of the title. It's how it resonates with you, which might include "not at all." I see two different interpretations. First is the evolutionary one, where the ancient ploughman is the progenitor of today's astronaut. We look back on him as "simple and unsophisticated" compared to the modern-day us, who are astronauts, but we owe him a nod as our ancestor. The second interpretation sees both roles in a present-day light. As stewards of our personal finances, we have dual roles as a ploughman and astronaut. The former involves our day-to-day responsibilities: earning a day's pay, spending wisely, paying the bills, etc. The latter (the one that might go ignored) has us looking to the stars periodically to contemplate our bigger universe and draw upon a deeper intellectual base.

Or we can see this in a third perspective. The amazing American dance choreographer and writer Twyla Tharp has written several brilliant books. In *The Creative Habit,* she speaks of different vantage points in the creative habit: zoom-in and zoom-out. Zoom-in is like the ploughman; zoom-out is like the astronaut. Think about a microscope and a telescope, both invented around the same time in the early sixteenth century.

And how about the tagline: The Evolutionary Journey to WealthNess?

One dictionary definition of evolution is "the gradual development of something, especially from a simple form to a more complex form" and typically refers to the impact upon successive generations. In science, there are four patterns of evolution, which are instructive to family finance:

- **Divergent**: where related entities evolve different traits independently in reaction to different environments or pressures. In personal finance, this suggests that the family financial genome across generations of family members can evolve in different directions. A spendthrift parent may beget an adult child who, in response to that childhood experience, grows up financially responsible.
- **Convergent**: where non-related entities independently evolve similar traits, different than their respective ancestors in reaction to similar environments, and thus grow more alike. In personal finance, think about the evolution of "loot bags" at a child's birthday party.
- **Parallel**: where non-related entities independently evolve similar traits, different than their ancestors, but the relative dissimilarity across generations remains unchanged. In personal finance, the global reach of fashion houses is an example.
- **Co-evolution**: where non-related entities inter-dependently evolve different traits as they interact with each other. Political structures impact personal finance: think, for instance, of China, the United States, and the Scandinavian countries.

Note that the last three involve the impact of non-related entities upon personal finance. Those "others" might include, for instance:

- The Jones family next door
- Other social peer groups
- Lifestyles promoted in the media
- The local culture
- Cross-cultural immigrant cultures
- Global cultural trends

And as for the word "journey" in the title? Journey is an evocative term in human life. It conjures newness, renaissance, growth, excitement, plus tension from the fear of the unknown. All of us are on our own journeys.

And last is "**WealthNess**." I introduce the term to mean:

> *A state of abundance of health and material possessions to achieve a life well lived.*

And that is what I wish for you, or you the couple, or you the family, or you the multi-generational genetic unit who needs to learn how to work together to achieve WealthNess. The journey there may be long or short, easy or difficult, depending upon where you are starting from. Like a trip, there is no journey unless you *want* to go, know *where* you want to go, and make the commitment to try your best to get there. The evolution part is the by-product of the journey. If you successfully embrace WealthNess, you will tangibly feel the confidence in your personal finance.

How This Book Is Organized

This journey is presented in six chapters, which are each further divided into sections. Each chapter closes with a brief summary of key points and concepts… totalling one hundred in all! Feel free to add your own to that list.

The chapters are as follows:

1.0 Invocation

This will set the stage for your call-to-action by drawing from a wide range of intellectual disciplines to incite and incent the pursuit of WealthNess.

2.0 Chrematistics (That's Greek for the Study of Wealth)

This chapter will help you to uncover your implicit philosophy towards money and to study its sources and purposes. Where does the elusive "happiness" fit in?

3.0 Families and Finance

Here, you will get under the hood to understand the family dynamics about money. How do couples play this out in a marriage? How do parents imbue money values upon their offspring? What are the family legacies of multi-generational WealthNess? This chapter also explores a concept called "family confab."

4.0 Financial Planning

Every one of us goes through life's stages in one fashion or another: birth, childhood, nascent adulthood, adulthood, career, family, retirement, death. How you progress through each one of these has a profound impact upon the work-in-progress called YOU. As you will see later, attitudes towards money are partially forged by age seven! Personal belief systems in adulthood are partially formed in teen-hood. The infamous Boomer Generation has left its mark on society at every step of its ages and stages and is largely in the retired stage now—what I call the fourth quarter. Except "retired" is becoming a bit of a dirty word. The biggest word presently attached to this generation is "longevity," so this chapter explores the longevity literature of the day to parse what retirement means going forward and proposes a substitute term: Re-living.

5.0 Investing

You may be a do-it-yourselfer, which obligates you to a fair amount of investing knowledge and also leaves your flank exposed to the famous Rumsfeld "unknown unknowns." Or you may hire professional advice, in which case it is still wise to have a baseline of knowledge in investing matters—certainly at the big-picture level. What is your investing philosophy? What is in the universe of investing strategy? What is safety and risk? How should you benchmark your investing success/failure?

6.0 Legacy

What will be the residual you leave behind? It is no coincidence that the term "residue" in your Last Will and Testament refers to the remainder of your financial assets upon passing. What about the residue of your non-financial assets? You can't start that process the day before you die—that's too late! And your Will won't adequately do the job for you. So, when do you start? And how do you start? We will start with financial advisor and author Nick Murray's **two questions**: Who do you love and what do you love?

Finding Your Pathway in This Book

As much of this book has been written ensconced at the base of an Olympic mountain, Whistler, I will borrow the ski-trail rating system to guide readers by degree of difficulty. I do this with the best of intentions to shield earnest beginners from becoming glassy-eyed and headed for the exit! Ironically, the difficulty codes vary around the world—and in some cases are directly opposite. So, I will use the North American protocol, of which:

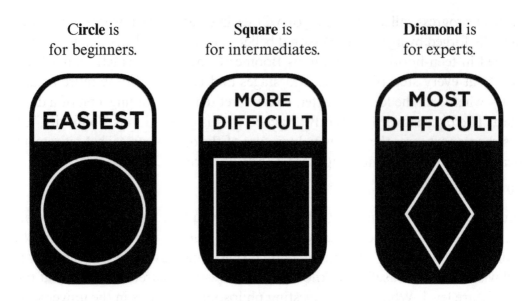

Circle will be the default for the book, and beginners should focus on this material. Stick with it, because your financial well-being is at stake, and you have much to gain. If your finances are in chaos, you need to face the reality that you are your own chaos, and it is you. When topics become more esoteric or detailed, I will identify the Square or Diamond. This gives licence to beginners to skip that material to avoid that glassy-eyed boredom. In fact, you might come back to it another day in the future, as your expertise and comfort grow (see following story about becoming a "sea anemone"). If you are skipping the "More Difficult" (Square) or "Most Difficult" (Diamond) sections, look for the next "Easiest" (Circle) to show you where to pick up reading again.

For intermediates, you already have degrees of financial wisdom and thus don't have to start from scratch. I hope the material here will extend knowledge that you already have, and also broaden your knowledge base. Embrace the Squares and, perhaps, venture into the Diamonds. You likely have the greatest gains to accrue of all three.

For experts, much of this may seem trivial. You might prefer to skim-read the Circles. For you, I have included some advanced topics and concepts that I have developed over the years, for example, "total saving rates," "return on contributed capital," and "the HFactor" (Diamonds), which might grow your financial wisdom. If you do take a "More Difficult" (Square) or "Most Difficult" (Diamond) detour, you will find an "Easiest" (Circle) to get you back on the main path of the book.

Home Bias

There are threads of Canadiana in the material. They appear in the contexts of the kinds of investment accounts, tax-smart investing, and government retirement programs. However, the bulk of the book's concepts are applicable to personal finance anywhere. While we will see lots of global cross-cultural research on happiness in Section 2.5, there is a paucity of such research in personal finance. Factors, including globalization, migration, and rising living standards will make this subject very topical as "mixed" societies evolve on planet Earth.

Connecting with the Material

All levels of readers have the opportunity to grow their financial wisdom. And that requires a four-step process:

- Recognize the problem
- Understand it
- Accept it
- Act upon it

As you progress through the sections and chapters of the book, you may find yourself wearing differing hats, which will impact HOW you respond to that material. For instance, in the Families and Finance chapter, your place in the Family Tree may cause you to wear TWO hats...seeing the subject from **two** vantage points. Further, the style of hat will change with the section. In the Couples section, I will introduce you to the normal distribution curve of couples' inclination to personal finance and the identifiers "RHTs, LHTs, and Ms." In the Kids section, I will refer to givers and recipients. In the family confab section, I will refer to the family generations: Presiding, Leading, and Following.

Deciding How Much Help You Need with Your Personal Finances

You may embrace the metaphor for personal finance as hiking in the mountains.

You may set your target to ascend the mountain in front of you. When you joyously celebrate that accomplishment, you are then surprised to see that mountain was hiding the one behind it, and you have to climb again. So might be the journey from a beginner to an intermediate to an expert. Alternately, you may be satisfied with ascending the first mountain only and seek professional expertise for the further ascents.

Do you feel you have strong stewardship applied to your personal finances? Who is the "team" that oversees this? You, your partner, your broader family, advisors in your world, others? Are there weak links in that team? If you seek professional expertise to advance your progress, what does the Venn diagram of your interactions with your advisors look like?

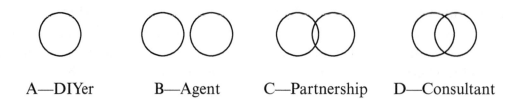

In today's world, lots of media ads encourage DIYers—Do It Yourselfers—to eliminate all those fees that advisors extract from your wealth. If you go this route ("A"), be aware of two important things:

1) Managing your personal finances takes a lot of time.
2) Be wary of the **Donald Rumsfeld Factor** (which we will cover later). Your biggest enemy here is "you don't know what you don't know." And perhaps more importantly, don't trick yourself into believing that what you **do** know is **all that is required to be known**!

You might choose to operate at the opposite end and use an agent ("B"), relying totally on your advisors whilst you get on with all the other demanding aspects of life. With humility, I do not seek to aggrandize my colleagues in the financial service industry, but I do despair and fear for lay DIYers. To run one's own finances on high octane requires understanding a massive collection of information/knowledge that I and peer professionals have spent many years in full-time pursuit of.

"Nonage" is a term that means the inability to use one's own understanding without another's guidance. Further, it is self-imposed if its cause lies not in lack of understanding, but in indecision and lack of courage/confidence to make these decisions on your own.

I proffer that the key is to find a good—nay, an excellent—financial advisor. They are out there! Here, you need to be aware of the risk that you have in choosing that advisor. There are lots of advisors out there, and the normal distribution curve applies. I recall the old joke: "Did you know that 33% of lawyers graduate in the bottom third of their class?" So it is with financial advisors.

As one of those advisors out there, I encourage many of you to consider partnership ("C"). This means that you need to accept the responsibility and burden of some degree of financial wisdom that you bring to the interaction between you and your advisor(s). You already may have this kind of relationship in other aspects of your life, e.g., health and your physician, or fitness and your personal trainer. All of these "advisors" act as cheerleaders/taskmasters who may hold your feet to the fire when your own discipline falters. This approach seeks a further refinement in its definition: how **BIG** is that intersection area of the two circles? Sorry! A small sliver doesn't count.

If you are an ace, you can largely manage your own financial affairs but need an occasional second opinion from a consultant ("D"). On the other hand, if the two circles almost completely overlap, you are a good candidate for going back to "A."

So, a purpose of this book for many of you is to gain enough financial wisdom that the Venn diagram intersection "C" is "big enough," such that you are a material contributor to your financial success whilst "partnering" with your advisor(s).

Aristotle in his book *The Politics* coined the phrase: *"A partnership for living well."* That's a concept that might be useful in your personal finance and across all of your life's vectors.

I have an electric-lift recliner chair in my reading room. One button tilts the back, and the other rolls out the footrest. I confess that this may sound silly. But I experience a brief, exhilarating joy each time that electric lift effortlessly raises my two legs to the horizontal in four seconds without any muscular effort from me! As a fifty-year industry professional, I hope that you might share that same uplifting joy as you gain confidence in the stewardship of your personal finance through some form of partnership.

Lastly, throughout the book you will also find "Sketches in Personal Finance."

Much of this book's material has been derived from my fifty years serving hundreds of families and thousands of individuals in helping them, in some small way, to choose their financial pathway. If you were a fan of the original *Law and Order* TV series, you may remember the closing line of each episode's intro, which I modify for this book as: "These are **your** stories…" in my "Sketches in Personal Finance."

Chapter 1: Invocation

Starting Your Journey to WealthNess

My mission in this opening chapter is to ignite your commitment to review the state of your personal finances. To do this, you will need to climb several mountains, with realistic self-assessments of:

- The state of your finances
- Your financial acuity
- Harmony with other decision-makers
- Your commitment and ability to change and, thus, grow
- Your ability to visualize new goals and the steps and resources to achieve them

This may be a big task. And we may pass or fail in chapter one! This Invocation will draw wisdom from a long list of people in diverse fields. Each of their quotes has the power to create an "ah-hah" moment that lands a perspective for our mountain climb, so bear with me as we set the stage.

"Money…" We all have our own unique relationship with money.

At one end of the spectrum are people who are totally obsessed by it. At the other end are those who totally forsake it and live a chosen life of poverty. The rest of us lie somewhere in between. That said, most of us don't deliberately **think** about our relationship with money; rather, we simply act it out day to day as we transact in the world of commerce—buying a daily cuppa at Starbucks, that irresistible new dress, or that hot car. We handle our philosophy towards money like we do our ethical values: we don't write them down somewhere—we live them through our actions.

In his book *Barking Up the Wrong Tree,* author Eric Barker notes: "Instead of behaviour following our beliefs, often our beliefs come from our behaviours." I think this is worth cogitating upon, and I encourage you to do so. (Sure…put the book down and go for a walk.)

Who's to say there is anything wrong with this cart-before-the-horse approach? I have two separate responses: one is introspective and the other is extrospective. We all have different inclinations towards introspection and self-analysis. A life absent of such internal analysis may be fine for some. However, our "values" constitute a "system," and all systems tend to have feedback loops, which are, by definition, either "positive" or "negative" feedback loops.

We tend to think of the word "positive" as good and "negative" as bad. But in the world of feedback, "negative" doesn't mean "bad"! Your furnace thermostat is not "bad," but it is a negative feedback loop. It keeps your house at a minimum temperature in the winter, and your air conditioning system keeps it below a maximum temperature in the summer. So, negative feedback systems are about "bounding." In the world of money, overdraft bank accounts and hitting your credit card limit are negative feedback loops, like air conditioning. Your excess spending habits are curtailed when the bank "cuts you off." Personal introspection is about a negative feedback loop. We test our actions against our beliefs to judge whether those actions fall within our bounds. If not, we (hopefully) ignite a call to action. So, if your money value system doesn't include expensive cars, but one day you contemplate buying a $180,000 Tesla, does your value system take the day off? Do you justify it within the parameter of contributing to the good of the environment, or do you buy a $40,000 Honda? This is a personal introspection owed to yourself.

Positive feedback systems are another thing. In mathematics, positive feedback is defined as a "positive loop gain around a closed loop of cause and effect." The feedback closes back to make the input larger, and so it re-cycles. Positive feedback can lead to system instability and potentially exponential growth and chaotic behaviour. An example in nature would be a stampede caused by a few cattle exhibiting distressed behaviour. In the world of money, a few distressed depositors or investors can cause a "run" on the banks or stock markets. And, as you will see below, even in a couple....

Sketches in Personal Finance

"You have your toys; I have mine."

This was the unspoken financial behaviour of a client couple spending money. She liked horses, and he liked expensive sports equipment. When one of them made a unilateral large expenditure (buying a horse), the other was justified to buy an expensive bike to "get even"...and the overdraft grew. Internally, their behaviours were a positive feedback loop (which, fortunately, were externally turned into a negative feedback loop by the bank).

Seeing the Real Picture

This invites us into the topic of "cognitive dissonance," a term coined by social psychologist Leon Festinger in 1954.

He described this as "situations involving conflicting attitudes, behaviours, or beliefs, which produce a feeling of discomfort leading to an alteration in those attitudes, behaviours, or beliefs to reduce the discomfort and restore balance." We hold many cognitions about the world and ourselves. A great deal of what makes people happy is living up to what they think they should be doing. When that clashes, a discrepancy is evoked, resulting in a state of tension. We are then motivated to reduce or eliminate it and achieve consonance, according to Festinger. He believed that we have an inner drive to exist in consonance, which he called cognitive consistency. As we may not like to experience internal conflict, we may limit our intake of new information or new thinking about things in ways that don't fit with our pre-existing beliefs—aka confirmation bias. Allowing cognitive dissonance to persist may promulgate future bad decisions or behaviours.

Not much has been written about what to do about cognitive dissonance. Neuroscience research suggests that the action of dopamine in the prefrontal cortex causes us to ignore evidence that challenges long-held views about our world, and thus subverts us from embracing cognitive dissonance and change. This is all part of the brain's game of energy conservation: trying to make decisions quickly and efficiently by building upon yesterday's experiences and assumptions to make today's choices, rather than from scratch. Ironically, dopamine acts oppositely in the striatum part of the brain, which responds favourably to novelty (change)! For most of us, the damming effect prevails over the novelty effect, and thus we maintain status quo. That said, research suggests that some people have a particular gene that causes dopamine to break down more quickly in the striatum, and thus promotes in them the novelty half of the equation.

So, we shall seek to fire up your striatum dopamine in the area of personal finance. We will dive into McLuhan probes, cognitive dissonance, and the term "WealthNess."

As a reformed accountant, I see cognitive dissonance like a variance in a business formula: "actual" minus "budget." If a business fails to achieve its budgeted profit, that is a negative variance.

As individuals, we are not inserting quantifications ($ numbers) into this formula, but rather qualifications, e.g., I aspire to be a moral human being. The problem for us is Festinger's confirmation bias. We each set our own budget (we define being moral), and we each self-assess our actual performance (I am moral). Magically, through that self-assessment our pursuit of being moral exactly meets our goal of being moral and, voila, no cognitive dissonance.

Cognitive dissonance realization can come from two different places: one "internal" and the other "external." External has us re-shape our beliefs simply as a result of new information. As economist John Maynard Keynes reportedly said: "When I am proven wrong, I change my mind…what do you do?" Internal is far more difficult as it requires us to recognize and address conflicts in our value systems.

Archeologist Robert Braidwood asserted that a culture must be ready for some evolutionary advance. So it is, too, for an individual, couple, or a family. So, you may need to create some internal cognitive dissonance to inspire pursuit of greater acumen in personal finance. In other words, what sets your "budget" and your assessment of "actual" in the cognitive dissonance equation? What are the markers for this?

Following are some warning signs of poor personal finance.

If you recognize some of these markers, this is a call to action…to change!

- Low/no savings
- Increasing debt
- Successful at saving but not at investing
- Lost sleep over money matters
- Not confident to manage your own portfolio but don't trust hired advisors
- No war chest for emergencies
- No silo for projects, dreams, vacations
- Avoiding paying the monthly bills
- Avoiding resource material on personal finance
- Absence of goals or disagreement about goals

Making a Change

Obsta principiis is a term used by ancient Romans, which translated literally means "resist beginnings."

Today, we might say, "Nip it in the bud," when talking about resisting the beginning of dangerous markers or habits. This means dealing with the "**present value of pain.**" Present value is a money term that most of us without business-school finance training get to ignore, although we understand it in broad terms. We can apply this principle to both quantitative and non-quantitative things. When we are faced with things we don't want to do, like financial management, we are experts at justifying procrastination. But there is some "cost" of deferring action over all those years. The future is fuzzier and less in our face; thus, we procrastinate. The present value of pain is the difference between the pain you will experience in the future **by not taking action today** versus the **pain you would face today** by taking actions you would prefer to ignore. The issue is that we discount that future pain so much that we justify doing nothing now and taking the easy pathway. But our discount calculation is biased to support our preference to maintain the status quo. In truth, the cost of doing nothing now and bearing the consequences in the future can be very high (like not saving for retirement).

Think of a "problem" you may have in a relationship (let's say the philosophy of money matters with your spouse). It is easier to not confront it today. But that can fester over the years and grow into a bigger quantitative problem (e.g., growing a line of credit balance). The cost of today's problem in the future may become much larger, and you may regret not addressing it before.

"Don't P.O.E.D." So spoke my high-school math teacher.

"Don't Put Off the Evil Day," he said…invoking us to start studying seriously for our final exams. This is equally applicable if our history of facing financial management is sketchy.

We might attach another word to ignoring cognitive dissonance: regret.

> *Regret is one of our most powerful emotional reminders that reflection, change, and growth are necessary…it's a call to courage and a path toward wisdom.*
> —Brené Brown, professor/author

Change can be viewed in a variety of ways. It can be: daunting, essential, healthy, exciting, annoying, a work-in-progress, trial-and-error, externally driven, or internally driven.

The ancient Greek philosopher Heraclitus said, "The defining feature of existence is change."

Truthfully, we all go through a plethora of changes throughout our lives:

- Leaving home to go to grade school
- Leaving grade school to go to postsecondary education
- Leaving the family home to start our own first home
- Joining the work force
- Changing jobs
- Finding a partner
- Having kids
- Moving to other locales
- Making new friends
- Divorcing

- Experiencing health traumas
- Losing friends and family
- Retiring
- Dying

We all do many of these things through life. So, take a bow...we are actually practised with change!

While some people revel in change and novelty, we all know the platitude about people being resistant to change.

We tend to repeat what feels comfortable and avoid discomfort. Change pushes us into the unknown. I frequently do an exercise in my classrooms, which you can do here. Simply fold your two hands together. Now...observe: Did you fold the right thumb over the left, or vice versa? Note that it was done instinctively. Now re-fold your hands to place the other thumb on top. Immediate discomfort! We just experienced Festinger's cognitive dissonance, without the cognitive! For fun and purpose, you and your partner might use that thumb-switching exercise as an avatar between you when one of you is "stuck."

> *There are two types of risk: the risk of going out on a limb and the risk of holing up in a safe place. Success comes from balancing between the two.*
> —Anne Marie Fink, author, chief investment officer

"Evolution" is perhaps just a fancier word for change. When we think about evolution, we think about Darwin. He did not coin the phrase: "survival of the fittest"—that was polymath Herbert Spencer. Darwin was about adaptation.

Hunter gatherers did not have a meeting one day and voted to "get off the road and settle down to grow stuff." Scientists suspect that climactic change occurred circa 10,000 years ago, which caused the environment to become agriculturally productive. The hunter/gatherer turned ploughman/farmer did not change the environment; it changed him. Conversely, the outer space environment did not change in the 1950s to enable the astronaut to breach Earth's gravitational force; we figured that out.

> *So how do we fix things? Put simply, by embracing the idea that intelligence is about adaptation. Sometimes we change ourselves to suit the environment, sometimes we shape our environment to suit ourselves, and sometimes we find a new environment when our current environment isn't working out. We need to nurture the*

adaptive intelligence that is best suited to identifying the need for such changes and developing the strategies for carrying them out.
—*New Scientist* magazine

Oxford professor Eric Beinhocker speaks of evolution as: "Differentiate! Select! Amplify! Repeat!" My own version of that as you embrace raising the bar of your personal finance is: "Observe! Assess! Adjust! Repeat!"

Investment manager/author Morgan Housel reminds us that we need to start with observation because: "You can't prepare for what you can't envision."

Chapter Two aspires to take you through a process to understand who you are and where you are financially. If you are a couple or a family, Chapter Three explores the extra complexities of joint financial matters. At this point, you should have a sense of the gaps in your pursuit of WealthNess. Chapters Four, Five, and Six will endeavour to achieve WealthNess by filling gaps in your knowledge to raise your comfort with personal finance.

Finding a Reason to Change

I think that one of the most important words in language is: **"because."**

Grammatically, it is a conjunction: a word that ties together two parts of a sentence, which are a "what" and a "why." Many communications stop with the What and skip the Why. Think about being told, "Do this!" versus "Do this… because!" In order to motivate the pursuit of a What—WealthNess, you must answer the Why as a make-ready condition, and that leads to Observe! Assess! Adjust! Repeat! The absence of a Why leaves the commitment floundering. Answering *Why with Because fills in the palette.*

Consider what John Kennedy said in September 1962 in Houston.

"We choose to go to the moon in this decade and do the other things not **because** they are easy, but **because** they are hard; **because** that goal will serve to organize and measure the best of our energies and skills, **because** that challenge is one that we are willing to accept, one we are unwilling to postpone, and one we intend to win."

Telling a twenty-five-year-old with zero net worth that they can be a "multi-millionaire" in thirty-five years, without much effort (other than discipline), might seem equivalent to landing on the moon in eight years. But it's true! Kennedy's speech writer, Ted Sorensen, quoted from William Bradford on landing at Plymouth in 1630, who said: "…all great and honourable actions are accompanied with great difficulties, and both must be enterprised and overcome with answerable courage."

Many years ago, I attended an accountants' convention in Las Vegas. The very first speaker, Ron Frantzen, said something I have never forgotten: "You can't talk yourself out of a situation you behaved yourself into."

The obvious follow-up statement is that one needs to **behave out of** that situation. One might convince oneself that fast-talking did the job and move on. But odds are, the other party saw things differently. We can even play this trick on ourselves when we rationalize some financial transgression such as an impulse purchase. We have to **act our way out** of that bad financial behaviour when the next such occasion comes along. We will only be successful the next time if we pause for an introspection and filter that experience appropriately. Observe! Assess! Adjust! Repeat!

Looking at the same idea with a different twist, Oxford professor Richard T. Pascale said: "It's easier to **act your way** into a new way of thinking, than to **think your way** into a new way of acting."

That is pretty profound. This resonates with author James Clear, who said, "The most practical way to change who you are is to change what you do. True behaviour change is identity change."

Every change agent knows that you don't **change** people, you **influence** people to change themselves. Further, being lectured to change doesn't make the grade; rather, learning is best from stories, analogies, and pattern recognitions.

These principles of adult learning may resonate with you, as they acknowledge that you:

- Need to know why you need to learn something
- Need to learn experientially
- Need context for problem-solving
- Seek immediate value

Knowledge is the precursor to understanding, which in turn is the precursor to wisdom, which I will submit, is the precursor to a good life. So, our journey together needs to be mindful of all of these. My mission here is to inspire you to make that pre-commitment. The challenge is to find the right "key" to open those doors. Appealing to your curiosity may be that very key.

The following quotes highlight the importance of curiosity:

> *Specifically, job one is to mobilize...curiosity...such that it is in search of alternate solutions.*
> —Richard Pascale

> *I have no special talents. I am only passionately curious.*
> —Albert Einstein

> *A person's curiosity is more state than trait. That is, our curiosity is highly responsive to the situation or environment we're in. It follows that we can arrange our lives to stoke our curiosity or squash it.*
> —Ian Leslie, author

That is another quote worth digesting for a while. However, you may need to be part magician to pull this off. Magicians perform amazing feats, which are always tricks on our cognition. In his book on curiosity and science, British science writer Philip Ball offers us the following: "One had to force oneself to find a subject fascinating, perhaps by means of consciously deciding to consider it wonderful." He also noted: "(One) needed to be sustained by a curiosity that was itself to some extent artificial: a manufactured, chosen state of mind."

In other words, if you were disinclined to personal finance matters before, relying upon your curiosity to counteract that may be an uphill climb. But there is hope! Author Ian Leslie has also said: "The closer you look at anything, the more interesting it gets." He adds: "Igniting curiosity is a potent strategy not only to motivate exploration but also to strengthen learning." Curiosity may be ignited by our **emotional** side and inspired by our **intellectual** (cognitive) side.

Author Mario Livio sharpens our appreciation of the curiosity to learn in his book *Why?: What Makes Us Curious.* He cites history's great polymath Leonardo da Vinci, who said, "Nothing can be loved or hated unless it is understood."

That one bites! Author Ian Leslie says that you have to understand personal finance before you are allowed to hate it. In our modern-day world, it is likely the exact opposite: we hate it because we don't understand it. Remember, science writer Philip Ball said that things get more interesting the more we delve in!

Learn Like a Sea Anemone

Here is a concept I ask you to embrace in order to ignite your curiosity about personal finance (or anything, for that matter).

Think about a visit to an ocean aquarium where you experienced an ocean-floor environment. The sharks and octopi and other fish are the show-stoppers. But quietly sitting attached to a rock are boring sea anemones. In their natural environment their tentacles pulsate in the ocean current, which washes various sea detritus over them: kelp, plastic bags, and little fish—the last of which is "food." All day, every day, the tentacles are sifting through everything that passes by, rejecting most and grabbing bits they like here and there.

Now, let's look at your brain, with 80–100 billion neurons attached to dendrites, and imagine those as sea anemone tentacles. Each "tentacle" represents something that you are interested in and have learned. When the world around you washes something across your neurons that you are already interested in, you grab that thing and add it to your world, enlarging that tentacle and increasing your understanding about that thing. When the current delivers something that you have not previously embraced, it washes by. In Livio's terms, we can't become curious about something we know nothing about. The duo of **curiosity plus pursuit of knowledge** makes a powerful pair.

I wish to offer you my own sea anemone story that got me through Physics 12 in grade school. In my senior year, I was obviously arts-bound, not science, for university (actually it turned out to be business school). I was obliged to take sciences through grade eleven but elected to take Physics 12 in my graduating year. I was very blessed in that my physics teacher was a Rhodes scholar, and we stayed in contact later through life. However, upon graduation, I earned a token 60% pass in Physics 12 (despite graduating with a "first class scholarship"), and that was the end of my science life. I think he and I implicitly had a deal: I will pass you if you promise never to take more science courses!

Now, roll forward literally forty years.

Until my late fifties, no article in a science magazine connected with any of my neuron tentacles; I would let it wash over and pass by. But then, I started forcing myself to read some of these articles, thus creating an ever-so-tiny new neuron on, for instance, genomics or the Hadron Collider. The next time such an article washed over my brain, it wasn't plastic detritus anymore but something that could be attached to that new, little neuron and make it a bit bigger. Heh, I know something about this! Today, I read a weekly science magazine and draw countless inspirations from the world of science to morph into my world of finance and life.

Lots of "plastic bags" wash over you, too, which you ignore (think: personal finance topics), because you have not built "neuron tentacles" for this unpleasant topic. So, I am going to ask you to become like a sea anemone and to sprout tiny little new neuron tentacles for "personal finance." Now, when information on this subject washes over you, that new little neuron will pop up and try to digest that information…and so, that neuron tentacle grows a little bit bigger each time. Voila!

What Is WealthNess?

We now will venture into the philosophical world of epistemology: the study of the nature of knowledge and what distinguishes justified belief from opinion. This book is about embracing your financial beliefs head on, however they have been formed, and answering positively to cognitive dissonance to bring you, your family, to a better place...the place I call **WealthNess: a new/revised chapter in your encyclopedia of life.**

Let's start here with the etymology of this new word. We are all familiar with the term "wealth"; that said, I suspect we would all write slightly different definitions. The *Oxford Dictionary* says, conventionally, "abundance of valuable possessions"...and more abstractly..." plentiful supply of a desirable thing." Deeper in etymological history, our word wealth comes from "weal" meaning "health or best interests." And "ness" associates with "well-ness." It means:

- A headland or promontory
- A measure of being
- Denotes action, quality, or state.

So, as noted in the Introduction, I shall define WealthNess as:

"A state of abundance of health and material possessions to achieve a life well lived."

Getting to WealthNess involves an evolutionary journey. Economist Edith Penrose wrote that there are two principal constraints to growth: the ability to manage complexity and the thirst for knowledge-gaining. She posited further that our success at the former exceeds the latter.

"Metabolism" refers to the chemical reactions within our body that convert what we eat and drink into energy. Metabolizing is the process of turning these "inputs" into good purpose. And so, we can "metabolize" the inputs of knowledge to the purpose of achieving successful personal finance. You are the gatekeeper to the resources of knowledge in personal finance, and that gate will swing open in the next chapter.

*We set out on your **evolutionary journey** to this better financial life by developing your WealthNess.*

This will require an intellectual financial journey: knowledge-gaining and embracing the complexity of that world. Causal learning must respond to three levels of cognitive ability: seeing, doing, and imagining. The "seeing" requires facing cognitive dissonance. The "doing" requires discipline and commitment. The "imagining" requires knowledge-gaining to fill information gaps so that you can envisage where you are trying to get to (chapters 1 to 3). "Financial responsibility" is the purpose of your goal, but you also need to identify the details of getting there at the ground level (chapters 4 to 6).

Understand that getting to the last page of this book will not achieve your WealthNess because:

> *Knowledge that does not change behaviour is useless.*
> —Yuval Noah Harari, author

> *Nothing is gained biologically from taking in information that is not put to use.*
> —Peter Godfrey-Smith, author/science philosopher

The ploughman came to appreciate the value of fertilizer and tools to enhance the crop. Knowledge is both fertilizer and a tool; it helps you solve problems and execute actions. You need to know what tools exist, then you need to have those tools…and know when to use the appropriate one. I am a gardener. One day I wanted to move a small bush from one flower bed to another. I applied a shovel to dig it out, but the ground was so hard, I couldn't break its surface by so much as an inch. I tried and tried, moving around the circumference of the plant. Dejected, I gave up. A few hours later, I saw a spade in the garage, with its pointy blade. Five minutes later, the bush was transplanted with the right tool!.

That's what we are going to do together in this book: build tools…hopefully the right tools. **This is a finance self-help book for the intellectually curious**. The ploughman also came to appreciate the concept of crop rotation, and so it is with our financial journey. We need to mix things…draw inferences from other places…transmogrify ideas and principles from a plethora of disciplines and wise people to the world of personal finance, including:

- Pathology and disease control
- Geology and tectonic plates
- Genomics
- Evolution
- Epigenetics
- Architectural design
- Human digestion
- Psychology
- Thermodynamics
- Ecology
- Magic

- Neuroscience
- Energy flow
- Entropy
- Chemistry
- Biology
- Meteorology

The busy Western world of the last few centuries has left little time to undertake reflection …about anything. Jesuit tradition encourages a regular examination of conscience: internal interrogation of your actions, desires, and motivations. And so, I encourage you to spend the time to reflect upon, and notate, your philosophy about money and gain voluntary control of your path to WealthNess through financial learning. Find time to mix with your own thoughts. Reading intellectual material prepares the brain and ignites the neurons to start firing and cross-firing—the result of which can be insights that aren't even in the subject matter of the actual material. Psychologists call this "priming."

Eventually, WealthNess takes on a spiritual tone. Look up the word "spiritual" in a dictionary; almost all the definitions have religious connotations. But the etymology of the word derives from the Latin for "breath" and is the thing that animates life. In a secular context, spirituality relates to relationships, values, and purpose, and attaining a sense of peace. I think that getting your personal finances in order—achieving WealthNess—may be a cornerstone of secular spirituality because it enriches your relationships, values, and purpose.

How to Proceed…

First of all, be mindful to make use of the ski-hill signs so that you don't become overwhelmed …or bored. Second, I would like to share a couple of concepts with you as a book reader. I read sixty to seventy non-fiction books per year. I describe them as being either "retail" or 'wholesale"; the former means being written for the general public, and the latter means written for experts steeped in the particular topic. I also describe them as "production line" or "custom"; the former means the reader can simply pick up the book at page one and buzz through to the end, and then move on. (Think about a car assembly plant.) In essence, your "job" as a reader of production line books is to be entertained and distracted. Custom books require the reader to slow down the speed of flipping the pages. Stop and put the book down at a particularly insightful section to reflect upon it. Your "job" while reading custom books is to learn and evolve. Thus, custom books **require a "reset" to your reading persona.** Don't read this book like a novel but like an **encyclopedia**. Your mission isn't to start at page one and keep going to find out WhoDunIt? on the last page. Review the table of contents and dive into whatever interests you on the day. The chapters and sections can inform on their own. You don't have to pick up the plot line from where you last read. As you become proficient with the bunny hill topics, you will feel the need to tackle the Squares and Diamonds.

So, in summary: stop…contemplate…consolidate…advance. Most importantly of all, take your time: digest…ponder…make notes…discuss with your partner/family. There will be no prize for speed-reading.

Draw inspiration from mathematician Lloyd Shapely who won a Nobel Prize in economics in 2012 and said: "I never, never in my life took a course in economics!"

*Lastly, the keen **reader**, in turn, should have an invocation back to the **writer**: "Take me to places that I have never been and introduce me to thoughts that I have never had."*

It's time to dream…

Enjoy!

1.1 Key Words and Concepts

1. Beliefs become behaviours
2. Cognitive dissonance
3. Change: Observe! Assess! Adjust! Repeat!
4. Igniting curiosity
5. Become a sea anemone
6. "Because…"
7. WealthNess: A state of abundance of health and material possessions to achieve a life well lived
8. Interdisciplinary insights from design, pathology, ecology, geology, magic, and more

Chapter 2: Chrematistics

Chrematistics *(from Greek): "The study of wealth as measured in money."*

Although not a popular term these days, it sums it up.

Tom Morris, former professor of philosophy at Notre Dame, and author of many books, including *If Aristotle Ran General Motors,* tells the story of his cross-legged, three-year-old son staring quietly back at the family dog. After a long silence between the two, the boy asks: "Dad, does Roo *know* he's a dog?"

A real piece of philosophy from a three-year-old! A ponderous existentialist moment for the dog?

Later, Morris tells of meeting a middle-aged woman who said: "Look, Tom, when I was eighteen and in college, we used to sit up late at night in the dorm and talk about all sorts of important things—life, death, love, meaning, God, happiness.... Now I am forty-five years old, and when I get together with friends all the conversation is ever about is what the kids are doing. We never talk about anything important. We all need a little philosophy in our lives."

This gives us all cause-for-pause to step back and contemplate our own journeys. Perhaps we too need to bring a little philosophy back into our busy lives.

*In this section, we will try to uncover your core **philosophy** about wealth and money.*

That belief system, perhaps undescribed, *draws* from your **root attitudes**, is *funded* by your **root sources** of wealth, and *drives* your **root purposes** with wealth. Your success is, at least partially, driven by (hopefully good) decision-making over your lifetime. The ultimate goals for a life well lived, I submit, are simply distilled to happiness and meaning.

We will visit each one of these in the next sections. Open your arms wide to embrace this.

Sections

2.1 Money Philosophy

2.2 Root Attitudes

2.3 Root Purposes

2.4 Root Sources

2.5 Happiness and Meaning

2.6 Good Decision-Making

2.7 Key Words and Concepts

2.1 Money Philosophy

What Does Money Mean to You?

"Money is dirty." So said an elderly, childless client of mine, throwing his hands up in the air, when he was drafting his final will.

Full disclosure: one of my aims in this book is to inspire you to enunciate to yourself what your **money philosophy** is. It is appropriate here to reflect back to the Invocation chapter, where author Eric Barker noted: "Instead of behaviour following our beliefs, often our beliefs come from our behaviours."

"Money" needs to be considered at three levels: academically, intellectually, and philosophically.

"Academically" refers to what was termed in the old days as home economics. You might call it the science of money. It behooves all of us to embrace a mini degree in finance, accounting, and tax in order to manage our financial affairs day to day.

"Intellectually" means that, regardless of what science of money we understand, we still need to **practise** that wisdom through our lives. Life is ultimately distilled down to the inner battle within ourselves: the internal conversations in our heads about what we should do, want to do, and what we ultimately do. This applies to our financial decisions as well.

"Philosophically" is a whole different level, and one that many of us never address. The word "spirituality" must follow closely behind it. I believe that money has a soul. OK…some of you are headed for the exits. But bear with me! The Britannica definition of soul in philosophy is "the immaterial aspect or essence." In ancient Greek thought, the soul "is the bearer of moral qualities" and of "all the vital functions that any living organism performs." You control your money. You control the good things it can do. Those things are "the bearer of your moral qualities" that you convey to the world around you. If it feels like your money controls you (and your family), you have a serious problem and really have some work to do.

Ideally, we all address these three levels from our own hearts and minds. Practically speaking, we can "sub out" the first one, the academic science of money, to other parties: accountants, lawyers, investment advisors, financial planners, etc. But the last two—intellectually and philosophically—must remain ours, and the locus of those is our brain. We make "money decisions" on a regular basis. Some of those decisions are quick and impromptu, and others are longer and deliberate.

The trick we need to understand here neurologically is: who is actually calling the shots? The default answer, of course, is "me," but it's more complicated than that.

> *The vast jungles of neurons operate their own programs. The conscious you...is the smallest bit of what's transpiring in your brain. Our brains run mostly on autopilot, and the conscious mind has little access to the giant and mysterious factory that runs below it.*
> —David Eagleman, author/neuroscientist

So, it's kind of like the operating system that comes preloaded in your new computer.

You know it's there but understand nothing about its programming. You turn it loose, and it does stuff for you to make life easier. But the truth is that the programming that might dominate your money decisions came from somewhere—genomically, inferentially, experientially—versus deliberate mental machinations in the moment. The subconscious brain can offer up an answer to your money decision in a fraction of a second, beating your more deliberate conscious brain to the finish line. The key is: how well programmed is that subconscious mind? Is it dominated by "bad-guy genes" that you unconsciously inherited? In this section, we seek to break the code of your unconscious brain.

Some of you will agree with my elderly client's statement and some will differ.

If you **agree** with his "money is dirty" view, I believe you will struggle unsuccessfully with money all your life: equally for having it or **not** having it. I ask you to embrace the mathematics concept of "substitution." You need to search your soul to contemplate what money achieves, not what it is. It is a base element, like a base metal. Alchemy has a long, and perhaps sordid, history of trying to transform base metals, like copper and lead, into gold or silver or, more loftily, even into a cure for human disease. I encourage your own journey as alchemist to identify what your money achieves. Jot down some answers, then review them to see if there is some commonality to what those achievements are so that perhaps you can categorize them in a philosophical way. That term, whatever it is, becomes your "substitute" word for "money" in my client's definition above. Then, you can finish his statement: "Money is..."—hopefully finding some purpose that is more healthy than "dirty."

For those who **disagree** with my elderly client's statement, I ask you also to proceed to complete the sentence "Money is...." before you advance here.

I believe that our own philosophy about money evolves; it's a work-in-progress. The philosophy of you, the young person collecting your first paycheque, versus you, the successful retiree with millions in the bank, will be different, at least in some of the markers. On the flip side, probably some (good or bad!) markers may stay with you through your entire life. If you are reading this as a young person, you can create your own interesting, longitudinal survey by documenting your philosophy as it evolves over your lifetime (watch for the later reference to a commonplace book). What a brilliant insight to share with your following generations (and likely a book of your own)!

I think that the long-standing definition of a "millionaire" as a person whose assets exceed $1 million is overdue for redefinition. When I was a kid back in the 1950s, and even well into my adult life, being a "millionaire" was a pretty rare thing. Nowadays, largely thanks to staggering real estate appreciation over the last thirty years, there are many, many "millionaires" under that old definition. A modern re-definition in the investment industry excludes the wealth of your residence and speaks of "investable wealth" over $1 million. To return to its historical rarity, I think that the next logical re-definition of a millionaire must shift from asset-based to income-based: an annual income in excess of $1 million.

Nouveau riche is a not-so-common term today from the early nineteenth century for people who recently became very rich within their own generation and like to show their wealth publicly—most commonly in their consumption habits. A *parvenu* refers to someone who has come into recent wealth but has not gained the prestige, dignity, or manner associated with it. Another French term, also from bygone days, is *noblesse oblige*—the obligation of nobility, meaning that great wealth comes with the obligation to give back to those less fortunate. Philosophically, this concept dates even further back to ancient Greek civilization.

The total **net worth** of the Earth's citizens more than tripled from 2000 to 2020: $160 trillion to $510,000 trillion, of which one third of the growth was attributed to China. (Note: there are slightly different estimates by different organizations.) Net worth includes financial plus real estate assets, less debt. There were estimated to be 58 million millionaires in the world.

The world has many problems these days. The severity, ranking, and validity of these problems are all subject to the personal opinions of the eight billion people on the planet. However, I would add another one, which is perhaps the **amoeba in the room** of world problems: that is the breadth and depth of wealth that has been produced over the last half century (or briefer), creating unprecedented numbers of nouveau riche/parvenu. Unfamiliar with wealth, many are deploying it like an impudent infant, when the world desperately needs them to come forward and contribute their wealth to solve our problems like wise adults. How quickly can parvenu mature? Compare this with the Derbyshire, England manor, Haddon Hall, which is 900 years old and still passing down through a family line.

During the last thirty years, the world economy has created a staggering number of nouveau riche and parvenu. These new wealthy people have not had the experience of time to have a philosophy of money that exists beyond "consumption" à la nineteenth-century France. How many generations forward will it take for these new wealthy to have sufficient experience with wealth to manage it with maturity and greater purpose—to have noblesse oblige? All of this underscores the importance of the material in this book.

Sketches in Personal Finance

Let's review some philosophies about money.

First let's look at a philosophy of discipline and heeding tomorrow. Simply summarized for now: $223,000 invested patiently by Larry over twenty-eight years became $1.05 million.

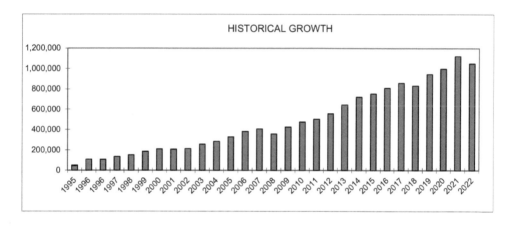

This simple graphic should be adequate invocation to inspire you to set in motion the process to build your own portfolio graph like his. Better still…share this with your kids! We will revisit Larry's portfolio later.

Now let's look at a philosophy of living for today. Here's a very different story.

A couple came into my office on a referral from a professional colleague. The husband recently retired from a career as a long-haul pilot. His wife had stayed at home through his career. From my previous experience with senior pilots, I knew three things: first, they are away from home a lot; second, they make a very high salary; and third, their work pensions are among the best of retired employees. In his working era, this couple pretty much could spend whatever they wanted to, and there was always money in the bank to pay the month-end credit card bill. But…not now! For this couple, that reality hit within six months of receiving pension cheques way lower than his salary.

It would have been useful to have the prescience ten or twenty years prior to develop a formal financial plan with a professional planner. I discussed having a plan made now so that they could see where the future indeed was taking them. This sort of plan costs $2,000 to $3,000. He said they couldn't afford that. Their main alternatives at this point were either a significant adjustment to lifestyle and/or a trade-down of their existing home to a lesser retirement abode. My final words to them were: "I am sorry…but I don't think we will be able to help you. We needed to be taking care of you twenty years ago in order to avoid what you are facing today."

There is no palatable *deus ex machina* (short of a windfall lottery or inheritance) that could save this couple. The solution, which needed a time machine, was that through his high-income working years, they ought to have tempered their generous lifestyle by deliberate extra savings that would have accrued a separate pot of wealth to support their retirement lifestyle. I phrase this as "**lifestyle averaging**"…meaning, through the high-income earning years spend less than you can afford, so you can spend more than you can afford on your retiree's income. The "spending less" part would be called "saving"!

This couple needed some of Festinger's cognitive dissonance earlier in life, but that wasn't going to occur within their own closed feedback loop. In short, someone needed to show them Larry's graph. Your take-away with this story is to encourage you to engage a professional advisor **early** in life. Don't procrastinate on this by convincing yourself that you are "small potatoes." Alternately, if you trust yourself as a DIYer, become that sea anemone and read books like this… and start saving.

Magician's Math: The "Wealth Effect"

Our philosophy about money can be driven by how wealthy we feel.

The urge to spend as a response to a sustained and unexpected change in wealth is a predictable human response. Economists have studied this so-called "**wealth effect**," in which an increase in wealth on paper directly causes households to increase their consumption and, correspondingly, decrease their saving. The wealth effect resulting from the periodic rapid appreciation of real estate assets has been a powerful stimulus to consumer spending and has increasingly captured the attention of central bankers. Wealth on paper doesn't put money in the bank to spend more, but higher property values give bankers extra comfort to create or increase mortgages or, more likely, lines of credit, which fund the increased consumption.

The empirical data on this subject is a bit sparse over time but worthy of attention. Economists Case, Shiller, and Quigley analyzed data from rising house values between 2001–2005 and concluded that household spending increased by 4.3% over the four years. The chief economist at Merrill Lynch estimated that the wealth effect from that home appreciation accounted for 50% of US GDP growth in the first half of 2005. *Case et al* updated their analysis to 2012 to include the ensuing housing crash through 2009 and observed the flipside of household spending dropping by 3.5%.

Stock portfolios can rise in paper value, too. Studies of the wealth effect caused by a rising stock market were inspired by the tech boom/bust in the equity markets. A 2001 paper published by the US Federal Reserve documented a dramatic behavioural response of wealthy Americans to the stock-market boom that prevailed from 1994 through 1999 and demonstrated that the magnitude of this response could account for the decline in the aggregate personal saving rate. At that time, wealth models showed that US consumers increased annual spending by about four cents for every dollar of additional wealth. After the bursting of the tech bubble, the Federal Reserve estimated that the resulting negative wealth effect held back consumer spending by about 1.5% in 2002 and a lagged impact continued to dampen expenditure growth for approximately two more years.

There are differences, though, in the wealth effect generated by increases in the **stock market** versus the **real estate market**. A 2003 Bank of Canada Working Paper found that for the US economy, the tendency to consume as a result of housing wealth could be an increase of as large as twenty cents per dollar. Homeowners view gains in real estate values as more permanent. In contrast, gains in stock prices are viewed as more volatile and not necessarily lasting. A 2004 study found that within one year, about 80% of the housing wealth effect is realized, whereas it takes almost five years for stock wealth to approach 80% of its long-run impact. More importantly, though, housing wealth has a broader reach. Stock market wealth effects are associated with older, wealthier groups; the top 1% of US stockholders control around one third of stock wealth. A greater proportion of the population, approximately 70% in Canada and the US, owns a home and this is spread more evenly across age and income brackets.

*Here is an **optional detour** for those who are game for a more academic angle on personal finances. (If you don't want to take this detour right now, jump ahead until you see the Circle/easiest sign.)*

Let's take a Diamond trail and infer wisdom from deep mathematics and a forgotten, great mind of the past. (Remember to skip this part if you are still on the bunny hill!)

Beauty

Almost a hundred years ago, Harvard mathematician George Birkhoff took his sabbatical year to travel around the Mediterranean Basin studying beauty… in art, music, and literature. He took his research home at the end of that year and, in 1933, published his findings in a book entitled: *Aesthetic Measure.* Being an academic, he felt that "beauty" needed a more erudite terminology…thus "aesthetic measure." Being a mathematician, he came up with a "formula" to define beauty:

$$\text{Beauty} = \text{order divided by complexity}$$

We lesser math whizzes associate a formula as a place to stick some numbers in and dig out the calculator. But we are stopped short to find keys on the calculator called "order" and "complexity." We can't perform quantitative arithmetic with qualitative values. However, a six-year-old introduced to her first fraction can help us glean some insight, nonetheless. The take-away is this:

In order to increase beauty in something, we need to:

> Increase the order, or
> Decrease the complexity, or
> Some combination of those two.

For instance, to make the book that you are now reading more "beautiful"—more appealing to you—I, your author, need to increase the order (structure) of what I am presenting, or decrease the complexity of what I am seeking for you to understand, or some combination of both.

For you, the object of the beauty that Birkhoff is informing you about is your personal finances. You might have difficulty **associating your finances with beauty**; but, as a financial professional for almost a half century, I wish to assure you that, indeed, it can be so! Your take-away from Birkhoff with regards to your finances is the same as mine in writing this book. Re-read the three points above and then consider:

- How orderly (structured) is the picture of your finances? Is it in chaos? Later, you will read the Investing chapter and encounter the metaphor of engineering and constructing a house.
- What initiatives can you take to make your finances more orderly?

Now let's look at complexity:

- Are your personal finances overly complex? Do you have unnecessarily complex structures in your world…perhaps due to well-meaning professional interventions? Contemplate whether such complexities **had** their purpose at a particular stage of your life which have since evolved.
- Do you have excess complexity due to "volume"—multiple bank accounts, loans, brokerage accounts/advisors, or holding companies?

Of the three points in the formula, the third is the most likely: a combination of order and complexity need some attention.

*Welcome back to the **book's main pathway**.*

For the map of your journey on the road to WealthNess in the following chapters, I would like to start at the root. "Root" is a seemingly elementary word in our language; however, it has several meanings:

- The part of the body of a plant that grows downward into the soil, **anchoring** the plant and **absorbing** nutrients (my emphasis).
- Origins
- The place something starts

Our money attitudes and philosophy are like Dr. Dolittle's imaginary creature the Pushmi-Pullyu; philosophy contributes to our attitudes and our attitudes contribute to our philosophy.

In the next chapter, we are going to break your money roots into three: **root attitudes, root purposes, and root sources.** So, the start of your journey to WealthNess is to examine the roots of your attitudes towards money. As you do so, consider the metaphor in the definitions above of a starting place anchoring you and of absorbing nutrients.

Also, keep Festinger's cognitive dissonance close at hand if you are going to grow through this process. The winner here is not just you, but potentially those loved ones in the following generation(s) whom you can inspire to create a **family journey** to WealthNess.

2.2 Root Attitudes

What Does Money Mean to You?

We are going to peel back the onion layers to uncover the root attitudes towards money that are implicit in your day-to-day personal finance. It is going to take some time to do this properly. I encourage you to bear with it, and do the work. We will meander in and out of some Square material, so if your eyes start to glaze over a bit, feel free to hit the fast-forward button.

Let's roll up the sleeves and start with the question: **how have you learned about money?**

To prepare for this, let's sidebar briefly to one of Canada's most interesting thinkers: Marshall McLuhan, who was world-renowned in the 1960s. In speaking of his own complex genius, McLuhan said, "I don't pretend to understand it: after all, my stuff is very difficult."

One of his favourite things was what he termed "a probe," which he defined as: "An investigation not for the purpose of an end-conclusion, but for the offshoot of new thoughts."

He further said, "Discovering an answer is not always the purpose of a question; rather, the pursuit of the process of discovering an answer." So, let's keep that in mind as you proceed.

We will dive into your root attitudes about money in the spirit of a McLuhanesque probe. Take the moment right now to jot down on a piece of paper your responses to **how you learned about money.** Warm up with the answer to a very simple question: did either of your parents teach you about money? I'll wait for you and pour a cup of coffee....

Welcome back. There are no right answers here, of course, but I shall offer the following:

- At the elbow of your elders
- By observation of the world around you
- By formal schooling
- By sheer self-determination
- By the School of Hard Knocks

How did our lists compare?

Let's follow that with a more specific probe: **Can you remember specific incidents or conversations that formed part of your attitudes towards money?** And did they emanate from positive or negative situations? Consider stopping here and writing down your responses.

Next sheet of paper.—this is a harder probe but don't avoid or procrastinate. **What's the most important thing in your life?**

I asked this in a room of forty people who had come to a course I taught. It was a bit unfair because it was only 9:00 a.m., they had just gotten seated, and did not want to be put to work. They came to listen passively. I pressed on....

"I ask you now, or later when you get home, to deliberately reflect on this. And I am going to add a caveat. Do not complete this assignment by writing: your partner, your parents, your kids, etc. Let us assume that, for most of us, this is universal. So, let us remove them from that obvious list, and force ourselves to mine a little deeper down the list. Be very honest with yourselves. No one else is going to read your list."

Now I ask you to sidebar and do the same thing. As before, there are no right answers here.

Here are my own personal answers:

- Paying attention to the triumvirate of mental, physical, and social well-being, and finding the time to nourish each
- Filling my world with intellectual stimulation and beauty
- Being mindful of the financial trade-off between today and tomorrow

Looking at your own list, evaluate how much time you spend on each point, and how much time you spend **avoiding** time on each.

Next, on another sheet of paper, complete this statement: **To me, money means...**

If you are a partner and/or a parent, keep going on that sheet of paper and contemplate these questions:

- How do your attitudes to money compare with your partner?
- How do your attitudes to money compare with your offspring?

Let's compare what money means to you with some academic research. In 2019, *Honchos, Coset,* and *Wernli* conducted research on this topic and published an article entitled "Culture, Money Attitudes, and Economic Outcomes." This was a survey conducted on 1,390 young (under age thirty) Swiss men and women. For starters, they stated that there is indeed a relation between attitudes to money and to actual financial practices. Maybe that is stating the obvious and maybe not.

They said, "We find that three main types of attitudes towards money co-exist: the prestige and power attitude, the money management attitude, and the goal-oriented attitude."

They identified money cognitively as an **agent** or marker for: achievement, status/respect, freedom, power, social facilitation, and its own end. They also categorized money with respect to four **behaviours**: hedonism, saving-orientation, solvency, and balance.

They reported that: "Culturally shaped attitudes to money are mostly linked to *savings and to indebtedness*." They found, for instance, a correlation between the prestige/power attitude and the propensity to take on debt and carry overdue bills.

As we each place our attitudes to money in the test-tube, we can reflect on these markers in the Swiss study. How do they rank in **your** importance? Endeavour to be honest with your self-assessments. Look at each one of these agents and score them:

Money…	strongly disagree	disagree	don't know	agree	strongly agree
Is my report card					
Gives status and respect					
Gives freedom					
Gives power					
Gives social status					
Is a thing unto itself					
Allows me to do anything					
Focuses my goals					
Sharpens discipline					

Also, this is a very useful exercise for a **couple** to undertake separately, then together. Furthermore, they might each answer it in the shoes of the other party (flush out that honesty factor). Better still, how brilliant it would be for a young couple contemplating marriage to undertake this exercise.

This is hard work. Be sure to do it! And take some breaks.

What do you see in the tabulation of responses? Were the highlighted values consistent with your upbringing or unique to you? Significant mis-alignment for a couple may be problematic.

Are you ready to dive in to this deeper? If so, take this detour. (If you don't want to take this detour right now, jump ahead to the next Circle/easiest sign.)

The root attitudes in personal finance can derive insight from the world of ecology.

"Trophic cascade" was coined by zoologist Robert Paine in 1980 to describe the powerful, indirect knock-on effects in an ecological environment triggered by the addition or removal of key components (e.g., predators) in the eco-system. Trophic cascades can have an impact on the entire eco-system. For instance, humans may intervene in some ecosystem to remove or reduce a certain trophic layer (predator). This has an immediate positive impact upon that predator's prey, whose population now grows in number. However, this then has a negative impact upon that prey's prey whose population declines, and so on along the next trophic levels in the food chain.

By definition, we all come from a family, regardless of its efficacy or longevity. The trophic cascade knock-on effect can impact family finance values. For instance, while growing up, your CFFO (chief family financial officer) may have had bad financial management skills due to, for instance:

- Disinterest
- Gambling habit
- Spending habit
- Entitlement attitude
- Substance abuse habit

This would have left WealthNess compromised, e.g., perhaps no funding for children's advanced education, which then potentially impacted their adult lives and families, and imprinted upon future generations.

*Another ecological phenomenon in nature identified by professor/biologist John Laundre is termed "**landscape of fear**."*

Fear of predation caused by the mere presence of a predator within an ecosystem is increasingly regarded as an ecological force that rivals or exceeds that of direct killing. The "landscape of fear" concept has been advanced as a general mechanism that drives the effects of fear that cascade from individuals to whole ecosystems. In other words, predators don't just impact their prey by killing, but also by their mere presence, or perception of presence, which causes more fear time, less eating, less robust health, less fertility, and avoidance of resource-rich areas that attract those predators.

Let's take these ecological concepts and apply them to financial ecology.

Here, the prey is you…your family, and the predator is financial mismanagement. Your day-to-day life is akin to the gazelle on the savannah. If the genomic imprint upon you from past family habits is financial irresponsibility, you aren't faced every minute with Ms. Lion (your banker calling you, past-due bills, credit cards over limit). But in your subconscious, this may create your own landscape of fear, where the knock-on effect causes anticipation of bad things. This creates subterranean stress, which can lead to health issues or a financially compromised golden age.

So, in our personal finance world, the potential "predator" is not a lion but **money worries**, be they perceived or actual. That landscape of fear can impact in the ways described above, both on the CFFO and the whole family—and even future unborn generations.

Next, our goal of multi-generational WealthNess is also impacted by a metaphor from the world of global disease control and pathology.

Let's start with some terms (which have become household words thanks to Covid).

- "Pathology" is the study of the symptoms of disease
- "Pathogenesis" studies the mode of development of the disease
- "Pathogen" is the agent causing the disease
- "Vectors" are the extending pathways of the disease

So, let's contemplate the term **"financial" pathology**, where the disease is some form of historical family financial mismanagement causing stress upon the present generation(s). Our job is to identify the pathogenesis, the pathogen, and the vectors related to the disease of this financial mismanagement. We need to ask:

- Who will undertake the role of pathologist?
- What will be the process to identify the specific pathologies?
- Is the current CFFO the pathogen or, in fact, just a vector, or "carrier" of the disease?
- In family history, is the true pathogen some **past** family CFFO who may, in fact, be long dead, but passed along the disease to the current CFFO?
- Do we need to focus, then, less on the pathogen and more on the family pathology in order to correct today's family's financial disease? The current CFFO may be the key contributor to reflect through deep family history to identify the pathogen.
- Who are today's vectors of the disease, and how do we inoculate them before they are stricken, or, if already stricken, how do we cure them?

What if **you** are actually a pathogen in the family finance disease? How can you realistically be the solution when you are the problem? First of all is coming to this realization. Over the entrance of the Temple of Apollo at Delphi are the Greek words: *Gnothi seauton* (pronounced no-thee say ow ton) translated as "Know Thyself." Second, get some professional help, either to address your own issues or to help you safeguard the next generation (see Family Confab section 3.3).

The term *epigenetics* in its contemporary scientific usage emerged in the 1990s, but for some years has been used with somewhat variable meanings. A consensus definition of the concept of an **epigenetic trait** is a "stably heritable phenotype resulting from changes in a chromosome **without alterations** in the DNA sequence."

The term epigenesis has a generic meaning of "extra growth" and has been used in English since the seventeenth century. Thus, in its broadest sense, *epigenetic*s can be used to describe anything other than DNA sequence that influences the development of an organism. For instance, lifestyle factors such as obesity, smoking, and alcoholism may trigger gene expression that might not otherwise occur.

> *In our world of WealthNess, can financial mismanagement express epigenetically to following generations from a family background?*

Why should we be interested in this?
Because the multigenerational management of money is important for all time to everyone of all income strata. As financial pathologists, we need to understand the attitudes about money for every family cohort alive: grandparents, parents, grown offspring, growing offspring, young offspring. To attack all of this may

require some family financial genome mapping across a broad spectrum, enquiring into family attitudes such as:

- Work ethic
- Laissez-fair? Lazy-fair?
- Pollyanna outlook
- Attitude to furthering education
- Attitude of entitlement
- Time perspectives
- Acceptance of investment and return
- Overall value systems
- Attitude cohesion/diversity

If you are having difficulty mapping the family financial genome, consider addressing questions like these to gain some insights:

- Does the family drive fancy, expensive cars?
- Does the Christmas tree explode with presents?
- Do the kids go out and find part-time jobs? Or are they accessing credit cards with no limits?
- Is expensive private school education within the reach of a family income?
- Are expensive holidays always the norm?
- Are there many family sacred cows regardless of the health of family finances?
- Does the family occupy multiple, and expensive, homes?
- Does the CFFO discuss money with the rest of the family?

After you have identified family traits, both good and bad, trace where they come from. What caused them? How widespread are they across the family? In family finances, if the CFFO is the incurable pathogen, how does a family member escape these epigenetic influences to build their own healthy attitudes to money? We will address this in more detail in the Family Confab section 3.3.

Let's stop and take a rest here. It could well be that these last few pages may be your biggest take-away in this book.

*Welcome back to the **book's main pathway**.*

The Intergenerational Effect on Wealth

The book The Millionaire Next Door by Stanley and Danko was published in 1996 with a catchy title and a plethora of insights about wealth.

Backed by research and extensive interviews of the wealthy, the lessons and inspiration of the book were for ordinary folks to learn how "ordinary" the wealthy are. The authors introduced several interesting concepts for WealthNess, starting with a brilliant sports analogy of offence and defence. The former is your income earning capacity; the latter is your spending habits. A shoot-out-the-lights offence often can't win a sports championship if the defence allows more points, and so; people must earn more than they spend. Sounds trivial, but it's not.

Stanley and Danko observed the key strategies of the wealthy:

- Live well below their means
- Choose financial independence over displaying high social status
- Plan, learn, and set goals
- Share these values
- Do not provide "economic outpatient care" for their offspring

Pretty down to earth. This final strategy leads the authors to delineate three classifications of accumulators of wealth: prodigious (PAW), average (AAW), and under-achieving (UAW). I think each descriptor speaks for itself.

We are all roughly familiar with the concept of financial compounding...which is a good thing. In fact, Einstein referred to it as "the eighth wonder of the world." Now, let's look at the concept of compounding in a different context: in a family of UAWs following behind the founding generation. Here, compounding can work against you. We first meet this family when the founding couple has started a family (let's say with one offspring) and has worked hard to be successful and create significant wealth. That family of three can enjoy a good lifestyle, hopefully bounded by the parents subscribing to Stanley and Danko principles, but maybe not. The offspring grows up, finds a mate, and they produce two offspring. Let's say that those two, and their chosen mates, have not built themselves for success and thus are UAWs. But they became accustomed to a certain lifestyle, which their offence skills are not able to support. What the founding generation does next is key: do they leave their offspring to find their own way? Or do they subsidize the offspring like welfare cases? If the latter, the wealth of the founding generation, which supported a good life for three, then must sustain six, then twelve, then twenty-four. This could all happen while the now-great-great grandparents are still alive.

You may argue that the scenario is unrealistic...for heaven's sake, somebody in all those adult offspring and selected mates ought to be an AAW or PAW! Maybe...maybe not. We didn't even build any divorce settlement math into the equation. How this scenario plays out is largely correlated with how the founding generation deals with it from the start. The Stanley and Danko research says that these couples choose **not** to provide "economic outpatient care." They cajole, inspire, or watch those offspring build their own abilities.

We can't be too clinical here, though.

What was the genesis of the founding generation's stewardship of their two offspring? Was it deliberate, inferred, or accidental? The likelihood is high that the wealth-creating founding generation was busy as heck building that success, never mind finding the time for their offspring's routine upbringing, nor the higher order task of forming the kids' financial acumen. How will those offspring respond to the earlier question: how have you learned about money? If you are a parent, the point here is if you make the time to deliberately steward your kids' financial acumen as the founding generation, the long-term "return on investment" will be enormous, and in so many ways.

Ready to draw insights from the world of science? Then take this detour. (If you don't want to take this detour right now, jump ahead until you see the Circle/ easiest sign.)

*Back to science and the concept of **entropy**.*

One definition of entropy is "lack of order or predictability: gradual decline into disorder." The Second Law of Thermodynamics states that the entropy of any isolated system always increases (i.e., declines into disorder). The collection of success traits exhibited by the founding generation of successful families ought to be passed on to the following generations. However, that Second Law of Thermodynamics tells us how difficult it is to swim against the current of nature's tendency over time. Some generation in the future is likely to be labelled the "Entitled Generation," thus marking the beginning of the end for that family.

The modern world of science is shedding light, literally, on the world of historical art. Famous paintings by van Gogh, Matisse, and Munch are losing their signature chromium and cadmium-based colours over time. Long thought to be a matter of exposure to light, science now has determined that it is **humidity** more than light that degrades the colour of these famous paintings. In the future, the gallery environments must control for humidity. This can act as metaphor for personal finance values degrading over time. The family must ascertain if, and how, the environment is inhospitable and/or unsustainable, and rectify this before too much damage is done.

On the other hand, there may be hope…according to astrophysicist/author Erich Jantsch, who said, "In chemistry, the term dissipative structures demonstrates that disorder can be a source of a new order; thus, growth appears from disequilibrium. **Confusion and chaos may not be the precursor to destruction but to regrowth and creativity**."

> *History is largely about energy flows being captured, contained, released, transferred, and subsiding. And new energy sources correlate with innovation. Major advances in civilization are almost invariably triggered by dramatic increases in the flow of energy through society.*
> —Steven Berlin Johnson

And so it may be, too, for individuals and families. Civilizations have reinvented energy from sticks to coal to oil to nuclear fission. Successful families must find their own way to reinvent the founding generation's success traits. Drawing from

Steven Johnson's observation, they need to create *new energy sources* to propel the family's life trajectories and to fend off family entropy.

In 2018, Professor Adrian Bejan won a Benjamin Franklin Medal for his pioneering inter-disciplinary contribution of the concept of **constructual law***, which states that any system tries to maximize flow.*

Metaphorically, *flow is anything that transports important things from one place to another*. While his discovery pertained to engineering and thermodynamics, it is applicable to social dynamics, economics, the human body, and business. For us here, it applies to multi-generational WealthNess. The better the flow of family values across time, the better the family. If family problems—like job loss, marital discord, or miscreant family members—cause inaction, flow decreases. If this continues unabated, pressure builds and the system, the family, fails. The CFFO must be the driving force to prevent family problems from festering unsolved. Instead, the CFFO must solve the problems wisely and kick-start increased flow to sustain the family organism. Remember what we encountered earlier in the Invocation chapter: *obsta principiis,* the old Roman saying meaning "resist beginnings."

*Welcome back to the **book's main pathway**.*

We can further draw wisdom from paleontologist Stephen Jay Gould, who observed that evolution is not a process of inexorable progress, but rather one of **contingency**. Cambridge professor Nicola Clayton adds a further footnote in saying that, evolutionarily speaking, **intelligence emerges in favourable conditions**. Both of these strike a chord.

For us dealing with personal finance, this advises us that:

- The financial plans we make should include contingencies for the unexpected (at time of writing, read "Covid").
- We need a healthy, not pathological, environment in which to make good financial decisions. If that healthy environment doesn't exist, someone must recognize this and motivate change.

In celestial mechanics, **"escape velocity"** *is the minimum speed needed for a free object to escape from the gravitational influence of a primary body.*

This informs us that, if epigenetics has burdened us with poor family personal finance, we need to cause enough change to **break away from that negative orbit.** If you want your offspring to lead a life of WealthNess, teach them the values that will engender WealthNess. Be deliberate about this. What does that mean? It means you need to think through and execute a "program" to achieve this. Keep reading.

2.3 Root Purposes

Finding the Real Value of Your Money

*Money needs to have a **purpose** in order to be deployed intelligently. No purpose… no strategy; no strategy…no coherent deployment.*

Jane Fonda and Lee Marvin starred together in the 1960s film entitled *Cat Ballou,* which was set in the American Wild West. Marvin portrayed a former gunslinger who had seen better days and was wallowing in alcoholism. Fonda had an agenda whereby she needed to reform him to his better days for her purpose. She was interviewing him on her ranch and asked him to display his present skill with his quick draw. His objective was to fire six rapid shots at a nearby windmill. He pulled his six-shooter from its holster and proceeded to fire a volley of six bullets, each of which caused a "twang" as the bullets hit the moving blades of the windmill. "Good shooting," she comments. "Actually, ma'am," he says, "I was aiming for the spaces!"

And so it is for your money's purposes. You need to know what you are trying to accomplish. You cannot declare after the fact that: "I was aiming for the spaces!"

Really, our **purposes** are (or should be) defined/derived from our philosophy and attitudes. We can reflect back on the Swiss study in the 2.2 Root Attitudes section, which identified purposes like status, respect, power, social climbing, report card, freedom, and, perhaps for some of us, wealth as an ends to itself.

Your lifestyle and related cost of living are at the front of the line of your root purposes. Many of the purposes identified in the Swiss study are contributing drivers to that number.

Cost of living is a complicated subject—perhaps a sacred cow—that drives the bus. If it is your habit to annually spend more than you make, then saving, investing, and legacy topics are very short chapters! Sometimes the "solution" is family welfare from the presiding generation. Alternately, your singular but complex job is to look at those Swiss drivers and dissect your spending in order to bring it down. It may require a tsunami impact on your lifestyle to re-align your finances with your expectations (remember the pilot in section 2.1).

When I am wearing my financial planning hat and preparing a formal financial plan, the big question that always falls back on the client to answer is: What's your burn rate? AKA your cost of living? It is usually very difficult for the client to answer this. Financially minded people frequently are the ones who actually track their spending and can answer the question. Most of the rest give up. This forces us to derive a very rough-and-ready proxy answer: How much did you make (after tax)? How much did you save (into saving vehicles)? We guess the difference is what you spent.

Way back in the 1500s, Bernardo Davanzati conjured the perspective of **value-in-use** *versus* **value-in-exchange**.

Still today, it creates a perspective that can be very salient in making financial decisions. Money is only an instrument, agent, or broker. It brokers the transition between the acquisition of the wealth and its disposition to answer some purpose, generating what economists call "utility," and we might call "having fun." The "return" on money as an instrument is always calculable and reportable. Once that instrument is converted into human utility, its value measure is no longer calculable or reportable, e.g., what was the "value" of that vacation? Of a new car? Of a kitchen reno? That seems like a silly statement. But perhaps it is not. The fast pace of Western society today has anesthetized the experience of gratitude for that conversion of financial utility to human utility.

Sketches in Personal Finance

Let's look at a story about value in exchange. My client became widowed in his mid-sixties. He and his wife had lived on a large (subdividable) lot. The house itself was 4,500 square feet and seventy years old. Living single now, he had to decide what to do. The property was large for one person. The entire outside gardens and interior needed renovations. But, upon sale, it likely all would be torn down and sold for lot value only. Simply said, every renovation dollar spent would be bull-dozed: value in exchange—zero; value in use—depends upon how long he resided there. If he did $100,000 in renovations and sold it two years later, the value in use cost $50,000 per year! So, the decision was: a) sell now b) spend the reno dollars and stay for a long time or c) spend little or nothing and leave in a few years. What would you do? He chose b) (and that was me).

You need to know what you want your money to do. To illustrate this, I was sitting in a boardroom meeting with my eighty-year-old client, whom I had known for many years. She was recently widowed and our mission that day was to address the redrafting of her new will. While she had raised two daughters, she was a bit unusual for a woman of her generation because she had worked through most of her prime years. Both she and her husband had modest income jobs, but they were part of the generation that knew how to save and knew how not to spend. She and her husband together had downsized from the family home to a nice low-storey condo development. From that modest background, today she was a millionaire, and an HNW (high net worth) investor, as she had a portfolio slightly over one million dollars.

I asked her again, "What's the money for?" She fidgeted a bit and looked blankly back at me.

"Do your daughters know what you are worth?" I asked.

"No," she replied.

This threw me off for a moment until I remembered a life-changing ah-hah I experienced during a week I spent on a beach in Mexico with my wife.

She and I resolutely spent a week every March somewhere in Mexico, during which my mission was to restore my energy, but it was also to do some reading. That particular week I had the pleasure and privilege of meeting author Nick Murray, also a New York investment manager. We didn't actually meet…I had fallen upon one of his books written to advisors, like me. In it, he instilled in me that all wealth ultimately must have a purpose, whether that be short term to buy a new car next year or long term for multi-generations into the future. Until an investor/advisor knows the timeline on money calls, he or she can't properly deploy the funds for the duration. And so, we should ask his question: **What's the money for**?

No doubt, Nick had experienced, like me, the blank response to that question. But he wisely provided me with a backup plan, and I responded by asking her two more questions: First, **"Who do you love?"** then, **"What do you love?"**

Answers to these two questions might unearth the answer to the original question. I say "might." In my own personal case, it directly led me to make two endowments to causes very dear to me.

Contrarily, Virginia Woolf cast some cold water on this when she observed that, "Our passions are uncharted."

Armed with enthusiastic intent, I returned to my client with these two clarifiers… and still drew a blank. However, I teased out that her beneficiaries were her two daughters. We will hear more about them below in the Meteorite Club.

So, over to YOU with these questions (take the moment **now** to do this). What's your money for? And if you are stuck:

> Who do you love?
> What do you love?

The simple, right answer, of course, is that money is different things to different people.

But the first answer likely is **me**, meaning **you**. The money is for you…in fact two you's: you and your partner; and You-Today and You-Tomorrow. You need to ensure that you have enough wealth to get through your lifetime in whatever style you desire, or is dictated by your circumstances, e.g., health. This is indeed **life's second-biggest question** and ought to be addressed with verisimilitude, rather than speculative conjecture. The truth should be found by undertaking a formal financial plan at some juncture in time…as discussed in Chapter 4.

After that may come us-the-many: the family that you wish to leave a legacy for the enrichment of their lives, and maybe for close friends. These speak to the "Who do you love?" question. After that may come the world, narrowly described as the community immediately around you (local hospitals and other local agencies) or more broadly described (causes around the world). These last two, of course, answer the "What do you love?" question.

Passing Your Wealth Forward

When we introduce others into the mix of our own wealth, be it today inter vivos or tomorrow upon passing, it adds complexity to our task of managing our financial affairs.

In his book *Six Dimensions of Wealth,* author James Hughes has captured this issue so insightfully. As we motion to bestow wealth upon a giftee, we need to be fully aware of what **persona** we are portraying in that exchange. Are we purely a benign neutral benefactor passing on wealth with no strings, only well wishes and love? Are we acting as facilitator to assist that giftee to accomplish some purpose, e.g., buying a home? Are we acting as influencer to encourage the giftee to achieve some purpose conceived or approved by us? Are we acting as a manipulator to force actions upon the giftee that they may not see as important? Or as a quid-pro-quo to tease out actions or behaviours unrelated to the giftee's deployment of said funds? "I will give you money if you quit smoking." Are we acting as avoider? "I failed to raise you to manage money well and be responsible. It is too late to change that, so I must keep you on financial life support forever."

My eighty-year-old client in the boardroom still couldn't get her head around "What's the money for?" In *The Cycle of the Gift,* James Hughes particularly speaks about how, in the absence of a proper process, gifts of wealth land upon the giftee like a **meteorite** hitting Earth. This is classically so when the family sits down to read the last will and testament of the dearly deceased. Often, the family had no idea what the elder generation had accumulated in wealth. Suddenly, now, they are wealthy!

Sketches in Personal Finance

Welcome to the Meteorite Club: They were two middle-aged women, each with a spouse, no children, long working careers, and deceased mothers who had been clients of mine. They lived five miles apart but never knew each other. But they shared the belief that it wasn't their money, but their mother's, and they both experienced the meteorite effect, as also described by Hughes. They had no idea how much they were inheriting. They each retained me as their advisor after the estate had been settled. A few years later, I sat with each of them to review their portfolio and finances. They both revealed the exact same thing: they hadn't touched the money because "it still wasn't theirs." It took many years before they felt comfortable "owning" that money. Now, they both are retired and dipping into their portfolios for travel funds and quality of life they didn't have before.

Another client received her seven-figure inheritance in her early sixties. Nearing retirement at the time, she had built her own savings of approximately $300,000. But now, the numbers were way bigger, and the quality of her new retirement life was dependent upon this new, larger portfolio. Unfortunately, the market wasn't kind in that first year, so her experience was not pleasant. It is common for investors to take the present and extend that forward. So, the rest of her future retirement was looking grim.

My point here goes back to the leading generation and its responsibility to the following generations. Make them familiar with the gyrations of a portfolio... prepare them to steward wealth such that the meteorite is not traumatic.

Sudden wealth often is dangerous wealth and, sadly, often temporary wealth. The stories of lottery winners are legion and infamous...and true. Meteorite wealth can be the same. This insidious problem with multi-generational stewardship of wealth is known as **Sudden Wealth Syndrome** (SWS), coined by psychologist Stephen Goldbart. It refers to the problems that people encounter should they suddenly come into large sums of money. The sources of such wealth vary from lottery winning to inheritance to speculative gains (in real estate or commercial ventures). SWS throws the first generation into the deep end, with a lack of grounding in money stewardship. Far too few take the immediate step to seek wise counsel. Aside from the risk of "blowing it all" (see endless stories about lottery winners), other impacts include fear of responsibility, dis-engagement from pre-existing social affiliations, and guilt about their good fortune. This segues quickly to a knock-on effect to the generation(s) following.

Your wealth may amply support your family for your generations forward ad infinitum...or until the meteorite really does hit! Infinity as a number is too mind boggling for most of us, except mathematicians, to ponder. Infinity as the duration of the wealth you have created in your life-time is **totally** incomprehensible. My clients find it overwhelming to contemplate their wealth transfer even only as far out as the **next** generation! In this matter, we are naturally more ploughmen than astronauts. "Just let me hoe this next row of dirt." But ad infinitum doesn't mean you have to be figuring out what your appropriate investment portfolio should look like in the year 2420. What it means is this: your following generation is the **agent** of your wealth for that next piece of Earth's history. They will be your stewards. And your astronaut job is to make sure they are equal to the task. Your will ought not to hand them a blind cheque. Beyond giving them a legacy of WealthNess, you also need to instill in them the same task of preparing their following generation.

The same principle applies here if you are a single person with no direct heirs. You are still leaving your wealth to **someone**—unless it is targeted to formal charities.

Chapter 3: Family and Finance and Chapter 6: Legacy will advance this topic.

2.4 Root Sources

You Are an Asset to Yourself

"Money doesn't grow on trees," my father used to say.

That said, one Sunday when I was little, my parents and I went for a walk around a little lake. A forest of deciduous trees grew right down to the lake pathway we walked along. I was walking a few paces ahead of my parents, anticipating the ducks at lakeside. My father was flicking small coins high over my head so that they fell on the ground in front of me. "Hmmmm," he said, "maybe there are money trees after all!"

Indeed…money doesn't grow on trees. The money we have has to come from some place. I think these places can be summarized into four sources: working, saving, compounding, and what James Hughes earlier termed as "meteorites." These are bolts of wealth that come to us gratuitously from external sources: gifts, inheritances, lotteries.

> *Assets are institutional vessels that capture and store human energy.*
> —Robert McGarvey, journalist

So, simplistically, wealth accumulation is the return on human energy. It could be said, then, that the life cycle process for most of us is about the monetization of human capital into financial capital, through the earning-and-saving cycle.

Working is, of course, the largest and most common source for most of us.

Your investment in yourself—education, experience, energy, opportunity, sacrifice, etc.—determines the earned income that you command in the work world. Get good at something! Preferably something you love. Define your skills more broadly…diversify your affiliations and experiences, e.g., travelling exposes you to other cultures, views, and lifestyles. "Investing" involves both human and financial capital. Expanding both can compound in a positive feedback loop: increased experiences may increase your skills, which may increase your earned income (and therefore your saving), which increases your financial capital, which may open doors to more work skills. Dennis Jaffe states that the neglect of human capital is the ultimate cause of the dissipation of financial capital.

When you sit down and list your assets and liabilities, you probably don't list yourself as an asset.
But, for many of us, we *are* our biggest asset. How do we ascribe a value to ourselves on that balance sheet?? Actually, it isn't that difficult. In the real world of finance, you can write a cheque to, for instance, an insurance company and,

in exchange, they will promise to pay you $x per month for the rest of your life. Valuing **you** is the exact opposite of that—your monthly after-tax paycheque can be valued today as the present value of that lifetime salary until you retire or die.

So, here we need to take a short course in Finance 101 and "present value tables." (These are readily available on the internet, e.g., www.accountingtools.com. There are four different tables for different purposes.) The finance table called "present value of an annuity" is the one you need here, which will provide a number that you multiply by your annual earned income to value your lifetime income stream as of today. That number may need a bit of finessing as you get pay raises, promotions, and new jobs over your working career—let's start with $50,000. To find that multiplier number on the table of rows and columns, you need two things: how many years you plan to work (that's **your** call! Let's say twenty years) and a "discount" rate (this is a bit fuzzier, but let's use 10%).

Go along the table on the twenty-year row to the 10% column, and you will see the number 9.3649. The product of that number times $50,000 equals $468,245, which is the value today of your career as an asset working for twenty more years. As each year goes by, you move up one row on the 10% column, and your future earnings figure diminishes…ultimately to zero when you retire. Now we have a quantitative number of human capital that adds onto your list of other assets, like your home and retirement funds at the bank.

If you are a closet accountant and like the idea of "capitalizing" your earned income annuity stream over the years, you might undertake an annual or periodic listing of your net wealth. It would be logical, then, over the years to assess the progress of your net wealth, i.e., what's the total? Taking it a step further, each time you might ascribe what the proportions are of, say, your human capital and your financial capital. As above, by definition your human capital declines as your "n" (remaining number of years that you plan to work) decreases. (Though perhaps not. Maybe you got that big promotion and raise. Maybe you work until age 80.) And hopefully, Mr. Stock Market has your financial capital compounding.

I worked up a sample spreadsheet of this that you can duplicate with your own data. I have only reproduced the first nine years for illustrative purposes, due to space constraint. The entire spreadsheet runs for twenty years.

The assumptions in this model are:

- You are presently age forty-five and will work twenty more years.
- Your starting values at age forty-five were: Home $1,000,000; mortgage $400,000; **RRSPs** $300,000.

- Your (or family) "disposable income" (your earned income after tax) is $100,000 and indexed at 3%.
- Your mortgage pays 5% and amortizes over twenty years.
- Your house appreciates at 2% over twenty years.
- Your investment return is 5% over twenty years.
- You contribute annually $18,000 to your RRSP and $6,500 to your TFSA

age	46	47	48	49	50	51	52	53	54
Home	1,000,000	1,020,000	1,040,400	1,061,208	1,082,432	1,104,081	1,126,162	1,148,686	1,171,659
RRSP	300,000	333,000	367,650	404,033	442,234	482,346	524,463	568,686	615,121
TFSA	-	6,500	13,325	20,491	28,016	35,917	44,212	52,923	62,069
Mortgage	400,000	387,053	373,443	359,137	344,099	328,291	311,675	294,209	275,849
"You"	836,492	844,745	851,007	854,918	856,071	854,001	848,178	837,998	822,775
Networth	1,736,492	1,817,193	1,898,939	1,981,513	2,064,654	2,148,053	2,231,341	2,314,084	2,395,775
Stats:									
Home,net	35%	35%	35%	35%	36%	36%	37%	37%	37%
Financial	17%	19%	20%	21%	23%	24%	25%	27%	28%
"You"	48%	46%	45%	43%	41%	40%	38%	36%	34%

The fruit of this spreadsheet is best depicted in a fairly simple graph, which shows the proportions of your three wealth sources—you, your home (net of mortgage), your financial investments—over the last twenty years of your working life (age forty-five to sixty-five).

Note that, at age forty-six, your human capital is almost 50% of your worth, and when you retire, that number shrinks to zero. At age sixty-five, your home and investments are approximately 50/50% of your wealth.

Keep an eye on the proportionate contribution of your house value over the years. The insane rise in urban residential real estate values in these recent years has been a welcome bump to net wealth. But it would be wise to track the percentage of wealth your home represents **across your periodic valuation periods.** Be wary of the statistic in the earlier discussion on the "wealth effect" in section 2.1.

The final graph summarizes the trajectories of your three sources of wealth over the twenty years. While "you" as an asset wanes to zero when you retire, your other sources wax.

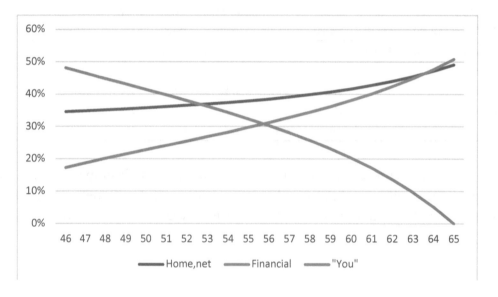

You might think that this human capital calculation is too "accountant-ish." But I think it is: a) easy to do and b) insightful in understanding the engine rooms of accumulating the wealth that you will need in retirement.

Factors to Consider When Considering Retirement

Let's take this one step further. Let's imagine that, for whatever reason, you desperately would like to retire early. While a formal financial plan is probably the best vehicle to address early retirement (more on that in Chapter 4), a revised human capital calculation with a smaller "n" may be insightful. We will speak to this topic, called the HFactor, in section 4.2.

Eventually, most of us reach stages in life when we ask ourselves:

- When **can** I retire?
- When **should** I retire?
- When **will** I retire?

"Can" refers to "freedom" date however freedom is defined. It might mean the year that your work pension fund is fully vested. It might mean when you can collect your work pension with no early penalty. It might mean when your financial plan says it is OK. It might tie into your partner's plans or health.

"Should" is more complex and less factual…more impressionistic. Is there an opportunistic time at work? Are you fearing the overnight transition to suddenly having no routines? Are you attached to the social and neural rewards of working? Is your health condition contributory? Is it attached to your partner's plans or health?

"Will" is the collection of thoughts, plans, circumstances, and conjecture which ultimately cause you to embrace the day. We will drill deeper into this in section 4.3 Longevity.

Continuing to make earned income may be about **security**. Your financial plan may say it is OK to retire now, but lots of longitudinal assumptions (like rates of investment return) are inherent in the financial math of that forecast. An extra working year will multiply the benefits. Why? Here are four financial reasons to keep working:

1) That extra year's income will buy the groceries for that year, leaving your financial capital untouched.
2) You likely will be able to add savings to your financial capital with some of the year's earned income.
3) Leaving your financial capital untouched leaves more money in the pot to compound during that year for future groceries.
4) Continuing to make earned income may become an addiction; in fact, I call it just that—the addiction of earned income. This is particularly true for high-income earners. There is a buzz from bringing in a lot of money. And it frees your conscience from having to be more judicious with your spending habits (back to the pilot, again, in section 2.1).

However, if you are a high-income earner, take note: the "system" works against you. Over their working years, high-income earners are treated prejudicially by the tax and pension systems in at least seven ways:

1) If you are lucky enough to be part of a company pension plan, the legislated contribution-math during your career builds a pension cheque than cannot be anywhere near your working salary.
2) If you are dependent upon "self-pensioning," the contribution math there similarly works against you, as you only can contribute to 18% of a capped salary, which is in the $150,000 inflation-adjusted range.
3) The contribution math to your government working pension is also capped to an inflation-adjusted income of approx. $65,000.
4) You won't collect the universal senior's government pension because it will be clawed back, effectively meaning that you never got it in the first place.
5) Tax-free savings accounts are capped at inflation adjusted contributions of $6,500 per year.
6) You are likely in a 50%+ marginal tax bracket on your income above, roughly, $220,000.
7) The new longevity of today's retirees means you may have a lot more retirement years to be funded. Whatever you have accumulated has to be spread thinner over a longer time horizon, thus leaving less per year.

Left-leaning people may say of this hardship: "Too bad; so sad. Society rules shouldn't be favouring the rich." But this isn't about favouring the rich as it is about treating them fairly. Sure, they would get bigger tax deductions annually from higher contribution levels, but that translates into higher withdrawal amounts through retirement that give taxes to the federal fisc later.

"Income averaging" is a tax term. "Lifestyle averaging" is my financial planning term that needs to gain familiarity amongst high-income earners. It means that we need to be thinking today about today and tomorrow. High income today may spawn a lifestyle that can't be sustained when we retire and trade our earned income for lesser pensions and investment income. That pilot couple in Section 2.1 needed financial wisdom, planning, and change management to deal precisely with this. So, if you are one of these people, understand you may need to lower your lifestyle now and increase your saving now to create a bigger pool of capital which, in turn, will create a larger investment income in retirement. In other words, by adding to your savings, you are sacrificing lifestyle today for a better lifestyle tomorrow. The alternative to this is either to accept that drop in lifestyle or draw down capital (i.e., your estate) to fill the lifestyle gap.

The Importance of Saving

*This brings us to **saving** as an inevitable root source in most of our lives.*

Economists define "saving" as: disposable income minus consumption. Let's start with some terminology: "saving" differs from "savings." Saving is the active verb for putting money aside, whilst savings is the noun for the pot of wealth resulting from your saving.

Analysis of longitudinal Canadian household saving rates is not particularly insightful. The annual rate since the mid-1990s has been 0–5%. The rate prior to that and back through the 1970s was always higher than 5% and for twenty of those years was double-digit. The reasons for the slide from double digits to less than 5% are no doubt multi-fold, but we think one aspect has been the consumer-driven society for many years. History has attached various labels to Western society—the Age of Enlightenment, the Industrial Revolution, and the Dark Ages to name a few. I think that sometime in the future our present era will be back-named the Age of Materialism. It is a common view in Western cultures today that people should spend. Governments encourage this to take the fiscal load off them to stimulate a distressed economy. And so, for instance, there are, on average, four credit cards issued to every man, woman, and child in America.

Economist John Maynard Keynes believed that people put very little thought into their saving decisions. He further believed that the saving function was not derived from the **saving need** but from the availability of unspent income. In plainer language, saving is at the back of the line, not the front. He said that, given the economic concept of "propensity to save," saving rates will increase if and when incomes rise. Modern research by Lusardi in the US, as well as others in Canada, supports this thought today.

> *Remarkably few people have a plan to save, even though it may be one of the **most fundamentally important aspects of life**.*

The term "income" merits further explanation. The metric used for the denominator in government saving calculation is "disposable income"—your after-tax income. We always need to be wary of that old saw: "Lies, damn lies, and statistics." We ought to be reticent in absorbing pure clean numbers just because they are numbers, especially when we try to intuit meaning to those numbers. So, for instance, the late, great economist Milton Friedman posited a different take on the denominator (the income) of the saving-rate calculation. He proposed "permanent income" as that denominator. He believed that people allocate their spending and saving ratio against this number. To the extent their incomes fluctuate ("transitory," per Friedman), they tend to adjust their saving, not their spending, component. It would be difficult to aggregate data for national saving-rate calculation when the denominator is a "fuzzy" number prescribed household-by household.

The term "saving" merits further explanation, too.

We all likely have our own definition flash through our mind when we see that word, and it involves transferring some of our hard-earned cash into some savings vehicle. But we also "save" when we reduce debt. Most of us have a mortgage in our lives, whose principal draws down monthly over the long amortization period… ending with the wonderful "mortgage burning party" when it is fully retired. Any other debt we have likely comes in two flavours: good and bad. Good debt would include a loan taken out, perhaps, to acquire an investment or business. Bad debt would include your credit card and/or line-of-credit balances that arose from consumer spending.

But how would you define saving for the retiree or capitalist who doesn't get up to go to work in the morning. Does the interest and dividend income earned, but not spent, count as that person's saving? Is the investment income earned and compounding in a pension plan account for a working person part of saving? Or do behavioural finance's "mental accounts" cause that person not to even think about this money until retirement?

*The importance of **framing** bears upon the act of saving; people find it easier to seek **external** goalposts than to establish their own.*

As a result, they are susceptible to societal cues which primarily tell them how much to spend and, secondarily, how much to save. The societal cue to save is indeed very abstruse. People are more likely to showcase the things they have bought than how much they contributed to their savings account. So, in the absence of their own plans, people's cues need to come from various other places—close peers, financial professionals, media, employers, governments, etc. (Here is where your **sea anemone tentacles** may be called upon.) Mandatory contributions (RPPs and CPP) and benchmark savings rates (18% of earned income for RRSPs; $6,500 per annum for TFSAs) are examples. Research by Thaler and Benartzi showed that people are pliable and can be coaxed into saving, and even into **accelerated saving**. Where a financial planner may not be able to convince people that they ought to have a formal financial plan, at least guiding them to a saving plan that requires them to stretch is a good half-victory.

Work in behavioural finance suggests that people work with different "mental accounts." Different pots of saving efforts are intended for different purposes—a house, a car, a new roof, education, vacation money, retirement money, etc.

Some may view this as a quirky way to approach household finance, but if it works—great!

I am very fond of mental accounts, which I call "silos," and I personally keep two such accounts in particular—for renovations and travel. I put funds into these accounts variously throughout the year. It is a great relief when renos or travel costs arise and—presto—there already is money put aside. I periodically also comb through my cheque stubs and visa statements to track how much gets spent in these two areas. Lastly, and importantly, I also periodically verify that my real bank account has a balance greater than or equal to the notional balances in these two accounts.

Think about your own silos…what are your dreams?

Ready to power up your understanding of saving? If so, take this detour. (If you don't want to take this detour right now, jump ahead until you see the Circle/easiest sign.)

What Is Your "TSR"? (Total Saving Rate)

I believe that there are in fact at least two saving metrics—"earned" and "total," and each is useful.

The first measure of saving—earned—is the more popular one implied by the government and in the media. It is the "sacrifice" one that economists call the propensity to save. I propose to call this **"earned saving rate" (ESR),** which is the saving put aside annually divided by annual earned (disposable) income, that being salaries, wages, and self-employment income. (In the case of incorporated entrepreneurs, it should also include annual retained earnings before tax.) Earned saving includes money put aside into "savings places," like pension plans, bank deposits, and brokerage accounts, and also should include "saving" applied to debt reduction, like home mortgages, as above.

I have coined a second measure of saving as **"total saving rate" (TSR),** which calculates a **broader measure of saving divided by a broader measure of income**. "Total saving" includes the earned saving above **plus** the investment income earned in your investment accounts (being interest and dividends and the realized and unrealized net appreciation in those accounts over the year), but also subtracts any withdrawals you may have taken **from** your investment accounts to fund life costs. "Total income" includes the earned income from ESR above **plus** the investment income earned in your investment accounts (the amount just calculated in the previous sentence). In other words, the investment earnings you leave untouched in your investment accounts is, in effect, **further saving by you**.

The aggregation of this information allows you to calculate your annual, **simple ESR and TSR**. But be prepared for a surprise. In a bear market, the annual return (and saving) from your investment accounts may be a negative number, meaning negative saving, and that negative amount may exceed the earned saving you are doing out of household income. As a result, it would be wise to calculate a second saving rate—long-term compound—for both ESR and TSR. This will smooth out the problem with negative-saving years and give you a good long-term benchmark of your saving discipline. (We will get deeper into rate of return knowledge in Chapter 5).

The following is an example of a chart that you can set up quite easily. It is drawn from real-life data involving a couple.

Year	2004	2005	2006	2007	2008	2009	2010	2011	2012	2013	2014
Earned income	137,414	120,198	167,445	180,701	190,860	140,771	129,853	140,395	158,464	128,157	106,164
Investment income	2,605	7,554	4,596	13,613	(11,916)	(20,527)	21,489	26,145	5,894	29,952	54,661
Mortgage paydown	18,192	20,100	20,475	21,225	20,008	-	-	-	-	-	-
Earned saving	14,738	22,997	42,938	32,125	58,174	32,634	21,090	31,233	9,297	22,084	23,118
Simple ESR	24%	36%	38%	30%	41%	23%	16%	22%	6%	17%	22%
Simple TSR	25%	40%	40%	34%	37%	10%	28%	34%	9%	33%	48%

The chart follows the years 2004–2014 during which the couple entered their peak earned income years and included a resolve to seriously save for semi-retirement in 2015. They started with very small pension savings. But, as their earned saving grew with contributions to their pension accounts, the reinvested return on saving grew, thus creating the difference between ESR and TSR. That said, you can see how bad stock market years (2008–9) contributed **negative** income, **lowering** the **simple TSR below** the **simple ESR**. They also paid off their mortgage in 2008, lowering the TSR in 2009. A further reality, not reflected above, is that, after 2008 the couple might deploy their former monthly mortgage payments into another investment account, thus raising their TSR.

Though this concept is not considered out there in the world, **the TSR truly is your saving rate** and, hopefully, can be a statistic that **makes you feel better about your saving effort**. Perhaps the Age of Materialism will pass into the history books while the new era awaits definition. While the Age of Materialism has us finding reward from internal and external recognition from the things around us—the cars, homes, fancy vacations, etc.—perhaps the new era will provide such satisfaction from bragging about one's "TSR"!

*Welcome back to the **book's main pathway**.*

Planning for the Future

So...when did we invent the future?

A silly question? In his book *The Long View*, Richard Fisher suggests: "Life had survived for billions of years **without us having the ability to picture the longer-term past or future**. When it finally emerged in the human brain, it was a new evolutionary invention."

Many today would opine that we are very planted in the present, tend to discount the past, and ignore the future. In fact, empirical research has uncovered an interesting thought: that **mentally processing our past aids us to project into our future**. Further from Fisher: "When people picture their future selves, the person they tend to see is something of a stranger."

Sketches in Personal Finance

> *Hi, Dan. Nice to meet you. **My name is Dan 2035**. I wanted us to meet, so you can get to know your future self. Only when that person becomes real to you will you appreciate what I am going to ask you to do now.*

Dan had an interesting story. He was age forty when we started this conversation, but I had already known him for fifteen years. As a young man in his twenties, he got a job working with the owner in a two-man retail hobby shop. They worked together for ten years when the owner decided it was time to retire, and he had been grooming Dan to buy the business, which Dan did. Dan ran it well for fifteen years and made a healthy income through his forties. At some point, I sat down with him in 2005 to discuss the long-term future.

As is common for people passing through life's stages, Dan and his wife were financially focused on raising their two kids and paying down their mortgage. Each had piled up six-figure RRSP room, and their existing RRSPs totalled $40,000. I encouraged them to embark on a ten-year program to age fifty: to a) use up all of this accumulated room and b) also make their ongoing **new**, annual contribution limits. This represented a hefty cash call over that decade. But they did it. And we celebrated that final catch-up year. Within five years of that, technological advancement and cheap competitors forced Dan to close the doors of a fifty-year-old business, and re-career himself at age fifty-five—not an easy task. But by then, the $40,000 had grown to $835,000, which further grew to $1 million by age sixty. It had been my job twenty years prior to act as his retired avatar to secure a significant call to action. After that, it was all thanks to him!

Earlier in section 2.2, we cited Adrian Bejan and his concept of constructal law, which states that any system tries to maximize flow.

Metaphorically, flow is anything that transports important things from one place to another. Previously, we talked about the flow of genomic family values, and how they are "transported" from one generation to another. Now, let's be more practical and talk about the **flow of funds**, which transports buying power from one time to another (including one generation to another). Over your lifetime, these funds are siloed and come in from: a) your labours b) income from your savings and c) blessings passed on to you from others. They go out to: a) fund lifestyle b) fund saving and c) fund your blessings, whilst you are alive, or upon passing, to the people and causes dear to you. That's it. Think of them in those six silos.

At stock points in your lifetime, you have accumulated certain pots of wealth, which I will call capital. These can be money in the bank, other investments, real estate, etc. These, too, effectively are siloed:

- Working capital: to pay your ongoing bills today
- Fun capital: to set aside for holidays, renovations, etc.
- Retirement capital: to pay your ongoing bills over the rest of your life
- Loving capital: your **present** worth to touch the people and things you love
- Legacy capital: your **future** worth to touch the people and things you love

The last silo merits further thought. It is the residual of your retirement capital upon death. That can be a "fill-in-the-blanks" number solely upon your passing; on the other hand, many clients have simply said to me: "The kids get whatever is left!" Remember Nick Murray here!

That said, according to author Eric Barker: "People who contemplate the end actually behave in healthier ways—and therefore may actually live longer."

So...there's your reward incentive to plan. If you wish to ensure that a particular sum is there for your inheritors, you need to work backwards whilst alive. This needs a financial planning forecast to find the right mix of "your today" versus "their tomorrow."

Sketches in Personal Finance

Later in Chapter 5: Investing, we will talk about "late-starters," but here, let's talk about "early starters."

Starting a saving program at an early age makes a huge difference. You can be the biggest beneficiary of Einstein's infatuation with long-term compounding. Here's the story about our Olympic athlete client. Her passion was snowboarding as a youngster, and she was good at it. She got onto the National Olympic Team, travelled the ski world at competitions, got a snowboard-producing sponsor, and did participate at one Olympic venue. All of this came to an end by the time she was thirty. However, unlike most of her peers who spent that decade of their life in school or travelling, she earned a handsome income, and saved a lot of it. The result was that she had accumulated investable assets of $376,000 by then.

If she left that $376,000 untouched for thirty-five years to age sixty-five, the account would grow (at 7%) to $4 million!! However, here is what really happened. With her twenties devoted to excellence in sports, her thirties needed to re-career with some supporting education, punctuated by family formation. The result through that next decade was that she needed to draw upon her portfolio to make ends meet. She drew the portfolio income out every year, with the result that, at age forty, the value was still approx. $376,000. Re-engaging the power of compounding to age sixty-five, now for twenty-five years, the account would grow to approx. $2 million—a drop by half. Taking away the compounding income from age thirty to age forty cost $2 million!

To be really impressive, compounding needs to pair up with the Law of Large Numbers.

I have to cheat a bit here. Definitionally, this law is associated with statistics, and says that as a sample size increases, the validity of the statistical properties is more closely realized. We need to float a **separate** definition associated with **finance**, which says, simplistically, as the numbers get bigger, the numbers get bigger! In the first scenario, at age sixty-four, our snowboarder's portfolio would be worth approximately $3.74 million. The income in her sixty-fifth year would be $260,000—several times the average industrial wage today. In the second scenario, the income in her sixty-fifth year would only be $131,000—only half! (Full disclosure: I sold the sizzle on this and didn't remind you about the impact of thirty-five years of inflation.)

So, our Olympian's amended message to you is: "Start early! Don't touch! Have a great retirement!"

Are you ready for a difficult angle on real estate investing? If so, take this detour. (If you don't want to take this detour right now, jump ahead until you see the Circleleasiest sign.)

Investing in Real Estate

> *Turn…Turn…Turn…To everything there is a season, and a time to every purpose under the heaven.* (Ecclesiastes 3:1).

Let's talk about root sources and the philosophy/purpose of our **retirement** assets.

In my adult lifetime, real estate has been the largest and broadest source of wealth accumulation.

"God isn't making any more of it." So said my father when I was just a little boy. Turns out that, of course, this wasn't his own quote, but he was the first one to introduce it to me. He has been dead now for thirty-five years, but if he was alive today to see what real estate is fetching, he would be incredulous. The family home he left on his passing was worth $175,000 in those days, and recently was assessed at the top of the speculative market at close to $5 million.

But…to everything there is a season, and a time for every purpose.

I cite clients who have directed all of their lifetime's wealth accumulation strategy to acquiring real estate. In their sunset years, their balance sheets are truly amazing, with massive net worth. But they are not comfortably off. Their retirement is fraught with cash flow constraints that impede the quality of their last years. The issue? In the Investing chapter, you will see that the return on an asset includes three elements: cash income, unrealized appreciation, and realized appreciation. When you buy 200 shares of a blue-chip stock, it pays a quarterly cash dividend. Over time, hopefully, it goes up in value on paper (unrealized), and one day you might sell, say, half your holding to realize half of the gain into cash. The dividends are tax-preferred with a tax credit, and the gain is also tax preferred, half of it being free of tax.

Sketches in Personal Finance

I had an eighty-five-year-old couple with $24 million in residential real estate, and a mortgage of only $1.5 million against that. That's a debt-to-asset ratio of roughly 1:17. But cash outflow to the $1.5 million mortgage was substantial every month, and the couple was always watching their spending.

When you own real estate, your monthly rental income receipts rely upon steady tenants, and you have costs to pay before you determine your free net rental cash flow. If it is a residential rental, you likely are constrained by law as to rental increases. Meanwhile, civic property taxes escalate at an alarming rate, which the landlord must bear. The beauty is that the property is going up in value (unrealized). Unlike the stock, you can't halve down by selling part of the property, thus converting part of the gain to realized. If you need cash, another downside is liquidity. A blue-chip stock can be sold any day, and you have the cash in your hands in a flash. Real estate markets can shut down and go "no bid" for months or years unless you are prepared to significantly drop the price.

But all of that is fine, depending upon your situation. While you are working, your earned income is buying the groceries, and you are happy if your rental unit can at least be cash-neutral after the mortgage payment, and meanwhile, it keeps going up in value! But when you become a retiree in your third or fourth quarters, it all may change. Now you need passive income cash flow to buy the groceries! The mortgage may be paid off by then, but odds are that there still isn't a lot of cash flow to live off.

In particular here, we must embrace the difference between **cash flow production** and **wealth accumulation**. Remember that the reward we get from any investment is some combination of cash flow (dividends, interest, rents) and, hopefully, appreciation in value. The latter is only realizable by selling the asset. Some assets have cash flow but no appreciation (think term deposit at the bank), some have appreciation but no cash flow (think gold bar), and most have a combination of the two…in varying proportions. In today's world, the cash flow production from stocks and bonds is, say, 2–3%.

What are you requiring your investable assets to produce for you?

If you have a good, steady job that "pays the bills," you aren't looking to your assets for cash flow; thus, unrealized appreciation is just what you need from those assets. But, the day you retire, things change. Your monthly paycheque is gone, but it might be replaced by a (likely smaller) pension cheque. In fact, you might collect a few pension cheques: one or two from the federal government and maybe some work pension(s). These are special, and I call them **"mailbox"** income, because they come at regular intervals (monthly) and in know-able amounts until you (or your partner) dies. But you still might need to tap your investable assets to meet your monthly bills and/or vacation/renovation/car budgets. You will be looking to the cash income provided therefrom to bridge the gap. If that sum is insufficient, now you potentially have a problem.

Let's say you need $40,000 one-off to buy a new car. You need to tap the wealth-accumulating assets to convert unrealized gains to realized gains (and assuming they are not losses!). Two issues now stare you in the face: first, are the assets liquid? Second, are they "divisible"? Your real estate asset certainly can't be sold in a few weeks (normally). In fact, there are some real estate market periods where there are no buyers at all. More importantly, your real estate asset is not fungible…meaning that you can't sell the bathroom for $40,000 to buy that car. You would have to sell the whole thing! This creates a third problem that you would cause realized taxable gain on the whole property, not just on the $40,000 that you need to raise. So, through life's stages as you are a working wealth-builder, real estate may be just the ticket. But when you transition to retirement, the goal posts may shift. Perhaps the elderly couple should have pared down their real estate holdings—what we investment managers call "asset allocation rebalancing."

A Diamond reader might point out that the property could be re-mortgaged or mortgaged up to provide some throw-off cash flow from the property. True! Remember that: a) the higher debt will raise the monthly debt service cost thus reducing the monthly cash flow available b) it is likely that the new/higher interest cost isn't tax deductible and/or c) if the property is held in a corporation, the extra draw to you may be taxable.

*Welcome back to the **book's main pathway**.*

Preparing for Life Transitions

The Ecclesiastes 3.1 quote above offers us further insights…this time for stock and bond investors.

Sketches in Personal Finance

Here is a couple who worked hard, saved, and inherited over their lifetimes, and retired in their early sixties with a sizable portfolio in RRSPs, TFSAs, and trading accounts. Through their working lives, they had applied "tax-smart investing" across the portfolio types, with equity orientation in their TFSAs and trading accounts and fixed income orientation in their large RRSPs (which would morph into RRIF income commencing at age seventy-two). With **no** employer pensions, their **portfolio income would be their pensions**. Thus, there was a fairly large annual draw from their trading portfolio through their sixties to pay the bills. The couple also sought to manage their personal tax bracket until the RRIFs kicked in. Here was the kicker: as mentioned above, the trading accounts which had to fund the draws through their sixties had been largely invested for decades in equities to grow. Funding those draws required periodic equity sell-downs for a decade. This exposed market risk and rebalancing issues. In this case, the issue was that the **construction** of the portfolios was built cleverly for the past and is good for the future, but it is not good for a "present" spanning between their retirement and their downstream pension funds.

So, back to Ecclesiastes, with apologies and modification: **to every asset there is a reason.** Also pay attention to the upcoming 4.2 Ages and Stages section. It may be hard to see or accept these transitions, as we humans tend to like things being the same. But strategies that may be right for certain stages in life may need to be reviewed and re-evaluated at other stages in life.

We are reminded of the ploughman plodding up and down the rows and the astronaut gazing up into the skies.

2.5 Happiness and Meaning

The Key to Happiness?

We would be remiss to discuss personal finance without talking about the "soft" stuff.

> *Happiness is…different things to different people…that's what happiness is.*
> —Lyric from "Happiness Is" written by Paul Evans and Paul Parnes

I remember these lyrics from a song when I was a kid. Maybe this is saying all that needs to be said, and maybe this section should stop right here…'nuff said? We'll keep going anyway. I will share with you many different takes on this subject, and you can see which, if any, resonate with you.

Start by reviewing your notes in the Root Attitudes section, when you answered the question "What's the most important thing?"—qualified as it was to exclude, for the moment, your loved ones. Think about how, or if, those answers circle back to contributing to your happiness.

Whether one's beliefs are secular or otherwise, according to Canadian author Mark Anielski: "We cannot deny our spiritual nature…. I find it curious that so many of us who live and work on intellectual planes often long to talk about our spiritual nature…and about the true meaning of life…and being human means to be in touch with that attribute."

Back to Tom Morris, former professor of philosophy at Notre Dame and author of many books: "Now I am forty-five years old…we never talk about anything important. We've lived long enough to have some real questions and maybe even some answers, but there's never any chance to talk about these big questions with other people."

Victor Frankl's famous book *Man's Search for Meaning,* published in 1946, said, in summary, that the most important thing was a "quest for meaning," and he identified three sources:

- In work (doing something significant)
- In courage (during difficult times)
- In love (caring for another person)

He weighed in on happiness, too, and said that it cannot be pursued, rather, it is derivative: "the unintended side-effect of one's dedication to a cause greater than oneself."

Mark Anielski is a leading commentator on happiness and has travelled the world to extol his wisdom and concept of **"genuine wealth**." According to him, the happiest people have a strong sense of community. Other important elements included mental health, physical activity, managing stress levels, and being married. Least important was household income! Here is how he weighed out key contributors: "Your well-being derives from your genetics, upbringing, and environment (50%), from social and recreational activities and meaningful work (40%), and from your income, possessions, and marital health (10%)."

Try scoring yourself on that….

He also said: "…I believe we value most about life: love, meaningful relationships, happiness, joy, freedom, sufficiency, justice, and peace."

Dr. David Blanchflower, economics professor at Dartmouth College, also studies happiness. He and others have found a happiness curve that is U-shaped across a lifetime, with the trough consistently being around age forty-eight around the world. This likely correlates with a "normal life cycle" of growing up, working, raising a family, and retiring. The family formation years are probably the most stressful, with growing kids, mortgages, and career responsibilities. The upsurge in happiness in getting older may relate to the accumulation of wisdom to deal better with life's travails and also having more autonomy.

The **experiences** of childhood years, more than **genetics**, may be the most important contributor to a feeling of wellbeing over a lifetime. We will pick this topic up in section 3.2 Kids and Money.

> *"The set point theory of happiness suggests that our level of subjective well-being is determined primarily by heredity and personality traits ingrained in us **early in life**, and as a result remains **relatively constant** throughout our lives. Our level of happiness may change transiently in response to life events, but then almost always returns to its baseline level as we **habituate to those events** and their consequences over time."*
> —Dr Alex Lickerman, *Psychology Today* magazine

Supporting this, in her book, *Atlas of the Heart,* Brené Brown cited Ian Leslie's belief that happiness is a trait, not a state: "Looking at happiness as a trait, researchers found that people's "usual" level of happiness is fairly stable."

The brilliant, late Hungarian thinker Mihaly Csikszentmihalyi weighed in on happiness, too: "I think in one sense, happiness is being able to do what you can to express who you are…. It could be physical, aesthetic, intellectual…. Most people that are happy are people who can do something well, that expresses their strength, their capacity, and hopefully they are kind of recognized."

*He used the term **autotelic**, essentially meaning self-directed.*

It is an activity that you choose to do, and it is so engrossing that it feels effortless, even though challenging to execute. The very doing of it creates a sense of full existence. The world of neuroscience weighs in with some interesting insights on this. Parts of the brain secrete dopamine, which makes us feel good. The dopamine that releases from the ventral part of the striatum causes a physical dopamine rush. Our autotelic pursuits release, instead, from the caudal and dorsal areas of the striatum, which light up when we are persevering difficult activities.

Another take on happiness is that it is about:

- Autonomy: the degree of ability to control our lives
- Connectivity: with friends and family, and in meaningful depth and openness
- Competency: to progress through life making good decisions

Now score yourself on that….

Another, cryptically short, take is that happiness derives from the excitement of creating a better future. This is topical at the time of writing as the world over deals with Covid and climate change. If the future looks dim, then happiness feels out of reach. We today can only modestly attempt to appreciate the similar feelings, caused by different themes, that our forebears experienced. In difficult times, we have to scratch all the harder to find a happiness lamp-post that we can throw our arms around for a sense of security and meaning.

> *When we change what has meaning, we change what we see.*
> —Kevin Ashton, author

Neuroscience research has studied the happiness buzz we get from the different ways we spend money.

It dichotomized between buying **things** versus buying **experiences**. It turns out that the dopamine burst lasts much longer with the latter and that people overestimate how much pleasure they get from material spending. If you are the spendaholic type and wish to "reform," there is no Spendaholics Anonymous treatment centre, so you have to self-diagnose and self-medicate. Try this: when you go on a spending spree, add up the damage and send a matching amount to a charity of choice. Either way, something good is going to happen. Either you curtail your spending to spare your bank account, or you make the world a better place!

Others have said that "contentment" is a better indicator than happiness.

Some alternate takes:

> *Success is not the key to happiness; happiness is the key to success.*
> —Albert Schweitzer, writer and philosopher

> *The pursuit of happiness has turned into the pursuit of pleasure, which has become the purpose of life.*
> —Stephen Green, author/UK politician

> *Perhaps the key to happiness (is) combining the right doses of excitement and tranquility.*
> —Yuval Harari, author

> *All those who are unhappy in the world are so because they desire their own happiness. All those who are happy in the world are so because they desire others to be happy.*
> —Shantideva, eighth-century Buddhist monk/philosopher

The Sanskrit language gives us a word for this: *mudita*. Curiously, the German language gives us another word, *schadenfreude*, for the exact opposite…where we find joy in someone else's misfortune.

A great deal of what makes people happy is living up to what they think they should be doing.

Yuval Harari further weighs in on this: "On the psychological level, happiness depends on **expectations** rather than objective conditions."

And that brings us back to Festinger's cognitive dissonance, which begs the question: where do the **expectations** (the happiness "budget") come from? Here is where it gets interesting. The happiness research has not found a clear correlation between income level and happiness, after a base-line income amount. The income/happiness correlation issue isn't about the amount of your income but its relativity. That then begs: relative to whom? Simple question…difficult answer! In simpler times, it may have been the other villagers in your small town.

Sketches in Personal Finance

My mother grew up in the 1900s as one of eight kids on a farm in rural Denmark that had been in the family since 1837. Late in the birth-order, she and her youngest siblings "got out of Dodge" in 1926 to come to the New World and ended up in Edmonton. There, life's relativity expanded to comparisons in larger venues, called cities. My point is that, in today's world, the elusive happiness expectation formed by relative comparison has exploded beyond the farm down the road. Thanks to modern technology, we have the other 8 billion inhabitants on the planet to measure against. How many "conveniences" existed for a home in 1837 compared to today? Every convenience that you don't have is potentially a mark against your happiness. Her forebearers in the nineteenth century probably didn't spend a lot of time thinking about happiness, and there certainly weren't polling agencies enquiring.

Happy Places

We all probably have read the global happiness findings in the press.

The four Scandinavian countries plus Switzerland always are in the top ten. Finland currently is number one. I agree with Harari's view above. Many of the results are based upon self-assessment surveys. In my mind, this brings us to the same place as the self-assessment surveys that report that everyone is an above-average driver! This, of course, is impossible. This takes us back to the earlier reference to Leon Festinger's cognitive dissonance. Happiness becomes the difference between one's expectations and (self-assessed) actual happiness. So, it's not really the Happiness Prize but the Cognitive Dissonance Prize. In fact, the Finn's national character is to be even-keeled and content with what they have. By contrast, with their "keep up with the Joneses" attitude, North Americans are unlikely to make the top ten.

Another take is the annual *World Happiness Report* rankings by country and by regions. Finland was once again number one. The attributes here are societal ones, which only partially correlate with ones that a family would conjure: social support, per capita GDP, healthy life expectancy, freedom to make life choices, generosity, and freedom from corruption. This list is in rank order of importance when comparing the average country score with the worst (Burundi).

The top ten include the five Scandinavian countries, four from the European continent (the Netherlands, Austria, Luxembourg, and Switzerland) and one Commonwealth country (New Zealand). The average population amongst the top ten is approximately 6.5 million. Amongst larger countries rank Germany (13), Canada (14), the UK (17), and the US (19). Of course, this doesn't infer that being small makes happy! But we might salute those three very large countries for ranking as high as they did.

A different take is the global *Best Countries* in which to live survey, conducted by the BAV Group and the University of Pennsylvania. Again, some of the Scandinavian countries (not Finland) and Switzerland make the top ten. Canada was number one for six years running but recently dropped a place to Switzerland.

Attributes were grouped in ten sub-rankings: adventure, heritage, culture, entrepreneurship/business, agility, movers, purpose, power, and quality of life.

"L'homme moyen" ("average man") was an eighteenth-century (literally) statistical character created by the Belgian Adolphe Quetelet for the purpose of measuring physical attributes. Many of these happiness surveys build a statistic that speaks for the "happy moyen"…the "average happy." But **none** of the citizens in a country will be THAT happy average person. These happiness indices rankings are useful for governments, think tanks, and societies. Behind the numbers, and understanding the structures of the nations involved, inferences can be made about economic growth, economic inequality, impact of immigration, welfare efficiency, social cohesion, and trust.

But they are of little or no use to you or me in assessing our own happiness and set point. I do think that one of your exposures is the crowd that you run with. Do you share their money values? Can you keep up with them lifestyle-wise and financially? My wife and I faced this thirty-plus years ago and parted company with best friends. If some of your "expectation inputs" come to you from your children's crowd, how do you manage that? Section 3.2 Kids and Money and 3.3 Family Confab could be beneficial, e.g., "My Family believes in…."

At the global level, the "GINI" coefficient is a measure of the economic disparity (defined by income, not wealth) across a society. A zero index represents total equality (meaning everyone has the same income) and 1.0 represents total concentration (meaning one person makes all the income in the country). The World Bank undertakes the periodic measure of this for all the countries in the world. The Scandinavian countries tend to have the lowest score (highest equality), while South Africa has the highest score (lowest equality) followed by China, India, and most Latin American countries.

Reflect on the UAW (Under-achieving Accumulators of Wealth) Family Compounding in the Root Purposes section 2.3. The GINI concept is interesting to contemplate in the multi-generational family environment. If the family has a high score (lowest equality), how does this impact the family dynamic and health? Why does it have a high score? Does this result from past mistakes in influencing the skills and aspirations of the following generation? Is it remedial? How would the rest of the family react to remediation by the leading generation?

Let's retreat from this heavy topic and contemplate some other beautiful aspects of life that may feed, not detract from, your happiness.

The Gratitude Effect

By dictionary count, there are approximately 170,000 words in the English language (and more, or less, in other common languages).

I don't know if you have spent time thinking about this, but I have four favourite words: **pleasure, privilege, blessing, and beauty.** I describe it as a pleasure and privilege to know someone in my little world and to serve them in some fashion… as a friend, an advisor. I also am very blessed that they choose to allow me into their world. Lastly, I think that the pursuit and creation of beauty is life's overarching purpose. That includes beauty in our immediate surroundings, beauty in our relationships, and beauty in the footprint we place upon the world around us.

I had a thought recently, sitting in my reading room: "That lamp is beautiful; I don't appreciate it enough!" Does an inanimate object appreciate being called beautiful? Probably not. However, Brother David Steindl Rast rescued my silly thought with: "Beauty seen makes the one who sees it more beautiful."

All my four words fit under the topic of gratitude. Let's see what modern neuroscience has to say about expressing **gratitude**.

Evidence suggests that expressing the gratitude we feel makes our lives better.

I interject that there is a pre-qualifier here: you cannot express gratitude unless you have felt/recognized it. The quality starts there or dies there. Gratitude produces a psychological boost, creating life satisfaction and even better health and sleep. Needless to say, the evidence finds a significant benefit to the recipient, too. The research also suggests that the benefit comes from the simple act of doing it; how brilliantly or articulately it is delivered is less important.

> *Evidence suggests that expressing the gratitude we feel makes our lives better. Gratitude produces a psychological boost, creating life satisfaction and even better health and sleep.*
>
> *Only when we change ourselves will society change.*
> —Vladimir Mukhin, Russian chef

Our busy Western world makes expression of gratitude rare these days. The quote is an invocation to each of us to "incite a riot" of positive societal change.

Sometimes we need to be deliberate in our expressions of gratitude.
The following are a few examples from my life. My wife and I spent four days in a downtown chain hotel in Prague. We had breakfast there every day. While we were there, the hotel hosted a physicians' conference, which caused the breakfast room to get very busy. We observed how effectively and graciously the restaurant manager handled the complexity each morning. On our last day, we

presented her with a bouquet of flowers in appreciation. We call this "random acts of kindness" (RaK).

After the Prague event, I decided the world needed to embrace RaK! If I have gained one piece of wisdom in my years, it is this: every brilliant idea I have ever had has already been thought of by someone else. So, for once, I exhibited wisdom and typed "random acts of kindness" on the internet. Lo and behold! There was already a world-wide organization doing this. My loss: another brilliant idea. My win: the work was already done. Go check it out.

When we are about to travel, we visit a local craft shop and buy several pieces of West Coast Indigenous art…mostly jewelry. We randomly give the pieces to people we meet along our travels.

Several years ago, my late wife and I travelled with another couple for a week-long experience at a cooking school in a spa hotel on the island of Ischia. The fabulous week was winding down, and the four of us had a dinner chat about coordinating our "tipping strategy" when we left. The hotel staff and management had been spectacular; slipping Euro notes into their hands seemed unsatisfying. Then we came up with the strategy of a hundred roses. On our penultimate day, we arranged for a local florist to deliver 100 roses to our room. At our last happy hour and dinner, we divided up the roses and each travelled around the entire hotel simultaneously delivering roses to hotel staff. This was a RaK that will never be forgotten.

More recently, our firm held its annual client appreciation weekend at a luxury hotel chain in the local environs. We had 108 attendees at the Saturday night banquet, spread over fourteen tables. We distributed stem roses around those tables. In my brief speech before dinner, I asked each table to determine who had the most recent birthday. That person was "it." All fourteen tables were charged with delivering the roses to all of the serving staff as they stood at-the-ready leaning on the outer banquet walls. Another RaK.

> *The customs and practices of life in society sweep us along.*
> —Michel de Montaigne, sixteenth-century philosopher

In the go-go Western world, society subconsciously engages in a consensual conspiracy, as value systems inexplicably degrade. We wake up one day and say, "How did we get here?" The present narrative for societal change in the twin backdrop of Covid and climate change may be ephemeral or founding.

How great would it be to see young kids volunteer to rake leaves or shovel snow for elderly neighbours for no compensation?

Yuval Harari weighs in one more time on happiness: "The second big project on the human agenda will probably be to find the key to happiness."

In closing, Vancouver publisher Pasquale Cusano had this to say about love: "Love is ultimately directed at the spirit of another, or the purpose we find in something. Love is life. Actions alone have no life; they are simply mechanical. There is nothing that will give you greater momentum than love—not power, fame, fortune, or ego. The more you love someone or something, the more fearful you become of the unknown. Nevertheless, choose love."

I have done what I said at the beginning of the chapter: I have shared with you many different takes on this subject, and you can consider which, if any, resonate with you. Philosophically, I believe that life is the giant inner battle within oneself. Addressing your attitudes and beliefs about the pursuit of happiness (or contentment or purpose) may be one of the most important things you can do.

Some time would be well spent exploring the happiness factor in your pursuit of WealthNess. However you slice and dice these various takes on happiness, it seems to distill down to one thing: attitude—the trait, not the state. We can interpret that as either delightfully, or annoyingly, simple.

2.6 Good Decision-Making

Factors That Influence Decision-Making

*OK! Let me start with a full disclosure: **I love good decision-making**.*

When we make good decisions, our lives are better and we are happier, and both of those states emanate out from us to those in our circle. But, truth-be-known... what constitutes a "good decision" is a subjective assessment in the eye of the beholder. So, let's try to give that assessment some rigour and consider:

- What defines a good decision?
- What goes into a good decision-making process?

This makes for a good Einsteinian "thought experiment" for yourself and your friends.

Good decisions find their roots in strong personal principles.

In today's busy world, few of us take the time to codify our principles—"**This I believe**"—which isn't to say we don't have principles. They just kinda float around in our subconscious. We do have a higher calling to cognate our principles if we are in a position of contributing to someone else's development: like a child, grandchild, employee, or mentee. I do a lot of mentor work with young people, and I encourage them to spend some internal time defining their own "Ten Principles" of engaging with life.

Ray Dalio concurs with this. In his book *Principles,* he opines: "And it's very rare for people to write their principles down and share them. That is a shame."

Attempting to be cryptically philosophical, life is a lot about making good decisions. Big decisions need to be made well and require reflection.

When faced with important decisions, I use two metaphors. First, is a dartboard. It is a shield against false urgency and the empathy gap (which will be discussed in a few paragraphs). Immerse yourself at Time Moment A to consider the issues and draw a conclusion—for the moment—which route you should go. Note this down, but do not decide yet. Metaphorically, you have thrown one dart at the board and where it landed represents that particular choice. Contrary to the game of darts, you are not trying to hit the bull's eye at the centre...just get onto the board. Now, leave it for a while and revisit at Time Moment B. Come to your second conclusion and throw the second dart onto the board, representing that choice. And so on through further iterations.

At some point you stop and look at the dartboard. How have the collection of darts landed? In other words, how are they distributed? If they all are tightly near to each other, you have an easy decision. If most of them are proximate, and there is, say, one outlier, probably you again have your decision. Lastly, if they all are scattered diversely across the board, you are stuck and probably need to go back to a different board: the drawing board! Of course, this works well, too, where the different darts aren't different decision iterations in time, but across your other decision-makers (co-workers, family, etc.)

My second metaphor involves your chin. I'm not kidding here.

With your fingers splayed open, note the distance between the tip of your thumb and the tip of your forefinger. When you place the tip of your thumb on your chin and rotate your hand, the tip of your forefinger will reach your forehead/brain. Now, hold the thumb steady and rotate the forefinger down. It will touch your heart. To me, this means that the lowly chin, which gets little press, is the centre of your decision-making, ensuring that all important decisions get checked by the heart and the head. So, my silly chin idea is a check-off to a well-rounded decision—both individually and in a group setting. On occasions where I chair meetings, I may close a discussion—before a vote—with my chin rotation. "Have we considered this from all angles?"

"Empathy gap" is a cognitive bias that causes us to underestimate the influences of "heart" matters in our decision-making. Professor George Loewenstein coined the term "hot-cold empathy gap." The concept is that our thoughts of the moment are "state-dependent." We are blind to how we would view the situation when in a different state (hot vs. cold). This is an interpretation of what I call the **tyranny of extrapolation**, where we assume that the condition state that we have observed in our decision today will carry forward unwaveringly into the future. That's also why the iterative trips to the dartboard help.

We need the wisdom to know when a decision should be approached with analysis and when with imagination. When called for, imagination is the gulf between the impossible and the possible.

We all need some time periodically to be like a truffle pig. Time to just "nose around in the dirt" to see what your senses can fall upon. Ferret around randomly in the dirt looking for something you haven't seen before. Get lost in the dirt for a while. You may emerge empty-handed, but that's OK. One time you will find a truffle.

Occasionally, you will catch an idea by the tail, but you don't really understand what it is until you catch up to the rest of it. The inventor of the loom named after him, Joseph-Marie Jacquard, famously invented it by the power of abstraction:

taking the essence of something else and applying it in another form (to create pre-modern punch cards).

As kids, we were mesmerized by the magic exhibited by magicians.

We remain mesmerized as adults, too, except we know that the miracle performed before our very eyes is some kind of clever trick that we haven't figured out. One of these miracles is called "magician's choice," or more formally "equivocation." The dictionary defines equivocation as "a fallacy resulting from the use of a particular word or expression in multiple senses throughout an argument, leading to a false conclusion." Here, the magician gives you the free choice to select a card for him. If you pick the one on the left, he says "OK"; if you pick the one on the right, he says, "OK, that's your card, I'll take the left one." While it appears to be your choice, his framing **after** your choice in fact always causes the choice to be the magician's, so he always knows which card will be his—the left one.

As adults, we make decisions all the time, some of them affecting our financial futures. It strikes me that in decision-making, we can be both the audience member and the magician. We in fact can trick ourselves because we know the result our heart wants, and the heart (the magician) tricks the brain (the audience member) by leading it to "buy" some false notion in the logical arguments leading to the decision.

Breaking a Decision Down

Our elementary school English teacher can come forward to help us, too, with decision-making. You might remember being taught to "**parse**" a sentence. In grammar, this means to break down a sentence into its parts and describe their syntactic roles. Syntax means the arrangement of words and phrases to create a well-formed sentence. In broader terms, it means to "examine or analyze minutely." So, we can parse a problem or idea to analyze and understand each constituent part of the whole idea.

Here is another way to look at the decision-making process.

I taught taxation over the internet, and half-way around the northern hemisphere, for fifteen years. For the chapter on tax "planning," I used the metaphor of a jigsaw puzzle on a rainy day on the cottage kitchen table. Mom opens the box and spills the 1,000 pieces onto the table. Some land face up; some face down. It turns out that last time the puzzle was made: a) some pieces got lost and b) some pieces from another puzzle inadvertently got mixed in, and c) the top of the jigsaw box—where the image appears—accidently ended up in cardboard recycling.

This depicts the world of decision-making. You have a problem that requires a decision towards a solution. You have a bunch of facts and knowledge (the jigsaw pieces). You don't necessarily know what the end result is supposed to look like (the missing jigsaw cover). Here is what you face to make your decision:

- Some of the facts before you are irrelevant to the decision and should be discarded.
- Some of the facts needed are missing and need to be found.
- Ditto re: the knowledge laid out before you.
- Your end goal may not be clear at the start, or even along the way, until the end.
- Generally, the sooner you can define the end goal, the quicker you can get there.
- However, sometimes it is good that the end goal isn't apparent at first; it may get redefined along the way

The first three points benefit greatly from grasping "omission and co-mission."

The first is identifying what information is missing and needed (jigsaw pieces lost). The second is identifying what information extant is irrelevant (jigsaw pieces added from a different puzzle). If you don't eliminate the latter, it can clutter and misdirect your process. The key point is that these two vital steps need to be executed in two separate passes, not one. They are different thought processes. They require different brain functioning…from different parts of the brain. The easier one—**co-mission**—is a blunt test of your familiarity with the subject matter in question. The harder one—**omission**—requires broken-field running by the brain: a deep search into your 100 billion neurons, each with 1,000 connections to figure out what is missing. It is easier to see what is there and that doesn't belong, versus what belongs that isn't there!

> *My secret had been I know what to ignore.*
> —Francis Crick, Nobel Prize winner

Peristalsis is the biological term for the important process of muscular transactions that your digestive system undertakes when you are processing nutrients. I think **mental peristalsis** is a good metaphor as we undertake decision-making. The facts, issues, and uncertainties surrounding your decision need to "work through" and be absorbed. Be mindful of the other benefit of bodily peristalsis: it separates the useful nutrients from the excrement. Similarly in decision-making, the passing of time might separate the valid decision points from the irrelevant ones.

Author Gary Klein introduced two interesting problem analytics. The first is "big picture"; he inspires us to turn things upside down for greater insight by deploying one simple, yet difficult, action. Look at any word or phrase and simply take the opposite of any of those key words, or insert a "no" or "not," and see what you get. We all can do this, we just have to train ourselves. Amazing insights can result from this trivial concept.

We all recognize the expression "the elephant in the room." It applies in a group decision-making milieu where there is a major problem or controversial issue that everyone knows about but doesn't wish to air. To not do so imperils the outcome of whatever situation is being addressed. To get a different sight-line on a decision at hand, long ago I applied this "Klein-ian" approach to identify "the amoeba in the room." This is entirely different! It implies something really small and seemingly irrelevant that might grow and similarly imperil a decision. Contrary to the elephant, the amoeba is not readily seen by the decision-makers. This invites a different neural journey to flush out the unseeable.

How about the word "no" or "not" inserted in front of a key word in the decision process? There was a marketing team addressing a new marketing strategy. One participant stated: "Our existing customer relationships are like Velcro." All nodded in agreement around the room, as they endorsed all the positive things being done. Was this truth or hubris? What if somebody simply restated: "Our existing customer relationships are NOT like Velcro." Seemingly trivial! Now the group enters a different neural journey seeking the negative things.

Klein's second analytic draws from his first. "Post-mortem" was already a phrase in language.

"Post" means "after," and the opposite of "after" is "before," or "pre," giving a new perspective. So, he introduced a very interesting second concept called "pre-mortem decision-making." This is essentially time-travelling à la the movie *Back to the Future*. Our norm is to operate in the present. We may seek context for decisions from the past, but it is counter-intuitive to do so from the future. And that is Klein's "pre-mortem." Decision-makers should put themselves forward in time, and then look back to the present day. A tomorrow scenario is assumed, e.g., yesterday's decision failed, and the decision-makers are writing the future post-mortem on why the action failed. The interesting concept is that, apparently, this flip causes our brains to process differently; we see different things. Pretending that it failed, followed by speculating why it failed, gives us further decision inputs today before we actually make the decision. Also, by assuming the failure scenario (which nobody wants), it gives licence to the participants to play devil's advocate without taking on the persona today of "idea-killer." This of course is cast in the business decision-making environment, but there is no reason why we can't use it in making our own personal finance decisions: Do we buy that cottage? Expensive car?

In society today, we tend to view procrastination as a negative quality. But it can be a valuable "character fault" if used wisely. Procrastination can bear the fruit of improved perception. Beware its flipside: the error of false urgency. Who/what says we have to make this decision by Tuesday? This is what salespeople do to convert the sale quickly.

> *In physics language, you might have the right observation but the wrong theory.*
> —Safi Bahcall, author/physicist

*A related trap in decision-making is being too focused on the **end result**, with not enough attention to the **process**.*

In 1778, Captain James Cook was exploring the west coast of Vancouver Island, and he came upon a large, sheltered bay that he could see was the home of a Indigenous settlement. As he was rounding the bay to sail in to meet them, the natives stood on the shore jumping up and down, crying, "Nootka! Nootka!" He was anticipating landing to meet them, and he thought they were declaring who they were. In fact, as he was working his way into the bay, there was a shelf of dangerous rocks below the waterline, that he hadn't seen. "Nootka" means "go around"! But he didn't understand. Fixation on the end—the goal or the decision—can blind us from due process to get there. This allegorical story has application for businesses "rounding the bay" and misunderstanding what their customers on the shoreline are telling them. Perhaps this can apply to multi-generational families, too.

I meld metaphors from fishing and nuclear physics to assist people with good decision-making. I call it: Fission—Fusion—Fishin'

In nuclear physics:

- Fission is about splitting things up: breaking down.
- Fusion is about bringing things together: merging into a unified whole.

Both produce energy but in different fashions.

And so it is in making personal finance decisions. We need to break down the elements of the decision—fission. Then we need to look at how it all comes together—fusion, and last—fishin'. In our pursuit of good decision-making, we can draw inspiration from recreational fishing. If you are a recreational fisher, reflect upon what you do, and try to morph it into personal finance decision-making. If, like me, you are not a fisher (I retired from active duty as a fisher when the last fish I caught was a seagull), let's imagine together.

Liken the different ways to fish to our approaches to decision-making. One fisher trolls…with a line in the water but moving about in the environment trying to find the fish. The angler fisher anchors in one spot and drops a line over, waiting for the fish to come to him. Then there is the fly-fisher, poetically made beautiful by the book and movie *A River Runs Through It*. This fisher becomes part of the environment itself, and casts and re-casts in search of the fish.

The decision maker can apply the same approaches:

- Fly-fisher: this is the same as the business strategy approach suggested by author Evan Dudek: make **many, small** commitments and see what pays back. So, we go out and make many small decisions by casting multiple times in different directions.
- Angler: we make one decision and throw that out to the world to see how it takes. If it fails, we pull up our stakes and try something else.
- Troller: we hedge a decision by testing it first (think focus group in the business world). If it works ("There's a whole school down there!") we stop there and harvest.

We can draw further wisdom on decision-making by asking simply: Why not…

> *When he makes a forecast, he also makes a list of the conditions in which it should hold true—as well as the conditions under which he would change his mind.*
> —Adam Grant, author

And what if…

> *His [Stephen Jay Gould's] point was that life is not a series of random events. Rather, it's a continuum of contingencies, meaning that each step along the way is contingent on what came before.*
> —Michael O'Brien, author

Thinking Differently

The most influential book for my personal life has been *The Iconoclast*, by Dr. Gregory Berns at Emery University, who is a neuro-economist, neuroscientist, psychologist, and professor of psychiatry. His wisdom in this book is useful to us in this section on decision-making. He says that iconoclastic thinking is neuro-based. Specifically, he suggests that the iconoclastic brain is different in three ways: how it perceives, how it responds to fear, and its social intelligence.

The iconoclastic brain doesn't see things differently; it perceives differently, which perhaps is a subtle difference to a layperson. It involves, for instance, not seeing familiar things differently, but rather seeing different things. This means exposing oneself to new things and environments. This forces the brain to work harder, creating new interpretations and connections, rather than energy cost-cutting by framing new things in light of previous experiences. We can achieve this by hanging out with new people and in different places, or more simply by changing our vantage point (e.g., Klein's pre-mortem).

I believe that the best decision-makers share a particular trait: how they see **constraints**.

They are able to recognize what the constraints are and not see them as constraints. It is truly a talent to challenge: "Why does X have to behave like X?" Rooms have walls, floors, and ceilings. An interior designer gives X treatment to the ceiling, Y to the floor, and Z to the walls. Why? I guess because they are perceived as different to each other. Why does a ceiling have to behave like a ceiling? I recently saw an ad in a design magazine. The Z treatment for the walls was wallpaper. Now we expect the ceiling to be painted X. But no, the same wallpaper Z ran up the walls and across the ceiling. And trust me, it looked cool!

Up until the 1960s/70s, on a hockey team the forwards were supposed to score goals on the other team, and the defencemen were supposed to keep their goal net empty. Then along came a guy named Bobby Orr: why does a defenceman have to behave like a defenceman? He reinvented the game and the position. He remains the only defenceman in NHL history to win the league scoring title twice.

Take inspiration from these two stories. Try to re-wire your neural network like a ceiling—or Bobby Orr.

Staying on the sports theme, for a fascinating insight, watch the Amazon documentary *This is Football* on the career of the world's greatest footballer, Leo Messi. Much of the game footage portrays him "just standing around." One might perceive him to be the laziest guy on the pitch, but his brain is taking everything in on the field…observing and processing. When he acts, things happen. He executes an economy of effort with an abundance of results.

Fear is a familiar aspect of being human.

Needless to say, there are many different forms of fear. Most of us are past the era of "fight or flight" to avoid being eaten by a tiger. But modern-day folks have many substitutes for the tiger. The amygdala is where fear and emotional responses are processed, and it has a long memory for bad experiences. Berns posits two ways to manage fear: **short-circuit** the creation of bad memories or **reframe to a non-emotional context**. Ambiguity aversion is the fear of the unknown. Risk aversion is more calculated. So, the trick is to morph ambiguity aversion into risk aversion. In essence, we exchange two four-letter words: "fear" for "risk," and deal with the situation more matter-of-factly. We will re-visit this in Section 5.3: Safety.

For fine-tuning our decision-making skills, it is always wise to mix with other people, as they provide different perspectives and perhaps uncover our blind spots. My personal views on group decision-making include the following suggestions:

- I encourage open brain-storming.
- If the environment is healthy, **there is no such thing as a bad idea: rather, some ideas just aren't good enough to execute**. This is fine-tuning, I admit, but I believe it is one that gives licence to free-thinkers and inspires creative solutions.
- Avoid egotistical ownership of the solution by one party. "Two half-wits: one fine brain" is always my mantra in group decision-making.
- Once you have settled upon a course of action, lock on that idea and guide it like a heat-sensing missile.

I would like to share a process that I have utilized in decision-making settings.

First, consider your reaction to two words: fantasy and rant. Most people react negatively to rant. Interestingly, I have found a dichotomy in people reacting to fantasy; half positive/half negative. Now, let me introduce a paranomasia, a play on words: **rantisize.** My definition is the opportunity, in group settings, for any participant to have "licence" for a limited duration to rant on some sacred cow they believe to inhibit the organization (or family)—a sort of "007 licence to spill" "without fear or favour" (my high-school motto). Each decision-maker will have a turn to rantisize without prejudice or judgment.

Personal Time-Outs and Neuro Archeology

> *Wisdom comes from three places: reflection, imitation, and experience.*
> —Confucius

The ploughman recognized the importance of being fallow…being left alone in order to restore fertility.

It is a busy world, and most of us don't take deliberate time to reflect. A larger extension of this is "mixing with oneself." That said, we spend 168 hours of every week of our lives with ourselves; there's just no escaping that. It has been estimated that we have 60,000 thoughts per day. It also has been estimated that we have closed-circuit internal conversations within our brain at the rate of 300–1,000 words per minute. Read that again. Do the math on that per hour for your waking hours that you are not externally engaged. Yikes! Will you or I live to see the day that some machine can be hooked up to our brain to read/write all of those conversations and then pass that transcript over to some researcher to categorize all of those thoughts by subject matter?

And so, I would like to suggest that you consider taking annual personal retreats to mix with yourself. I call this Zero-On-One. I do so for three three-day jaunts per year in the fall and spring. I drive two hours to a nearby spa resort and get the same suite every time: the hotel has come to refer to it as the Hemingway Suite. I pretty much barely leave the room and eat my meals there. A key is to prepare at least a little bit for what you plan to do as you may need to bring some resources. I read…I write…I think…I take naps…. I also collect thoughts between trips in a file.

One of my old friends told me that he could never get away with such a retreat—his wife would be convinced he was off to have an affair. Affair enough! How about a compromise where the couple "retreat" together but separately. I think it is important to have time with oneself. Maybe have two rooms? A large suite? Some joint time together? Try it. Experiment! Make it work.

If a selfish escape is a non-starter in your world, you can achieve private time in smaller doses. I regularly spend twenty to thirty minutes sequestered in my infra-red sauna or a hot bath (hint: lock the door)…and by the way…bring a pen and notepaper. It is very seldom that I come away completely without any interesting thought to develop. The Japanese have a word for this: *hikikomori*—a sense of physical isolation at home.

When you gear your brain down in this milieu of mixing with yourself, you may be surprised to see what flushes out and comes to the surface. But you also need to mix with others' thoughts, too, to spread fertilizer on your fertile mind. Pick your favourite medium in today's world—books, podcasts, etc. Become a "mind mixologist"…an intellectual hunter/gatherer.

That's a segue to the not-so-common-anymore **commonplace book**. These "memo pads" of thoughts, ideas, and knowledge were common in the seventeenth century and beyond. Isaac Newton's commonplace book is held in the Cambridge Library. *The New York Times* gave this idea a resurrection in an article in February 2021. My modern version is a **commonplace i-Phone Note file**, where I collect words, ideas, and quotations. Several parts of this book hatched in my commonplace notes.

I thought one day that I had coined a new term: **neuro archeology**.

But of course not! Cognitive archeologists Renfrew and Malafouris beat me to it. However, I define the concept radically differently. Theirs is "interactions between brain, body, and world over cultural and evolutionary spans of time" (Wikipedia). My definition involves you as your own neuro archeologist working with tools to mine the depths of your own "ancient" memories. A personal retreat creates the environment for quiet private time where neuro archeology digs around to identify pairs and patterns that might lead to innovative thought.

Here's an example. When I was eight years old, my family was invited for family dinner by a distant-but-very wealthy relative, who lived in a mansion. After the meal, we "adjourned to the parlour," where the lady of the house, an amateur concert pianist, played her grand piano. After that, she played a vinyl of a German/Russian tenor…very high-brow for an eight-year-old. Now, fast-forward fifty years, and I am in a taxi with friends driving from Positano to the Naples airport. The cab conversation got into music of bygone eras, which, for some reason, caused me to remember that night. I had had no interaction with the world of that tenor since that evening; this was the early days of the Beatles! For the duration of the hour cab ride, I withdrew from the conversation and put on my neuro archeology hat to unearth that guy. And I did! It felt like a eureka moment. (For the old timers, his name was Ivan Rebroff.)

My point here is that, in mixing with yourself in these retreats, you also knock on the door of your Old-Self, too. Our 100 billion neurons are believed to each have 1,000 linkages to other neurons. When you tap the shoulder of the Ivan Rebroff neuron, that one is connected to 1,000 more…perhaps other old storage memories, which may provide insight to mix with your brain of today. That is what these famous people did with their commonplace books—a mixing bowl of ideas across time.

A final metaphor I use here is the cross-hairs in the scope of a rifle.

Like me, you may never have held such an instrument, so let's imagine. When you look into the scope and are trying to hit your target (which here is a good decision), you see the cross hairs align to give you a true point of aim. Then pull the trigger—that is, you are ready to make the decision. If the cross-hair lines have not come into focus yet, your decision is still fuzzy and you should retreat and regroup.

In closing, develop a passion for good decision-making. Most of us are not good decision-makers by nature, but rather by nurture. Like the survey of people as drivers, we probably all consider ourselves to be better-than-average decision-makers. Become a student of decision-making—grow some anemone tentacles. Your inner self will know when you have achieved this.

2.7 Key Words and Concepts

9. "Money is…"
10. The New "Millionaire"
11. Wealth Effect
12. Beauty = order/complexity
13. Spend some time reflecting on what your root attitudes are to money, and where they come from
14. Plot the family line—backwards and forwards—of these attitudes
15. Is there a family pathology?
16. Is there family welfare?
17. Complete the Swiss questionnaire and reflect on those answers
18. What's the most important thing?
19. What's the money for? Who do you love? What do you love?
20. Working, saving, compounding, and blessings
21. The addiction of earned income
22. Lifestyle averaging
23. Total Saving Rate
24. Silos of capital
25. The power of compounding meets the (Financial) Law of Large Numbers
26. To every asset there is a reason.
27. What's happiness got to do with it?
28. Good decision-making and dartboards, chins, jigsaw puzzles, time-travelling, nuclear physics, rants and jaunts, commonplace books, and neuro archeology

Chapter 3: Families and Finance

Historian Henry Adams defined politics as the "systematic organization of hatreds." I proffer the definition of family finance as the "unsystematic organization of family finance."

Personal finance for a single person is hard enough. Add a partner or add a family and the complexity compounds. For a couple, non-alignment of money philosophy invites a lifetime of financial challenges or, ultimately, separation. For a family, failure to pass on healthy money philosophy invites lifetimes of inter-generational financial welfare. Alternately, passing on an unhealthy money philosophy perpetuates financial challenges across generations.

I will suggest in this section that parenting is the genome of society, and that there is a financial genome inherent in every family.

For the pursuit of WealthNess, there needs to be an iterative process whereby:

1) Each partner in the couple needs to address their own money philosophy
2) The couple needs to find a reasonable alignment of those two philosophies, and
3) The parents need to deliberately, and consistently, convey that philosophy to the next generation.

Simple, huh?

In the family context, I introduce three terms to classify the generations: **Presiding, Leading, and Following.** The presiding generation is always the most senior living generation. The leading generation is the one that stewards the family financial and other decisions. This would normally be the presiding generation, but it may become the next generation when the presiding generation loses mental capacity or the energy and will to lead. The following generation(s) are the younger ones that follow.

As we progress through the three sections in this chapter, be mindful of your take-aways from the Chrematistics Section.

Sections

3.1 Couples and Money

3.2 Kids and Money

3.3 Family Confab

3.4 Key Words and Concepts

3.1 Couples and Money

Working Together as a System

> *There's a lot of internal feelings related to money because money can also reflect the power and the balance of the relationship.*
> —Lauren Papp, director of the Couples Lab at the University of Wisconsin, Madison and author of several studies on marital conflict

In this chapter—families and finance—"personal" finance will be renamed "family" finance.

Everyone comes into a marriage with one past relationship they cannot leave behind: the one they have with money.

It's a deep, complicated past liaison with a lot of history, and often goes unacknowledged in the relationship. Money is not just currency. It comes with emotions attached. Fights about money, therefore, are not just about having enough, and sharing it equally; they strike at the essence of people's fears, hopes, and desires. It's no accident that people under financial pressure get divorced much more often than people who aren't. Studies have shown that money is the most commonly reported squabble-starter for couples, and the source of the most heated arguments. Too often in relationships, as Ray Dalio said in Section 2.6, people's principles aren't clear, including principles about personal finance. But handling finances together—and navigating the hazards therein—is an essential ingredient to a successful long-term union. Ignored it may be the amoeba in the room that grows to elephantine proportions.

In physics, two particles can act in unison and become a system. They behave like one object, although they are separate. It is as if they sit on opposite sides of a teeter-totter slide: when one side is up, the other responds implicitly. They act in this unison despite no communication between them. Einstein famously weighed in with his frustration to comprehend this phenomenon, which he described as **"spooky action at a distance."**

Some couples are blessed with an almost implicit mutual understanding about family finance that never need be spoken.

They react beautifully to each other's actions; they just get it...Einstein's "spooky action at a distance." They are rare, to be sure. Think about games. Think about bridge and your partner, where your cooperation across the bridge table cannot be achieved by oral communication, but rather by each of your **actions**: "I do THIS, which I believe helps us to OUR GOAL, and now it is YOUR turn to interpret what I did and make the next move wisely." So, this couple plays out their shares of family finance transactions, both spending and earning, with only **implicit** communication. Contrast this with the Sketches in Personal Finance couple in Chapter 1.0: "You have your toys; I have mine." Have you wondered if there ever has been a study on successful married bridge partners and correlated them to successful family finance?

For the rest of us, healthy, successful family finance is about conversations and assigned responsibilities.

My forty-plus years of sitting with couples and talking about family finance has brought me to the **normal distribution** *curve (with apologies to non-statistics-trained readers).*

The normal distribution curve was "discovered" by mathematician Carl Friedrich Gauss in the early nineteenth century, and popularized, related to coin tosses, by Seventeenth Century mathematician de Moivre. To keep it simple, it says that two-thirds of observations fall into a middle range of outcomes around the mean, with one-sixth falling (lower) to the left and one sixth falling (higher) to the right. This has been found to apply throughout nature.

I have observed it in the context of couples' inclinations to financial management. The mean in the middle for two-thirds of couples, "M" is that one of the couple is naturally inclined to financial management. The left-hand tail, "LHT," for one-sixth of couples, has **neither** being inclined to financial management. Lastly, the right-hand tail, "RHT," for the other one-sixth has **both** of the couple inclined to financial management.

So, which are you?

Let's revisit the Prologue and the graphical insights from Venn diagrams. Imagine two topics: family financial management **skill** and family financial management **inclination**. So here is an exercise for you and your partner: On separate sheets of paper, draw a circle for each of these, with the size of the circle depicting **your own** self-assessments. (You could repeat this exercise, except this time draw the circles for your assessments of **your partner**.) Here's an example:

Next, compare the sizes of each pair you have drawn with that of your partner, and then move each pair of responses together to describe how much **overlap** there is between them— that is, in a Venn diagram. Below, in the circles on the left, there is not very much overlap, meaning that they don't share a lot of the same skills…say, understanding their insurance coverages, having investing acumen, etc. In the circles on the right, there is a fair amount of overlap, meaning they share a lot of financial inclinations…say, budgeting, monitoring bank and loan balances, etc. This simple exercise may help the couple assess where they are on that normal distribution curve.

For instance, the Venn diagrams above likely depict an M couple. For LHT couples, both likely would have very small circles of skill and/or inclination. For RHT couples, all circles likely would be large. Another couple may have large inclination circles but small skill circles; they are good candidates to keep reading.

At first thought, one might intuit that the right-hand tail ("RHT") couples are the best off, with twice the fire power, but not necessarily. Depending upon the couple, it could create disharmony as they both position for control. Clearly, however, the left-hand tail ("LHT") couples have a problem. In the absence of self-realization and appropriate remedial action, LHT couples likely are destined to a married life of financial turmoil. Regrettably, my observation is that remedial action is very difficult to embrace. At least one of the couple needs to sprout some anemone tentacles for personal finance. And so…being in the middle ("M") may be the best place.

In the Introduction, I wrote about the ploughman, who might take care of the day-to-day financial responsibilities, while the astronaut would keep an eye on the bigger cosmos of family finance. The M couples, the ones who have **one** person in charge, still need to pay attention to the different ploughman and astronaut roles. By this, I mean that the spouse who stands aside ought not to totally abdicate from any involvement. There must come some big decisions in a couple's life—astronaut moments— and that's the overlap on the Venn diagram.

I am reminded of my dear friend's explanation of managing family finance through forty years of marriage: "When we got married, my wife and I made a deal. Whenever big financial decisions came upon us in life, she would be the one to make them. I would take care of all the small decisions. And, in forty years, we haven't yet faced a big decision!"

How does a couple dichotomize routine versus big decisions...ploughman vs. astronaut?

What happens when big decisions end up in a tie and one votes "yes" and one votes "no" on a potential action? Often, the result of a tie means no decision, and that is, in fact, a "no" decision. The couple should delve deeper, probably on paper, to explain the basis for their choices. Is the issue a matter of absence of facts or unreliable facts? If so, perhaps the couple can pursue better data. Is the issue one of different risk profiles? Is the issue one of scarce resources (money) and/or disagreement on the allocation of those scarce resources? By this I mean: perhaps the "no" spouse doesn't necessarily dislike the "yes" spouse's idea, but has an undisclosed other agenda, which would be denied due to insufficient resources to do both.

Another solution is to look externally, perhaps for a "tie-breaker" or mediator or sounding board. This is a good time already to have a trusted advisor at your disposal, e.g., your accountant, investment advisor, or financial planner.

Do you remember the Rock-Paper-Scissors game from our childhoods? (I doubt whether modern-day video gaming has bothered to digitize it.) If it wasn't part of your culture or generation, here's how it works: two kids together shout out 1-2-3, and then show their hand either as: a) a fist (rock), b) two forefingers forming a V (scissors) or c) flat (paper). The concept is that paper can cover a rock, scissors can cut paper, and a rock can smash scissors. Whoever wins gets to enjoy some *schadenfreude* by inflicting a slap on the wrist of the loser. If you are bad at this game, after a little while, your wrist will really hurt and become beet-red.

My wife and I used a modified version of this to facilitate family decisions (without the slapping part)—usually around vacation destinations.

Here's how it worked (and it did). We would be thinking about next winter's sun fix location. We would agree on a list of six or so. Let's say, Maui, Cancun, Disney World, Vale, Cabo, Phoenix, and Aruba. Then, we would stand together in the living room...very close...and face-to-face. We would jump up and down, counting one-two-three, after which we each would shout out our first location preference. "Cancun...Maui." If we both picked the same location on the first jump (that never happened!), the decision was made quickly. Now we would each re-evaluate with the second jump, bearing in mind info we got from our partner's first choice. "1-2-3...Aruba...Cabo." Hmmmm...still not there. But so far, a) neither has elected a ski vacation and b) neither has elected for a theme park week and c) both have chosen water-based locations over the desert. As we dig deeper (and remember that we live in the Pacific Northwest), the first of us was expressing the desire for a water vacation that required a major south-easterly commute; the other chose a closer commute west or south. Third jump. "1-2-3… Cabo….Maui." The first of us has capitulated to the shorter commute; the second has flipped between American vs. Mexican milieu. We're almost there! And so it goes. Parents might even find it fun to enjoin the kids in this family exercise.

Silly…fun…but effective.

Sketches in Family Finance

This first story is about a family pathology. For the past thirty-five years, I have had this couple as clients. They have become dear friends, and we have travelled together on more than one occasion. Both of them were entrepreneurs in very different industries. They separately took on pioneering financial ventures in those two fields, each of which lost a fair bit of money. They acted responsibly during those financial campaigns to promise each other that there would be a cap on the financial hemorrhaging, at which time either of them would throw in the towel. Unfortunately, such happened for both of them. But it took a while to wind things down, and along the way, one of the couple got reinspired to give it another try, with further investment. This prompted the other spouse to propose likewise. That brought them into my office to talk about things, when I said, "What we have here is a family pathology that needs to be controlled." We discussed the past histories of both ventures, the couple's present state in life, and the alternative futures facing them, both as a couple and as actualizing selves. They went home. They called me back. Both businesses came to an end.

This second story is about what should be considered at retirement. "Congratulations on the end of a journey, and welcome to the beginning of a new one." So started an interview with a couple in their early sixties. She was an entrepreneurial health professional, and he had just sold his forty-year business for a handsome sum. What lay ahead? If this book had been finished then, I would have sent them off to read it, in particular, the chapters on children, legacy, longevity, and transition. In the meantime, I encouraged them to sit down separately, and then together, to think about:

- The next twenty-four months
- The following two to five years
- The period "80-x," where x = their current ages
- The future sources of purpose
- Their following generation(s)

- Their passions, and the "agencies" out in the world that serve those passions

This begins to build a road map for the transition through their third to their fourth quarter. (For more on this, see section 4.1.)

Are you ready to embrace a concept in psychology to strengthen family finances? If so, take this detour. (If you don't want to take this detour right now, jump ahead until you see the Circle/easiest sign.)

Now imagine a couple, or a family, with the goal of financial comfort (or maybe just saving enough for a vacation).

They may not choose to talk about family finance, perhaps because it always leads to conflict and stress. And so, instead, they both play out their share of family financial transactions, both spending and earning, without direct communication. How well does that work out? In bridge, it is not a given that your partner will correctly interpret your bid as was intended to cause you to achieve your goal. Some people are good at bridge; some are not. The one family member who is inclined to financial management may resonate with the idea of WealthNess, but the other partner may remain unengaged. Might this deter the potential of growth and evolution of family finance?

Let's dabble a bit in a psychology term: **Gestalt**, which a dictionary defines as: "An organized whole that is perceived as more than the sum of its parts."

The "parts" here are the individual members in family financial decisions; the whole is the family. As family members individually embrace WealthNess learning, the WealthNess of the family will increase. But the gestalt effect is that good family finance decisions will feed off the previously unengaged member now contributing positively to those family decisions. Good decisions are now shared successes, and bad decisions no longer evoke finger-pointing at the lone decision-maker.

Ready to take a brief deep dive into Newtonian physics for insight into how a couple's money philosophy affects their WealthNess? If so, take this Diamond detour. (If you don't want to take this detour right now, jump ahead until you see the Circle/easiest sign.)

CHAPTER 3: FAMILIES AND FINANCE

The Importance of Being on the Same Page

Next, let's turn to Newton's first law of universal gravitation from the year 1687 to see how it impacts the power of couple finance:

$$F = G\frac{(M1 \times M2)}{r^2}$$

We will look at this to appreciate the exponential power to grow WealthNess thanks to the combination of the couple's growth.

For Newton:

F = gravitational force of attraction

G = gravitational constant

M1 and M2 = the masses of each of two objects

r = distance between the centres of the two masses

His theorem states that every object attracts another object with a force that is proportional to the product of their masses and inversely proportional to the square of the distance between them. Newton's law was superseded by Einstein's general relativity 200+ years later but is still materially valid. (Side bar: Newton's G was determined as a decimal, of which the first ten numbers were zero! Only at the eleventh decimal did it prescribe a value.)

For those of us who "dropped out" after Physics 10 in high school, our lone take-away on this was that Newton's apple (M1) fell **because** it responded to the gravitational pull of gravity from Mother Earth (M2). In physics, then, force is any interaction between two masses that, when unopposed, can change the motion of the objects in both magnitude (i.e., acceleration) and direction (a push or pull). In the absence of interaction between the two masses, there would be no force. Lastly, science recognizes that both living and non-living things can be affected by force.

Okay, enough physics! What's the point? I don't know how much couples discussed family finance in 1687. But Newton's First Law gives us guidance today on the complexity of family finance in the context of the **interaction of a couple**.

For us, M1 and M2 are the two partners. The M in this context includes a range of personal financial attributes each partner has: proclivity towards "home economics," education, income-earning ability, stability of earned income sources, health, work satisfaction, degree of knowledge about money matters, etc. Like Newton's G, our G is a big thing out there that we don't control: the economy. That might involve the global economy, the more local economy in your country or area, the industry sector that you work in, etc.

What is r? "r" is the correlation of money philosophy between the couple. This r has a value somewhere between zero and one, where one is complete agreement of the couple on money matters and zero means they are completely opposite. It is squared to accentuate the importance of cohesion of the couple's money philosophy.

So, what then is F? It is the health of family finances: what I have termed WealthNess.

So, Newton's unbeknownst First Law of Family Finance is:

$$F = G \times (M1) \times (M2) \times r^2$$

Let's copy/paste the gravitational explanation above, and substitute terms for family finance. You can glaze over the Physics 10 lesson above, but this is the important take-away:

The **health of family finance** (F) is the interaction between a couple that, when unopposed (i.e., benign economy "G"), can change the financial success of the couple in both magnitude (size of wealth accumulation) and direction (success or failure). In the **complete absence of alignment on money** matters between the two partners (r = 0), there could potentially be no financial success. Each of these elements taken together: G, M1, M2, and r define the success or failure of a couple's financial lives together, and you see how important r is.

So, like Birkhoff's earlier Beauty algorithm, the formula is not something that we try to ascribe numbers to solve an equation. But rather, it is a set of qualitative descriptors to help us understand **what** can effect success in family finance. Thus:

- Like gravity, no one can de-couple themselves from the economy around them. As it bends, surges, and lurches, we must periodically respond with our own adaptations and (Stephen Jay Gould's) contingencies.

- If you are a couple, then the couple's personal financial skills (M1/M2) multiply and compound the ability to create WealthNess.
- If the couple's attitudes towards money (r) are highly aligned, then selecting and attaining goals will be facilitated and WealthNess will grow nicely.
- If the couple's attitudes towards money (r) are **not** aligned, then the strength of their personal financial skills (M1/M2) is mitigated. If the r value is in fact significantly divergent, then the strength of high personal financial skills can largely be negated in the pursuit of WealthNess.

The main take-away in dragging you through Newtonian physics is the **last** bullet point.

*Welcome back to the **book's main pathway**.*

Where Do You Stand as a Couple?

So now it is time to figure out how all of this applies to you and your partner and what action is needed. Here are some steps to get you started.

- Identify and acknowledge which couple you are on the normal distribution curve.
- If you are an LHT couple, address this ASAP to secure a trajectory to WealthNess. Identify all the family financial tasks and figure out who will do what. Given that neither of you is inclined to this, the optimum solution likely is to divide and conquer the tasks, rather than draw straws and the loser is "it." If you can't see a pathway, get some help and promise to take the advice. Create some specific short-term goals in order to create a quick positive feedback loop. Be like a heat-seeking missile to pursue this goal.
- If you are an M couple, you are in a good place. Remember: being an RHT doesn't mean being more than an M. You might dabble in Square and Diamond concepts that catch your interest. Like the RHTs in the bullet below, you likely have a need to deal with Family Confab issues in section 3.3

- If you are an RHT couple…congratulations! Pick and choose from the various Square and Diamond concepts that I have shared. I have a hunch that the chapters on Family Confab, Longevity, and Legacy issues may be your only weak spots. With the success you have achieved to-date, strengthening the family values towards WealthNess is likely the amoeba in the room.

The cryptic take-away for you is to underscore the importance of:

1) Talking about money
2) Aspiring to having relatively like-minds related thereto.

These are unlikely conversations on a first-date or on the way down the aisle. But find the time.

3.2 Kids and Money

It Starts with the Parents

Let's start off-topic. The very first adult book I read post-university textbooks was written by the late Lyall Watson, and I re-read it forty-five years later to retrieve this quote for you. It actually may be relevant to this section by giving us one of those deep, poignant moments when we are blessed with some ah-hah serendipity (with apologies to educators).

He said: "Children have a very powerful sense of the propriety of certain things. They believe that rocks and houses are alive, that bears and elephants have feelings, and that it all matters. Every child of five knows everything there is to know, but when they turn six, we send them to school, and then the rot sets in. I wish there were some way of reconciling formal education and natural knowing."

What's the most important thing?

I often ask people this question. We can fill a library with books and opinions on this topic, and there is no universal right answer, nor can there be one single thing in rank order that supersedes all others. Our life on this planet is far too complex for such distilled simplicity. But, nonetheless, I am going to proffer my answer: **Parenting is it and it is the genome of society**. In biology, the genome is the complete set of genetic material in an organism. It contains all of the information needed for a person to develop and grow. The sum of all parenting—family-by-family—makes up who we are as individuals and, thus collectively, as society.

The term **"meme"** crept into our lexicon in the last generation. A meme is an idea, behaviour, or style that spreads by imitation from person to person within a culture (family) and often carries symbolic meaning.

Eighteenth-century philosopher/economist Edmund Burke said that society is a partnership of the living, the dead, and the yet unborn. In the current backdrop of climate change, that thought becomes even more profound than when he said that. We can make the same statement about families. We don't associate the word "climate" with families, but a climate is about an environment, and a family unit is an environment. Therefore, I think we can contemplate climate—and climate change—in the family environment, too. The go-go economic machine since WWII has impacted Earth's climate, but also that of families. We ought to be looking at the impact of that climate change for family systems with as much concern and conviction as the planet.

> *Money, genes, race, and schooling account for only one third of the correlation between opportunity and success.* ***Parenting style***

*contributes very little, but **parenting behaviour** contributes a lot, as does social capital.*
—Eric Beinhocker, author

That is profound! Please put the book down now and go for a walk to reflect upon Beinhocker's powerful insight.

…Welcome back.

It is difficult to make your kids good with money when you yourself are not.

Beinhocker emphasizes the importance to parents of "doing the work" to understand their own money philosophy and attitudes (back to Chapter 2). Do you remember the very first advertisement that pressed your "want" button? Was it a toy? A game? A plush toy? Do you remember how old you were when that happened? If yes, now you remember when your attitude towards money was starting to formulate. Do you remember how your allowance scheme worked with your parents? How you made your very first dollar working for someone else? More moments in the formulation of your attitudes towards money. And those attitudes are endemic in your money behaviours.

We need to revisit epigenetics, discussed in Section 2.2. Root Attitudes, in the context of parents and child-rearing.

We all are familiar with "genetics" (DNA and the double helix) and may cite the longevity and health conditions of our elders as markers for our own prospective longevity and health. But "epigenetics" is a newer and different beast. According to the US Centers for Disease Control and Prevention website: "It is the study of how behaviours and environment can cause changes that affect the way your genes work. In other words, epigenetics means that ***gene expression* changes without changing the actual genes themselves**. Unlike genetics, epigenetics is **reversible** and does not change your DNA sequence, but it can change how your body reads a DNA sequence."

Examples of such behaviours and environments include obesity, diet, smoking, alcohol, stress, environmental pollutants, and even working nightshifts. "Epigenetic inheritance" means that these impacts can be passed on to offspring **undeliberately.**

I think it is very important for a modern-day parent to contemplate the forces of gratitude and entitlement amongst young people. I think they represent conditions alike Einstein's quantum entanglement in Section 3.1 Couples. Except, this time, it is about two qualities, not two people. So, for kids, a high sense of entitlement corresponds with a low sense of gratitude. It is as if these two qualities sit on opposite sides of that teeter-totter slide: when one side is up, the other is automatically down.

Pay attention to these matters from early on. Otherwise, the parent-child relationship may become a bottomless pit in which to unsuccessfully throw endless love and money.

Talking About Money

Although the term is credited to the Danish philosopher Orsted in 1811, Einstein was famous for his **"thought experiments"** (which produced one of his most famous contributions to science as he mentally chased a beam of light). A thought experiment is "a hypothetical situation in which a hypothesis is laid out for the purpose of thinking through its consequences."

It also could be said that the purpose of thought experiments is the **means**, not the **ends**, i.e., your real objective is not necessarily to get the right answer (back to McLuhan probes in Section 2.1). I think the more interesting aspect of thought experiments is neurological wiring. You are presented with something so totally off the wall that your brain has no previous experience from which to draw. So, it is forced to spend the extra, precious energy to tackle the problem by seeking new connectors.

And so, I proffer that you expose your offspring to thought experiments.

Make it fun but think about the wiring you are inspiring, and inspire them to think BIG. Start this early in their lives and make it a reflexive habit to have these conversations. Find teachable moments in the day-to-day: "**What did you think about** …?" Make sure that some of these questions are about money and gratitude and happiness.

*When you want to have that discussion about money and wants-and-needs, be deliberate about **where** you conduct that.*

In today's busy world, all family members are constantly on the go, including the kids off to ballet, sports, music lessons, etc. Sitting around the family dinner table together may be the exception, not the norm that it was in my generation. My advice is this: don't have difficult conversations with your kids around the family dinner table…pick another spot. Let that family environment be sacred to positive family interaction. The right place might be by creating a family institution of "going for a walk" (best in a nature setting) for these discussions. And bottom-line strategy: don't do nothing!!!

The late Harvard professor Clayton Christensen in his final book cited research by Risley and Hart on the subject of parents communicating with their very young children. Apparently, parents speak in a range of 600–2,100 words per hour with their child. Developmentally, it is not so much the volume of words spoken, but rather the subject matter and tone. They termed richer, adult-like interactions "language dancing," which invoke deeper thought processes within the child's brain, which in turn developmentally produce a cognitive advantage for the child.

There is that old truth: You don't change people, you influence them to change themselves. There is a strategy that might be effective, called proxy questions: a more delicate way to probe into someone's life. Essentially, the issues you are trying to address become "objectified" for the conversation. You might view it as presenting in "third person" instead of "second person," to use the grade-school grammar metaphor.

> *Stop asking kids what they want to be when they grow up.*
> —Adam Grant, author

Grant calls this a second-person-singular question that puts the pressure squarely on the child. Kids learn what adults want to hear: "I want to be a doctor…I want to be a rocket scientist, etc." More genuine answers may result from re-framing, for instance in third-person-singular: "What do you think a young person your age should aspire to be in today's world?" Or change the timeline: "What do you think you would like to be doing when you are retired?"

"But…I'm just a KID." That was the response of my fifteen-year-old great nephew when I gave him a book to read on personal development. On the one hand, we ought not to steal or crush the beauty of childhood from a child (as per Lyall Watson earlier). On the other hand, while I have zero formal education in psychology, only in the School of Life, I believe that the teen years are extremely formative to the future value systems of the adult. But they recognize that they still are kids, and adulthood stands far down the road.

> *If you want to build a ship, don't drum up people to collect wood and don't assign them tasks and work; but rather, teach them to long for the vast and endless sea.*
> —Antoine de Saint Exupery, twentieth-century French author

Let Children Practise Being Grown Up

When young people express a "want," endeavour to help them build a process towards that purchase to instill deliberation over impulse. What are they going to do with it? How often will they use it? Is there a past lesson to draw upon from a previous purchase decision? Give some context, by way of comparison, to the magnitude of the proposed purchase. Recall Section 2.5 Happiness and Meaning, which posited that experiences yield more happiness than material things.

In my youth it was fashionable with some parents to assist, but also to inspire. They called it matching! I wanted a bike. "Save up for it!" they said. Whatever I saved, my parents would match. It was kinda like buying a bike on sale for 50% off.

Don't allow "being a kid" to become a career choice for your adult offspring. The last couple of cohort generations have experienced inflation: **maturity** inflation… A lot of kids don't "grow up" until their late twenties now, adding an extra decade to "child-rearing." Society as a whole engages in a consensual conspiracy to retard the maturation of today's youth.

> *Jumping from failure to failure with undiminished enthusiasm is a secret of success.*
> —Science Team at the Hadron Collider

Modern education has taken the position that children should be shielded from the pain of failure. The reality is that adulthood doesn't work like that. So, let them learn to fail, and fail often, and perhaps even fail spectacularly…whilst the stakes are small in youth. Remember: A diamond is a chunk of coal that did well under pressure.

If you are a parent, you may quickly associate "safety" with that of your offspring.

If you have young offspring, safety probably takes a physical tack: "Look both ways before your cross the street." "Let me hold your hand." "Don't run too fast, or you'll fall and hurt yourself." Over time, your offspring grow older, and you don't worry about those physical dangers so much. But then they enter teen-hood and, in today's world, you worry about their psychological safety in the world of peers and social media. Then, as young adults, you worry about their financial safety: Can they get, and hold, good jobs? Will they find good life partners? Does that couple struggle with fertility? And then, its full circle to worrying as a grandparent: "Look both ways before you cross the street." Or it is: "Oh My! The kids are getting divorced."

Years ago, I bought a reconstructed New Orleans gas lamp (converted to electricity) that I placed at the bottom of my driveway.

I bought this special electric bulb that mimicked the flickering of a gas light. One day, my new neighbour appeared at my doorstep and said that her three-year-old daughter would get scared whenever she walked by it flickering in the dark at night, and would I change the bulb? As a parent, you may be horrified with my response. I told the mother that perhaps it was a good thing that children learn how to deal with being scared by something as innocuous as a light-bulb. No life will be completely devoid of some form of trauma. Life skills, like self-reliance, openness to new experiences, and resilience need to be learned. We are blessed with practice enduring small things in order to be better prepared to endure big things.

> *Research shows that stress inoculation training—in which people learn to cope with anger, fear, and anxiety by being exposed to stimuli that cause these feelings—is effective in creating emotional resilience.*
> —Arthur C. Brooks, author and Harvard professor

As a parent raising kids, you contribute to their safety by way of the values you bestow in them, be that deliberate or inferred. The approach to child-rearing has changed radically, and in barely one generation. Western-society parenting has evolved to a "safety net" approach, where kids are protected and where, to use the Garrison Keillor line: "All the children are perfect." A philosophically different approach is to provide kids with **springboard, not safety net**, assistance.

In my lecturing, I often state that attitudes towards money are formulated by the mid-teens. Academic social scientists have declared me wrong. That age is ten, which coincides with their brains beginning to master second-order reasoning. If you are now on the other side of that child's age, you, the parent, need to think early and fast about how you may mould or contribute to your children's attitude towards money. And when I say the word "money," I also mean the word "spending," because the two are inextricably linked. A lot of life's progressions are determined for many of us by just fumbling along. A lifetime is a long time, and there seems to be plenty of time to make mistakes and make up for them later. But not with this. Zero to ten will go by in a flash. And then…it's too late. So, parents need to be more proactive in having a strategy here.

Creative Financial Training for Your Kids

And so, I introduce an interesting collection of ideas from David Owen, a journalist with *The New Yorker* magazine, in his book *The First National Bank of Dad*. He first sets the stage with some observations, then he proposes a wild and interesting idea—the Bank of Dad, a financial institution destined to lose money.

He opines that: "To a kid, a savings account is just a black hole that swallows birthday cheques…they perceive that parentally enforced money restrictions are not intended to promote saving but rather to curtail consumption."

Parents wish their children to behave with their money with mature sobriety, often even more so than they do themselves! "Long term" to a five-year-old does not have the same association as it does to a parent. In Owen's estimation, a fair metric of long term for a small child is probably a month. "To be attractive to a child, saving has to make life better for the child—and the benefits have to be tangible." At current interest rates in regular financial institutions, the interest earned on $100 in a year might be enough to buy a chocolate bar. This is insufficient to learn the rewards of saving and deferred gratification.

Instead, The National Bank of Dad would take in deposits from his young children and pay them—are you ready—**5% per month**! Compounded, that comes to 70% per annum. This turned them into instant accumulators of wealth. As soon as they could see their saving was generating a meaningful reward, frenzied spending and instant gratification were less interesting.

Owen's bank also functioned like a regular bank, where withdrawals could be made. He left withdrawable cash in a special place in the house, and the children could draw on it on a honour system and have their "account" debited.

Over time, as money accumulated and wants developed, the young children also learned valuable lessons about "buying well"—getting value for money and not buying based upon infatuation of the moment. These traits aren't so easily learned spending "other people's money." The philosophical issue at hand is that of control.

> *Children need to experience, within the limited confines of youth, the importance of the feedback loop of spending and of saving. They need the opportunity to make wise and foolish decisions in order to hone their decision-making skills.*

Over time, however, Owen discovered that he had seeded too much success! The children's savings were growing significantly, particularly after they were old enough to make some outside pocket money to invest. The 5% per month compounding rate was starting to take its toll. So, he "renegotiated" the rate to 3%. This system carried on for six years until the children entered teen-hood, at which time another clever scheme kicked in, and the Bank of Dad closed its doors.

As the children entered teen-hood, other grown-up lessons needed to be experienced, and they needed to be weaned off 36% rates of return at the bank. So, Owen graduated from banking to a stock exchange. He became the brokerage and clearing house for his children to undertake real, albeit simulated, stock investing. In essence, he became the other side of the transaction in all of their trades. He had a simple idea to tie it to the real world yet make it do-able: all of the real stock prices were divided by one hundred! In other words, the share that traded on the real market at $80 would trade at the Dad Exchange for eighty cents. The account also functioned like a real one because low rates of interest (no longer 3% per month) were paid on cash balances, phantom dividends were credited, and any bond or mutual fund could be bought. Owen started the process by seeding their accounts with approximately $250 spread across six blue chip stocks. After that…it was into the deep end! The author was largely hands-off in the area of investing advice, choosing instead that the children learned themselves.

Hopefully, Owen's family also has a philanthropy philosophy and strategy, even if that involves donating $100 per year. Start a family process where the kids contribute to (and maybe even decide) which charities will be supported. Teach them to research these organizations on the internet. Flush out/create passions for causes with these young people.

It is not likely to see your fifteen-year-old sign up for an online university course in finance, but there are other ways to advance their experiences. For instance, you might prevail upon your investment advisor to donate a half-hour to them. It's also a good time to dust off the old globe you bought for them years ago and spin it around to show the breadth of the planet and global investing. They probably are learning in school about environmental matters—introduce them to wind-farm tech companies. They also are probably more adept on the web than you are—challenge their Google skills to look up wind farms and do some research. Investing insights also can be learned from their vantage point. My wife and I own a large dog and a very small dog. We always laugh when the little one sees that the shortest distance between two points involves walking between the four legs and underneath the large dog! From our vantage point we don't see it—from hers—it's obvious. Similarly, young people too have plenty of perspective as mini consumers…pet shops, clothing chains, technology companies, etc.

In summary, Owen's two ideas are creative and interesting, and worthy of consideration.

Influencing Through Storytelling

Gutenberg, the inventor of the printing press in the fifteenth century, obviously made a huge contribution to civilization. But his great achievement inadvertently acted out an old concept in mythology, which says that **you can't create something new unless you kill something old**. He killed family "story telling." For all-time before that, wisdom and knowledge were passed on from generation to generation by stories around the fire.

My client, who was a grandfather, had grown up as a young boy in Nazi Germany. He had written stories about his experiences then, which he wanted to share with his grandsons, including a Christmas story about escaping Hitler Jungen training to find his way back home to his mother in the dead of winter. But his son said "no," he didn't want to have his kids hear that, and the story died in the trash bin.

Long before the printed page, telegraph, telephone, television, and internet, telling stories around the family fire or dinner table was a prime means of communicating family history and, implicitly, family values. Family story-telling is not so common anymore, if for no other reason than it lacks a locus in which to occur. In the post-television era, we get our "story" fix from the world of television shows: our stories are not **our** stories, but rather stories of fictional families on the screen. And, in the post-Hollywood era, we are inundated with an infinite number of stories available to us in that medium. Our heroes may become Bart Simpson rather than Grampa Bill.

The Family Narratives Lab explores how people remember and narrate life's events.

They conducted research on a child's emotional well-being. The number one predictor? Take a guess. **They determined it was whether the child knew their family history.** Family story-telling bonds the family unit and contributes to the identity and development of the child. Historically, a lot of family story-sharing happened around the meal table, or afterwards in the family room. But, in today's modern family, time-tempered meals are uncommon, as there is usually some soccer practice, etc. to get the kids to. And family room time together is displaced by video games and screen time. It might be valuable to visit their website.

To be fair, the decline of storytelling has been a two-way street: the young don't want to hear it (too busy on their devices) and the old don't want to tell (too busy in modern-day life). I would aspire that the Family Confab section will provide a renaissance to inter-generational story-telling, perhaps through the medium of a family treasure book, with contributions from all generations. This book captures family events, history, beliefs. It is part scrapbook, part "operating manual," part dialogue box. In the overall proceedings of Family Confab, it may be clever to appoint someone from the young generation as custodian of the Family Treasure book. In the modern world, and with family geographic dispersal, it may be wise to make the book digital.

Now, let's overlay an amazing story from 2016 at Penn State University, where some students were invited to "write letters to their freshmen selves covering what they wish they had known back then" (when they started their college career). The responses were aggregated and ended up on a website that became very popular for other incoming freshmen, and it was duplicated at other universities. To be grammatically correct, this was a shift to "first person," not to "third person," but the principle is the same…avoiding "second person."

What's the point here? You, the leading or presiding generation, can exercise your impact and influence in "first person." Again, that old truth: **You don't change people, you influence them to change themselves.** Take the time to write down your own short stories that bear upon family money philosophy and pass them down. Aspire to be ego-less in this process: be willing to show yourself as the hero or the goat in these stories. Aggregate these over time, perhaps into a small book. Or perhaps send out periodic "instalments" to the following generation. Encourage response and feedback, perhaps positioning that as them helping you, not vice versa. This can flow into the Family Confab concept introduced in the next section.

Money And Grown-Up Children

> *Every generation has to start again from zero. There are no certainties about the future. We must always have our antennae alert to the way things are changing.*
> —Carlo Petrini, founder of the Slow Food Movement in 150 countries

Petrini's philosophy is certainly in extremis and unpalatable to parents today.

In fact, the opposite is likely to be more common: "I don't want my kids to have to experience what I had to." The long tail of history—across cultures—has proven that the old adage "from "shirtsleeves to shirtsleeves" in three generations (the Dutch say from "clogs to clogs") is an historically guaranteed phenomenon as sure as the sun rises. In very recent history, the middle class has exploded across many regions of the planet. There has been insufficient time and effort for that presiding generation to absorb the reality of their new wealth and to embrace multi-generational WealthNess. This "climate change" in the family unit ranks in urgency with the Earth's climate issues, In fact, they are correlated.

According to Dirk Junge, author and former wealth advisor, the presiding generation has "the chance to sustain not just family wealth, but also to pass on the values and education (the following generations) need to find success and satisfaction in their pursuits."

The values that I am speaking of include:

- Spending wisely
- Investing wisely
- Giving back (and the transference of those values forward)

Let's start by visiting some well-known people in the upper wealth category and see what they think about multi-generational WealthNess transfer:

- Thirty-year-old New Yorker Thomas Gilbert went to jail for killing his father when his financial support was reduced.
- The rock star Sting announced in 2014 that none of his six children would be inheriting any of his estate.
- Daniel "James Bond" Craig joined the list with a similar pronouncement in 2021.
- Fashion mogul Peter Nygard found himself and his wealth in a high-profile divorce case in 2002, challenging a monthly child maintenance payment of $68,000. The plaintiff ultimately was awarded monthly maintenance of $15,000 while the defence cited "affluenza," a paronomasia coined in the 1950s by Fred Whitman from "affluence" and "influenza."
- Warren Buffett is of course famous for his official estate strategy of leaving "enough money so that (children) feel they can do anything, but not so much that they could do nothing."

There are two opposing schools of thought on children born into financial privilege. The glass-half-full says, "**May you be blessed by the curse of inherited wealth**." The glass-half-empty says, "**May you be cursed by the blessing of inherited wealth.**"

My observation in life is that when a situation develops between two people, the "blame" is very seldom all on one side, and more likely to be proportionate. So, if your grown child has not developed financial responsibility, and you choose a final shot over the bow by leaving them little or nothing in your estate, you likely are blind to some degree of your own proportionate blame for their shortcoming. We need to be critical thinkers, not simply consumers of sensational press. The emphasis in these high-profile stories isn't necessarily about how these offspring should learn to make it on their own. Rather, we should also ask all those famous world "Names" what they did or didn't do in raising their children to instill sound financial values. Who is to say that, properly trained, those inheritors couldn't be great custodians of wealth?

Sketches in Personal Finance

"I only am concerned with my son." Thus spoke an elderly, wealthy client to my suggestion to prepare his following generations for a large inheritance. He had only one child and two grandchildren. His position was that it was his son's responsibility to oversee this issue with his grandsons. But, for starters, he **wasn't** addressing the issue with his son either, aged sixty. Secondly, by the time his son inherits from his dad, the grandsons will be in their thirties and have missed critical years of money-minded-ness. Is he falling back on my other client's opening line in Section 2.1 Money Philosophy: "Money is dirty"? If so, we may need to reference back to that section to refresh on the "soul of money."

In my experience, the following generation manages their family finances in **their current reality,** not based upon some **prospective future event**. They can't practise on a "shadow" portfolio or a "shadow" lifestyle. With the presiding generation's new longevity, it often means today that the following generation is inheriting at upwards of age sixty-five to seventy. This leaves scarce little time to gain experience with WealthNess, which may require some learning mistakes to be made along the way. Reference back to the Section 2.3 Root Purposes, in which we discussed Sudden Wealth Syndrome: the adjustment problems afflicting individuals who suddenly come into large sums of money, such as through a lottery or inheritance. Becoming suddenly wealthy can cause significant stress to an individual. Symptoms include feeling isolated from pre-existing (and perhaps jealous) friends, guilt over good fortune, or an extreme fear of losing the money.

The reality is that much inter vivos, inter-generational assistance happens these days. Part of the success of this is situation-specific…in how each party handles it. We are inspired by James Hughes. In two books, Hughes has left a remarkable and beautiful invocation to all of us as givers and as recipients. Both books focus on the transaction between these two parties. Each must understand the role of giving and of receiving.

To distill his wisdom to its finest essence: "How can we give and receive in ways to enhance growth and freedom rather than subsidize dependency and entitlement?"

His position is that we don't take the time to understand what transpires between the parties when there is a gift. Both parties have responsibility here. The giver must do more than "sign the cheque," and the recipient more than cash it. He says that the act of giving quickly disappears into the ether without an echo. In fact, what is required is to understand the spirit of the gift. The giver ought to self-reflect upon the reason for the giving and put themselves also in the recipient's shoes. The action of giving cannot stand on its own without words attached that communicate the giver's intent. The recipient must experience gratitude, not entitlement. The recipient might have responses that the giver did not intuit. The spirit of the gift should neither be a bribe nor a penalty payment. That said, both parties must recognize that no gift is truly free. In fact, Hughes cites that in Iroquois culture the gift is believed to have a spirit of its own. So, aside from our persona as a giver, our gift acts as an instrument: a sword that we wield to fight our battles or a shield that we use, similarly, to save us from harm from battle.

Sketches in Personal Finance

I was in a meeting in our boardroom with my seventy-five-year-old, retired academic scientist client. We had worked together for over thirty years. He was a major global force in his field and was still doing a bit of consulting around the world, which he did through a small company he owned with his grown stepsons. We were discussing how to distribute the year's corporate earnings, and he directed me to declare $10,000 dividends to each son. With cheque book in hand, he had me fill in the two cheques, which he then signed and asked me to mail to the boys. At that moment I remembered James Hughes.

I went to my desk drawer and pulled out a selection of greeting cards. "David, pick one card for each son and take a moment to write them each a note. I will address the envelopes while you're doing that."

He cried. He did it. We did it. And he died a year later from cancer. His boys remain clients of mine today.

Practising WealthNess

There are tidy, small ways to help grown children practise wealth. A young couple with kids today has three fundamental saving pots to work on: the kids' education accounts, the parents' pension accounts, and tax-free savings accounts. The presiding generation might assist annually with these contributions.

Sketches in Personal Finance

I first met Graham, an engineer, forty years ago when he was president of a charitable organization and approached me to serve as its volunteer treasurer. I did, and we both served on that board for a few years. After that, we exchanged Christmas cards for twenty years until, one day, he phoned me and later he and his wife became clients. Ten years after that, he sadly passed away from cancer. His wife was now custodian of a fairly large portfolio....another meteorite! The couple had two grown children, each with a career, a spouse, no kids, and little in the way of financial assets. Mom sold the family home, changed cities, and moved in with her daughter. Her financial picture was healthy. The kids had not been drawn into their parents' financial picture while Dad was alive but were now cognizant (a second meteorite). I flew over to her new home, and we spent the afternoon talking about her money. She agreed that: a) she had more than she would ever need and b) the kids ought to get used to having wealth. So, she committed to an annual, modest wealth transfer to each child to fund their annual pension and TFSA contributions. She called this "test-tube money"! The passing of their dear dad also rang the bell on each of the couples to start preparing for their own retirements. Each couple is still with me and has a portfolio of approximately $300,000 and has started to add their own saving contributions.

My early years in practice in the late 1980s coincided with the beginning of the tectonic shift in real estate prices. The impact was that grown-up kids could not aspire to raise a family within the large city urban communities in which they grew up. The knock-on effect was the start of inter vivos wealth transfer from parents to their offspring. The now-grandparents did not wish to see their children and grandchildren living far away in an affordable, small town. In many cases, this worked out well. The nuclear family remained close, and the kids enjoyed further price appreciation in their homes. Sadly, some of those young marriages did not survive, and the resulting divorce brought the financially supporting parents into court to "protect" their loan investment from their now-ex-in-law.

I think that most uber-wealthy people understand that the wealth they pass on likely will continue for generations immemorial. *Credit Suisse* somehow arrived at a statistic in 2021 that there were 56 million millionaires on the planet (defined to have assets exceeding US$1 million). My point is that there are many wealthy folks who aren't uber-wealthy but will nonetheless pass on significant wealth that, too, has the likely potential to continue for time immemorial. It is extremely difficult, bordering on impossible, to have such folks grasp the concept that their wealth will be forever (ignoring the likely climate issues and the less-likely meteorite). In their minds, it "expires" on their passing…because they no longer are custodians. However, there is **only one thing they need to do to hedge the family's infinite future:** instill financial responsibility—WealthNess—in the following generation. That's it. Trying to conjure what their investment portfolio is going to look like in the year 2220 doesn't matter. None of today's companies in the S&P 500 will even exist then. Many of the countries in the world may not exist then. You, the presiding generation, need only leave this one major legacy.

3.3 Family Confab

Inspiring WealthNess Across Generations

There is the old saying: We don't really know what a hammer is until we encounter a nail.

We can morph that a bit to: We don't really **appreciate** what a nail is until we **own** a hammer.

The punchline to family finance is that the following generations need to be prepared for wealth. It may resonate with you if I suggest that the following generations are stakeholders **today** in **your** WealthNess.

Everything we have shared so far in the previous sections of Chapter 3 is a segue to now.

If you are part of a family in the traditional sense, then all of your work through Chapter 3 needs to transmogrify to those who will succeed today's leading generation. (I am going to capitalize Family in this section to emphasize its importance.) Successful WealthNess **should** pass forward to succeeding generations "until the meteorite strikes." Failure to pass on appreciation of WealthNess to the following generation dilutes or nullifies all that the leading generation accomplished. It is probably safe to say that passing forward a WealthNess philosophy is harder work than making the material wealth itself.

If you are single with no children, and your inheritors are other relatives, e.g., nieces, nephews, etc., then I believe you still have a duty to share your values with them. If you are single and charities will inherit the bulk of your worldly wealth, then you can skip this section.

> *The health of a Family at any time is the reflection of the consciousness of the Family.*

This is my own adlib from a quote by Hazrat Inayat Khan, a twentieth-century Indian professor of musicology. It rings the gong to multi-generational WealthNess.

In 2015, I conjured a concept I called Family Confab, which could become the medium for extending the concept of WealthNess across generations. "Confab" is not a commonly used term in today's language. It derives from Latin and means:

- A chat together
- An informal private conversation/discussion
- A meeting of members of a particular group

The purpose of Family Confab is: to inspire a healthy and successful approach to WealthNess across Family generations by having all Family members actively engaged in that process.

The goals of Confab include:

- Leaving a lasting, positive impact on generations far into the future
- Mitigating money worries and thereby reducing stress
- Building a coherent Family philosophy towards life and WealthNess
- Building a Family culture where difficult subjects are able to be discussed and differences are addressed

Family Confab is a major undertaking and, thus, elevates to a higher ski trail.

Detour to:

A Family Confab needs a family leader to be the champion and driving force. This should be the presiding generation, unless they are very elderly, in which case the leading generation should lead.

Family Financial Genome mapping

LiDAR stands for Light Detection And Ranging.

A LiDAR system bounces laser pulses off subterranean objects on Earth to locate and measure them. LiDAR shares many common elements with radar, but the wavelength of light is thousands of times shorter, which allows super accurate results to be delivered very quickly. LiDAR has many commercial and industrial applications. But it also has been a boon to archeology. LiDAR-equipped planes can fly over ancient lands overgrown by nature and geology over hundreds or thousands of years. LiDAR allows the area to be mapped, allowing geologists to visualize what an ancient settlement looked like, further contributing to understanding better that civilization itself.

Now, let's slide LiDAR over to Family Confab and uncovering/mapping ancient Family attitudes towards money. An archeologist flying above such overgrowth without LiDAR would be hard pressed to guess what was there; it is too hidden.

Similarly, my Confab invocation for you and your family to flush out Family values is equally difficult. So, we need some tools....

Family financial genome mapping may be a good place to start.

A Family financial genome map is a set of philosophical landmarks that identify the foundation of how money is viewed, as you worked through in Chapter 2. **Genome mapping** enables scientists to compare the genomes of different species, yielding insights from comparisons. Similarly, the Family financial genome map also needs to look outside the Family to compare to "norms." Some "disease genes" may be systemic in the surrounding society; like cancer is to a physical genome, entitlement is to a financial genome. What might this involve? Family members might generate a series of questions whose responses speak to the underlying financial psyche of that person, which contributes to the Family financial genome.

For example, do you agree or disagree with these statements:

- "I believe that my children should learn to support themselves and expect no inheritance."
- "I believe that financial problems always sort themselves out, and don't require remedial action."
- "I believe in putting a significant portion of income into savings throughout a working career."
- "I don't believe my kids should work at menial jobs through school when they are going to be professionals one day."
- "I figured out money on my own, and my kids should do the same."
- "My Family and I deserve the things we have."
- "My Family and I have a consistent concept of what constitutes success."
- "My Family and I have a consistent concept of what constitutes happiness."

Next, consider:

- Who in the Family line had the gene for **profligate spending**? Or **parsimony**? Or **industriousness?** Or **laziness**?
- Where and when along the Family line did prosperity develop? Or decline?
- What values caused either of those?
- Where along the Family line did social responsibility develop? Egocentrism?

All of these responses should be written down, aggregated across all Family members and compared. Inconsistent Family responses can be identified and investigated. The Family Financial "disease genes" can be identified from their root source and addressed. Family Confab aspires to sustain the information flow about family culture across the cohorts.

In the long history of un-hygienic medical practice, the birthing process often not only took the life of the newborn but also the young mother. In the mid-nineteenth century, the Austrian physician Ignaz Semmelweis fell upon the possibility that puerperal fever could be mitigated if the attending obstetrician practised hand scrubbing. His hypothesis was soundly rejected by the medical community, even though he was supported by the famous Florence Nightingale. Scrubbing-up did not become accepted practice until after his death in 1865. Further, it was not officially incorporated into the American medical system until the 1980s.

Is there something similar in the Family financial practices…something incredibly obvious, once seen; something that might invoke pushback and denial from family members; something that actually could be huge if corrected?

Creating a Family Values Statement

We met Mark Anielski in Section 2.2 Happiness and Meaning. He directs his concept of genuine wealth to the **community** level: "A genuinely wealthy community is one which has articulated its values and lives life accordingly. Such communities work in a spirit of collective and shared responsibility, or stewardship, to ensure that the various conditions of well-being that add to quality of life are flourishing, vibrant, life-giving, and sustainable for current and future generations."

> *There is no power for change greater than a community discovering what it cares about.*
> —Author Margaret Wheatley

Now re-read both of these quotes about **community** and substitute the word "**Family**" for "community." Family Confab should result in defining its statement of Family values. **"This Family believes in…"** which would include, inter alia, financial values.

The following questions might provide some ignition for the fire:

- "What are our individual and collective goals for the next year…for the next five years? How will we work together to attain them, and what plans/sacrifices will this require?"

- "Do we/should we practise the silo school of home economics by putting money away regularly for specific purposes (vacation, major purchases, renovations, education, retirement)?"
- "How do we manage life's never-ending one-time annual costs (house and car insurance, property taxes, mortgage bonusing, pension contributions)?"
- "Are we victims of the 'wealth effect' when house values keep going up?"
- "Are foreign real-estate investors driving up real estate prices a bigger asset to us than our own human capital in earning a living?"
- "How much fortitude do we have as a Family to lean into the Joneses Phenomenon?"

Family Confab should explore what Dr. Dennis Jaffe calls a "Family constitution," and result in developing a Family "treasure book" where family members of all ages contribute their thoughts on what the family does well, what it does poorly, what the family values are, what is given and what is taken back, etc.

Family treasure book section topics may include:

- This Family believes in…
- This Family supports its members by…
- This Family is good at…
- This Family is not good at…
- I support this Family by…
- This Family is blessed by…
- This Family's beliefs are reflected to the outside world through…

As you work on your family value statement and Family treasure book, keep in mind that each Family member/generation needs a role, some way of contributing:

Grandparent cohort:

- Influencing the Family's societal capital
- Inculcating the Family's spiritual capital
- Contemplating their legacy
- Protecting Family cohesion
- Transitioning their own fiscal management

Older parent cohort:

- Transitioning from high-cost time of life to high-saving time of life

- Address Tharp's focal length: zoom-in and zoom-out (as discussed in the Introduction)
- Judiciously managing out-patient care for younger generations
- Influencing the Family's societal capital
- Managing their financial capital
- Leading the Family capital

Young parent cohort:

- Initiating the culture of Family capital
- Inculcating the value of human capital upon younger generation
- Forming Family financial capital
- Financial role-modelling for younger generation
- Seeking purpose
- Building resilience

Older child cohort:

- Investing in their human capital
- Developing attitude to societal capital
- Developing altruism and gratefulness
- Developing purpose
- Attuning the older generations to shifting societal values
- Being mindful that their adult values are already forming

Younger child cohort:

- Understanding that their attitudes towards money are already being developed

The child cohort might become the coordinator and custodian of a Family treasure book. A family retreat might make a positive work-and-play environment. To keep things manageable at the start, the Family might target some specific outcomes to work on.

Communication is obvious and critical. Couples and families need to discuss financial matters overtly, not just by playing out behaviours (as Eric Barker warned us in the Invocation Chapter). This is critical throughout the evolution of a multi-generational Family, and the nature of the conversations needs to change as the offspring age and mature.

The concept of rantisizing in Section 2.6 should be fair game in the Family Confab environment.

Family Confab likely should morph into a tradition. There will be a lot more heavy-lifting in the inaugural event, and subsequently, more of an update/review. Somebody needs to take notes. The concept of personal retreat in Section 2.6 might inspire a family retreat for Confab. One of my clients had a multi-decade institution of family camp. Unlike the Las Vegas ad, what happens at Family Confab retreat needs to find its way home. Fundamental Family Confab values might get "coded" into expressions that work their way into day-to-day life.

In summary, your response to this section may be "Oh my gosh! That is way too much work!" I ask you to consider:

- The **known costs** of undertaking this: Who in the Family has the time? The skill? The stake? It involves moving out of our Family comfort zone.
- The **unknown benefits** of undertaking this: Remember here the all-important concept that we shared in the Invocation chapter: the present value of pain. The "pain" is what can, and does, happen to families that fail to prepare future generations to steward money …to build a family philosophy for the ages. But this pain may be in the future, maybe even distant future! Maybe soooo far in the future that the presiding generation can't begin to fathom it. When discount rates meet the long term, the value today indeed seems small. But odds are high that pain will hit every family eventually.

Remember also our visit with Stanley and Danko in Section 2.2 and their concept of PAWs, AAW, and UAWs.

It is always fun to see "little" kids display adult thoughts.

I remember hearing a five-year old declare that his favourite food was sushi. I don't think I even knew what sushi was until I was at least twenty! But the experience is even sweeter when that youngster displays **adult financial behaviours**. My neighbours have three boys—aged eight, ten, and sixteen. Last summer, I was away for a week on a business trip, and I hired the two young ones to keep my precious garden watered. When I got back, I was intending to pay them. But their dad intervened with his own Family lesson about give-and-take: "Don lets you use his pool—this is your appreciation back." So, I was pre-coached that the boys were not going to accept my $25. Instead, I developed a back-up strategy for our meeting. I told them I accepted their gift of time, but I ought not to benefit financially from their kindness. I proposed to still part with my $25…but to a charity of their choosing. That led to a long story about charities and choosing the one(s) that meet your passions. That led to much conversation in their family living room…during which the eight-year-old left the room. He returned and gave me $5 to add to the pot. I made a donation of $500.

I would love to hear how your little ones grow and give at Family Confab.

*Return to the **book's main pathway in the next Section**.*

3.4 Key Words and Concepts

29. Where are you in the couple's normal distribution curve?
30. How do the couple's financial inclinations and skill-sets overlap
31. Is there a family financial pathology?
32. Parenting is the genome of society
33. A family is an environment and subject to climate change
34. Parenting behaviour conveys much more than parenting style
35. Teach your kids to embrace thought experiments, including financial scenarios
36. Where, when, and how do parents convey financial values?
37. Kids start developing money attitudes very early
38. Bank of Dad: a practical tool to inspire the saving habit
39. How do we restore family story-telling?
40. The obligation of the presiding generation to embue WealthNess/money-minded-ness in the next generations
41. Bank-rolling "test tube" money-minded-ness by the presiding generation
42. Gifting a "nail" to appreciate a hammer
43. On gifts, gratitude, and entitlement
44. The health of a family at any time is the reflection of the consciousness of that family
45. Mapping the Family Financial Genome/identifying financial pathology and disease genes
46. A Family Treasure Book can create an open forum to advance Family WealthNess
47. All generations have a role in Family Confab

Chapter 4: Financial Planning

If you don't know where you are going, any road will get you there.
—Lewis Carroll

I hesitate to rehash this much-quoted quote, but it is so pristinely correct. I hope that by the end of this book, you will plan to have a **plan**…perhaps a series of mini-plans that advance you wisely through your financial life.

The term "**economics**" derives from the Latinized Greek *oeconomica*, which meant **household management**, and was about managing household accounts. "Home economics" today has morphed to the study of food, nutrition, and health, and "economics" is a PhD-level academic endeavour, which effectively still studies "household accounts," but in **aggregate** for a whole society.

Personal financial planning is a nebulous term to most people, and meets resistance:

- I am too young to need this!
- I am too old to benefit from this!
- I don't have enough wealth to apply this!
- I'd rather be golfing or gardening!
- What can it do for ME?

What does it *mean*? In this chapter, I proffer different takes on personal financial planning. They will vary in their degree of difficulty to execute and, accordingly, in their efficacy over a lifetime. I take this approach for the purpose of hoping that you will find at least one simple approach that works for you now…and maybe you will "graduate" to more complex ones over time. The key in the moment is not so much the means, as it is the end. Your goal is to raise the bar of your financial management now. Momentum can be gained by small wins.

Getting your financial house in order is neither too big nor too futile a project to embrace. Let's try a baseball analogy: "runs" are what win a game.

Runs are easily defined as getting a player safely to home plate. However, how that is achieved is what makes the game. One batter can step to the plate and take one pitch and blast it out of the park—that makes a run. If other players happen to be on base at the same time, they too will score. Alternately, a runner may be on third base and a line drive to right field allows the player to come home, even though the batter may get thrown out at first. Finally, a batter may get to first, and the subsequent hitting strategy is to advance that runner around the bases. The ultimate drama, of course, is the bottom-of-the-ninth grand slam homer!

And so it is with a multitude of financial planning, tax, and investing strategies. If you look at them from the wrong perspective, you may say: "Pass—the benefit is too small." I will counter that doing a bunch of small things—hitting a bunch of singles—advances your goal of WealthNess. Embrace every one of them.

*Life's **biggest** question is: "How long will I live?" Life's **second biggest** question is: "Will I have **enough**?"*

Financial planning follows two forms: modular (which I will call Ages and Stages) and a formal six steps. The latter is a detailed process that produces a long-term prognostication and plan for the remainder of one's life. It should answer life's second biggest question. Modular planning follows the timeline of one's progression through life from early adulthood to retirement and legacy.

In this chapter we will go under the hood of the following ways to raise your bar of financial planning:

- A role-play into the future
- S.I.T.
- A periodic financial checkup, called Ages and Stages, as you progress through life
- A formal financial plan

Chapter 4

4.1 Preparing for the Future

4.2 Planning for Ages and Stages

4.3 Financial Plans

4.4 Longevity

4.5 Key Words and Concepts

4.1 Preparing for the Future

Know What Is Ahead of You

Life's second biggest question is: Will I have enough? The late John Bogle was the famous founder of Vanguard and the author of many investing books, including *Enough,* in which he spoke about the accumulation of wealth. **He believed that "the heart of a family is not its money or power but its values."** He described his blessings as:

- Innate frugality
- Common sense
- Propensity to save
- The miracle of compounding
- The value of a balanced portfolio

Let's turn to a former political figure for some guidance on "enough." Donald Rumsfeld had a high profile in US politics, particularly when he was Secretary of Defense. He was unfairly ridiculed for his "We don't know what we don't know" speech. Here's what that concept would look like in a matrix:

	AWARENESS	
	You Know	You Don't Know
KNOWLEDGE You Know		
You Don't Know		

Now let's take his matrix, modify it, and apply it to the world of personal finance. Our horizontal remains the same: **Awareness**; however, our vertical changes from **Knowledge** to Bogle's **Enough.**

Take a moment to decide which cell describes your confidence with your long-term finances. For instance, the top left square would mean "I **know** that I will have **enough**."

	AWARENESS	
E N O U G H	You Know	You Don't Know
You have		
You Don't Have		

Next, I have ascribed letters above to each of the cells. So, for instance, box A means "you know that you have enough," box B means "you don't know you have enough," etc. Identify your letter.

	AWARENESS	
E N O U G H	You Know	You Don't Know
You Have	A	B
You Don't Have	C	D

If you are in box A…congrats! However, you might wish to probe further and ask yourself if you have more than enough, and, if so, so what? You can decide to do nothing in response to this state, or you might start to think about how your "excess" can be directed, now or upon your passing, to some "good" in order to make an impact. You also might be wise to survey the worlds of your beneficiaries. Are they ill-prepared for your meteorite? Will you cause a trophic cascade, as introduced in Section 2.2 Root Attitudes. It is easy to say, "I don't care; I'll be dead," but this is the wrong legacy to leave in your wake. Your action call may be to prepare your beneficiaries to steward that wealth into future generations. See Section 3.3 Family Confab and Chapter 6: Legacy.

If you are in box B, perhaps ignorance is bliss? Maybe…depending upon your personality type. If you are the "half-full" type, perhaps you can safely stumble along on your present path and do just fine. If you are the "half-empty" type, then this uncertainty condition probably is not good for your health. You would be wise to get some competent opinion to affirm your financial health. If you are the chronic worrier type, then even this probably won't help much, as you will conjure future disaster scenarios.

If you are in box C, you may be living in the landscape of fear, as introduced in Section 2.2 Root Attitudes. This is not a healthy place either, for you or those connected with you. You need to commit to action, and may need an outsider to lead, direct, and cheerlead. You need to assess how critical your timelines are. If time is still on your side, modest behaviour change may get you to a better place. If time is against you, you really need to get at it. Make a plan, commit to its execution, and monitor your progress. Recall *obsta principiis* and the present value of pain in the Invocation Chapter. Embrace Stanley and Danko's concept of offence and defence, discussed in the Section 2.2 Root Attitudes.

When people come to me in this quadrant, I reach out to shake their hand and say, "Hi, allow me to introduce myself…I am the Smiths 2050." That future person needs some standing in your today world to make the need for action real and urgent. More on that in the next chapter.

If you are in Box D, you are a crisis-in-waiting. In his famous book, *All I Really Need to Know, I Learned in Kindergarten*, Robert Fulghum told a story about watching the neighbourhood kids playing hide-and-seek. He went on to talk about one particular shy kid, who was very excellent at hiding, and the rest of the kids could never find him. The author's advice to the kid was: **Get found, kid**. And that's my advice to you: **Get found**! Get help! Take action! Re-read the earlier discussion on cognitive dissonance in Chapter 1: Invocation, and, in particular, remember Morgan Housel's: "You can't prepare for what you can't envision."

Armed with your "Rumsfeld" classification, let's proceed through the rest of the Financial Planning Section accordingly.

Sketches in Personal Finance

The easiest thing you can do to kick-start a lifetime of good fiscal management is to embrace the following graph, reproduced from Section 2.1, where its purpose was to inspire and give hope. Here, we are more analytical in learning what Larry accomplished…

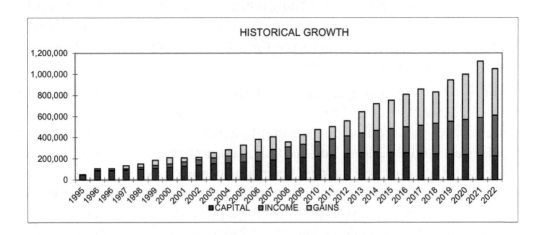

Larry was one of our very first clients when we opened our doors in 1994, and this succinctly summarizes his financial life history. He was age 40 at the time. He retired at age 60, and the plan we created had him live off other sources of wealth through his sixties, so that he would draw from his retirement account starting at age 70. This graph shows the growth in his retirement account, which he contributed to annually through all of his working years. The **bottom bar** on the chart represents his accumulated contributed savings over those years. The **two upper bars** represent the accumulated investment income (appreciation and cash income) earned over those same years. Note that the two portfolio income bars are fairly similar in size over those years. As you can see, the portfolio grew to $1.05 million in twenty-eight years, and approximately only one-quarter of that came from his own saving; the rest was earned investment income. So, becoming a "financial millionaire" only required a lifetime saving of $223,000.

The Discipline of Saving

A key element of successful personal finance draws upon discipline—that same discipline that gets you to the gym, that pushes you from the dessert table. For some of us, discipline challenges are met easily; for others, not so. Discipline is often called upon "in the moment": you eat that tart, or you don't; you go to the gym, or you watch television. Your decision on any given day may depend upon your mood that day. A stepping-stone to discipline is forming habits.

Create some financial habits.

Psychologists would call these "rituals," which give us a sense of control which, of course, then reduce our anxiety. There is a further benefit of rewarding our sense of self-discipline, leading to successful pursuit of goals; in our case, **financial** goals. These rituals ought to be specific, repetitive, and carried out!

What they are is actually less important. The breadth, depth, and frequency of your financial habits may vary according to your self-classification as beginner, intermediate. or expert. Those habits will evolve as your personal finance skills grow—think of the sea anemone tentacles. As a pathway to personal finance success, self-enforced saving schemes (e.g., automatic deposits) are second only to Einstein's astonishment with the power of compounding. The checklists that follow in this section may offer a starting point for your rituals.

Creating "structures" may interject a sort of third party to answer to. In my world of personal finance, I call these mental accounts "**silos**." I was on a tourist cruise boat on the Danube when I met Richard T. He told me how he saved up the funds to pay for vacations…in $5 increments. Literally every day, he would empty his pockets of loose change and bills under $5 into a jar! That's a silo.

When my wife passed away, I inherited a pension of hers of $600 per month. I arranged to have that deposit go straight into my retirement saving account. That's a silo. Another client of mine receives quarterly bonuses at work. He puts part of each cheque in the bank towards travel and house renovation accounts. That's a silo. The point here is to set up some structure that operates outside your momentary discretions and pays it forward to a **future you**.

There are various other attitudes out there towards personal finance—both bad and good.

A client once asked me this rhetorical question: "Doesn't everybody live off their line of credit these days?" This may not sound very profound, but **job one is to spend less than you make**, and we call that saving! In truth, for some people that is profound. I have a client today who was making $500,000 a year back in the 1980s, but he was spending $502,000. At age 80+ today, guess what? He is still working.

Then there was the Texan with "a tall hat and no boots" versus the accountant with "deep pockets and short arms."

Role-Playing into the Future

The reality is that money is the ultimate scarce resource for most of us.

Personal finance ultimately starts at the wallet: every expendable dollar in our pocket has a multitude of potential claimants. Some of these choices are trapped in the **today/tomorrow trade-off**. When you sit down with yourself to make these decisions, actively (and metaphorically) place another person at the conversation table—you in the year 2035! It is too easy to give this "person"—the retired YOU—no voice in today's financial decisions. We saw this with Dan in Section

2.4. The result of that meeting was the couple's commitment to themselves for 2050. They agreed upon an aggressive saving strategy which had them: a) contributing their annual, new RRSP room every year plus b) catching up their unused room over the next five years.

Now let's do a SIT Review. By **SIT**, I mean that you need to understand that, in managing your personal finances, you have THREE roles—as **Saver, Investor, and Taxpayer**—that make the SIT acronym.

Role One is the **Saver** and that means spending less than you make. Some money needs to be put aside from today's income to finance tomorrow's living costs. Ideally, this is achieved with a steady, monthly diet of contributions to your saving vehicles. If you leave it to a once-a-year act, like RRSP season in February, the cash cupboard may be bare at that time, and saving may not happen.

Role Two is the **Investor**, as you now must put those hard-earned savings to work in that savings account by selecting appropriate investments which, like you, will go to work each day to make more money for you. Too many people make that annual deposit, and then walk away until next year. That deposit may sit in cash, earning a pittance in a bank savings account or perhaps in a one-year GIC earning less than the rate of inflation. Too many people think that their job is finished when the **saving** part has been done. But the job has just begun when you plunk down that contribution to a saving vehicle at your financial institution. That money can invest in a wide variety of opportunities, literally around the world. Thus, the investor can build a powerful savings account that should be successful at accumulating wealth over a lifetime. Recall in Section 2.4 the chart showing the life-time **build-up of financial capital** as the **human capital declines** through until retirement.

Role Three is the **Taxpayer**. Here, you need to understand how taxation contributes to your personal financial decisions. At the saving moment, this includes understanding which type of account is most suited to your life goals: a TFSA, an RRSP, a RESP, or a "regular" account. This decision turns on what you are saving for—which silo: a new car, a house, education, retirement, etc. Each of these goals has a different timeline, and different accounts would accordingly be more suitable. Your tax bracket—both now and in later years—also comes to bear in choosing the right account vehicle. Lastly, **tax-smart investing principles** need to be understood and applied to your investing earnings, so that you are placing the right kinds of investments in the right kinds of accounts. More on that in Chapter 5: Investing.

Sound complicated? Well, in truth, it is. But it all starts with some knowledge and good intentions…and with periodically **applying the wisdom of "SIT."**

4.2 Planning for Ages and Stages

Modular financial planning

> *All the world's a stage, and all the men and women merely players; they have their exits and their entrances; and one man in his time plays many parts.*
> —Shakespeare, in *As You Like It*

And so it is for personal financial management: which player are you at this time, and what's your role if you are part of a family?

Modular financial planning is about having a series of **mini-plans and strategies** as you progress through the stages and cycle of life.

I have borrowed from the sports world and use the term "quarters"; thus, roughly dividing the life cycle into four stages. The duration of each quarter is arguably twenty to twenty-five years, thus representing a life span of eighty to a hundred years—that being somewhere between what life spans are today and where futurists are predicting them to be in the future. I am loath to ascribe names or life states to each of those quarters, because to do so would unreasonably attach labels. Rather, I simply refer to them in chronological order as first, second, third, and fourth. For those who attain significant longevity, there is a fifth quarter…overtime! Also, which quarter you are in is not determined by your age but, rather, by the pace and direction of your own life trajectory. The connection between age and life phase has shifted many times for humankind (and most particularly in modern times), as life expectancy has trebled from our very early days on the planet.

It is one thing to pay heed to what you need to do in each quarter; it is another to pay attention to your **transition** from one quarter to the next. Transition is just another word for "change," which we spoke about in the Invocation chapter. This must start with acknowledging that shift from one to the other, which isn't easy because the quarters aren't demarcated by our numerical age in tidy twenty-year brackets, but by our own particular life progression. Also, we like things to stay the same, so the easy default is same old same old.

Author Bruce Feiler offers us wisdom on **life transitions**: "The number of disruptors a person can expect to experience in an adult life is around three dozen."

He suggests that ten percent of these are significant—what he calls "life quakes." The average length of a major life transition is around five years. "Mastering the skills to pass through life quakes becomes all the more acute." He further posits that approximately half of all transitions *are "voluntary." He then goes on* to state: *"People who exhibit agency have been shown to be happier and healthier and have a higher quality of life."*

So…what is that?

Agency is: "the feeling of being in charge of your life; knowing where you stand, knowing that you have a say in what happens to you, knowing that you have some ability to shape your circumstance." Along with agency, belonging and cause are also important.

Let's review each of these quarters with a checklist of financial matters to address. Remember that modular financial planning is a life-time progression of mini-plans: resetting new goals and timelines. Along the way, let's also pay attention to the **transition issues** between quarters.

The First Quarter

The child and teen-hood stages of life were largely discussed in Section 3.2.

Social scientists say that **attitudes towards money are formulated before children hit grade school.**

We typically don't get a lot of formal education in managing our own finances. More likely, we get "on-the-job" training, starting with the role-modelling within our family home as we grow up. Some parents deliberately include money education in their parenting: others don't. For the teach-by-example group, sometimes the role-modelling lessons are good, and sometimes they are bad. Outside the micro level of the family home, there are also macro-level impacts being exerted on the child at the societal level. These are more often bad than good. The evolution of the rise in living standards in the developed world has produced the most broad-based middle-class in the history of this planet. With this comes succeeding generations who have acquired ever higher base levels of "entitlement," all of which costs money. High baseline expectations tend to significantly raise the baseline of financial outgoes, which leaves less for tomorrow.

Second Quarter

Now is the time to put someone in charge as the Family financial officer. If you are single, you are it. For couples, remember the normal distribution curve in Section 3.1 Couples and Money.

Home acquisition is a complex matter for today's young folks. If you do acquire a home, mortgage reduction is likely job one. *Other important considerations are*:

- **Budgeting is a classic way to keep control of personal finance.** This requires some attention to detail, both in collecting the list of outgoes and aggregating the results. This works well for some but not for most others. For the latter, discipline can nonetheless be attained by some "reverse financial engineering." The incoming monthly cash flow ought to be skimmed off the top to those higher purposes—silos (e.g., for debt reduction, retirement saving, a sinking fund for a new car, etc.), leaving the rest for day-to-day living costs each month.

- **Credit card mismanagement needs to be short-circuited** by: a) limiting the number of cards one has and b) keeping a credit card limit to a reasonable level (and undoing any unilateral limit increases "graciously" bestowed by the credit card companies). The undisciplined should run the other direction quickly from the line of credit financing now so widely available from financial institutions because it permits a never-never land of interest-only payments with no principal reduction.

- **Starting a family?** Use RESPs! With the competition for your scarce saving, your newborn's post-secondary education seems way far off. But you can't beat the upfront 20% rate of return that results from government matching. Even if you metaphorically put the funds in a sock after that, you are still ahead. Don't procrastinate too long—there are only so many years to contribute, and there is a limit under the rules as to how much catching up can happen as your child gets older.

- **Treat your finances like a garden.** If you enjoy gardening, you might do all of the work maintaining it yourself and read garden magazines to know what to do. If you don't enjoy it, you farm it all out to a landscaping company. If you like gardening but are time constrained, you figure out which tasks to job out and which to do yourself. Do you keep the easy tasks, like lawn cutting, or the harder tasks like bed maintenance? So it is with personal finance. Do you have the time, interest, and skills to stay abreast of tax law and stock markets? If not, sub these out to professionals. If you sub these tasks out, choose your advisors carefully. Find ones who are ethical, disciplined, and don't drive Porsches. Trust them, but stay in their backyard, so you know what they are doing for you. Select the structure of your Venn diagram relationship with them, as discussed in the Invocation chapter. Empower them with a philosophy statement of how you wish to pursue your financial goals (e.g., risk profile), and monitor that they are doing so. Remember your sea anemone role in the Invocation chapter.

You can't ignore probability statistics—like mortality tables—so prepare:

- Make sure you have prepared your will.
- Remember that your retirement savings obligations aren't finished when you make the annual RRSP contribution. So, manage your investment strategy wisely. Over a lifetime, the investment returns will contribute far more to your retirement lifestyle than your saving contributions.
- Avoid non-sensical tax deductions, like various tax shelters.
- Dedicate time to tax and financial planning regularly.
- Pay down non-deductible debt first.
- Review the adequacy and need for life, disability, and critical illness insurance coverage over your working lives.
- Create a forced savings plan to secure the saving discipline.
- Review and reassess the risk profile of your investment portfolio.
- Review the success of your portfolio at least annually.

Third Quarter

There are many financial matters in common between Q2 and Q3, as people pass their way through life at different paces.

Make sure you have a plan to use/retire all of your RRSP contribution room once the mortgage is paid down and/or the kids are out on their own and before your retirement. This may require some massive contributions in later life but find a way to do it. Use TFSA room as a second level of savings once your RRSP room is caught up.

- Get a proper financial plan by the time you hit age fifty to fifty-five.
- Organize your savings **plan today** for long-term income splitting in retirement.
- **Coordinate the investment strategies of your portfolios** to contribute to long-term income splitting, including principles of tax-smart investing.
- If you start saving late in life, don't pursue a "home run" risky investment strategy to try to catch up lost ground.
- As you draw down the education funds for your college kids, watch your equity exposure.
- Transition focus from debt reduction to wealth accumulation.

This might be the quarter in which you are dealing with "lottery" winnings in the form of a bequest from a maiden aunt or your parents. The School of Behavioural Finance suggests that you will treat this money differently from the salary you bring home each month. Apparently, **we create "pots" for different sources of incoming money as we do for spending pots** and apply different templates of financial management to them. The truly disciplined will apply all of this found money to some higher, long-term purpose while the undisciplined will "blow it" on some toy or treat. I think some middle ground works—apportion the found money to reward some "todays" and mostly "tomorrows," and be reasonable with the proportions.

This is also the time to prepare for your transition into your fourth quarter.

I call the immediate years leading up to retirement: **anticipension!** Forethought and planning are critical and, surprisingly, often lacking. If you didn't get a financial plan done in your early fifties, you need one now. The biggest question in life becomes: will there be enough? The today/tomorrow trade-offs still exist, albeit with a smaller timeline than before. In the absence of professional third-party analysis to provide guidance on this, couples may disagree on a subjective assessment of this question, and that incongruity will hamper and haunt them until it is sorted out. The range of questions are classic: how long to remain at work? How rich will the discretionary part of retirement be? How much is left for the next generation?

Remember that the older you are, the less time you have to benefit from Einstein's famous compounding.

For most of us, the fourth quarter will involve the transition from working. The financial aspect of that was, hopefully, addressed with the creation of a formal financial plan. The non-financial aspect is a whole different matter, which brings out the accountant in me.

Contemplate the following qualitative equation:

$$\text{Retirement} = \text{Quitting your job plus Y}$$

Now, solve for Y, which is all the rest of your life that now needs filling. "Retirement" hasn't really kicked in until you solve for Y.

Sketches in Personal Finance

On a Monday morning whilst writing this book, I got a call from a fifty-four-year-old male client who had been a crane operator for twenty-five years. He'd had a particularly bad day at work and told me he wanted to quit and retire… preferably by Friday. The good news was that we had previously done a formal financial plan for him and his wife, but it needed a quick re-visit and update. Also, coincidentally, his last parent had just died, and soon he would be inheriting half of her wealth. The revision of the plan, and the pending inheritance, provided support that financially he could retire. His wife, the same age, was going to keep working for a while. I spoke with her privately, and she confided that she was worried that he was not prepared for retirement and had no "latent" hobbies. I ran my equation by him. His answer for Y was "no more stress from work." Hmmmm.

I was a junior grunt auditor doing my articling in the late 1970s. I spent a lot of time in the Accounting Department of a large client corporation doing "ticking and bopping." One late Friday afternoon, the normal routine was broken. "Larry" in Capital Accounting was retiring that day, and the controller presented him with a retirement gift in front of the whole accounting floor. "Speech…speech," was called from the audience.

Larry was a quiet guy and not accustomed to public speaking. But he rallied and gave his "retirement speech," in which he said: "Many of you have asked me what I am going to do in retirement…well [and he paused at great length], I don't really know what I am going to do in retirement, but I DO know what I am NOT going to be doing. I am NOT getting up at 6:30 a.m. and catching the 7:15 a.m. bus at the corner and arriving at work at 7:45 and leaving the coffee room to sit at my desk at 8:00.…"

And then he sat down. I have often wondered how life played out for Larry.

And so, I encourage you to work on solving for Y.

I ought not to dip my toe into solving Y for you!! My role is to aspire to convince you how important this is. That said, I will give you a "hint." I believe that Y = Purpose! That still leaves open a broad range for interpretation, i.e., it might be your purpose to sit on the couch all day and watch TV. "Purpose" may be too heady a term later in life for some, to whom I offer a gentler alternate word: "interests."

Fourth Quarter

Think about your new role and purpose:

- Consolidate your life's experiences and wisdom.
- Stare down your own cognitive dissonance.
- As your presiding generation parent ages, you may need to fill into the role of leading generation.
- Be very prudent about fiscal management as your earned income era draws down.

- In grandparent-hood, be mindful of the WealthNess values you portray to those young grandchildren. Establish a healthy persona of ally and mentor and tell stories.
- Also, be wary of my friend's grandmotherly statement, "I want to spoil the heck out of them!"
- Remember the old joke: Grandchildren and grandparents have a common bond: they share the same enemy.
- Provide backup support and guidance to the parent generation's portrayal to those young children.
- Think about the very fine line between exerting control and promoting freedom.

This quarter is a time for planning and action. Let the following checklist be your guide:

- **Map out your incremental cash flows year by year** until **full maturity** for all your retirement income sources (usually age seventy to seventy-one).
- Compare these incomes at various ages to your cash needs in early, mid, and late retirement.
- **If there is a shortfall at any point**(s), consider different ways to bridge the gap.
    - Electing for early CPP for either or both of you
    - Drawing down your non-sheltered investment capital before drawing on your RRSPs
    - Withdrawing lump sums from your RRSPs
    - Working part-time
    - Converting non-productive assets, like a recreational property, into cash and investment income
- Carefully consider your **employer's pension income options** when you retire with respect to last survivor options.
- Try not to touch your RRSP until you are required to at age seventy-one.
- That said, make use of the low marginal tax rates until age seventy-one; perhaps deregister some RRSP income.
- Elect the **younger spouse's age** to determine your minimum RRIF payments.
- **Split your CPP entitlements** to improve income splitting.
- If you sell your home, or trade down to a smaller one, have the **excess proceeds invested by the lower income spouse.**

- If you own an **unproductive asset**, like a cottage, arrange that the higher income spouse owns it.
- Review the risk profile of your retirement investment portfolio and its ability to produce cash flow for calls.
- If you have money to spare, consider helping your children with house acquisition, their RRSP contributions, or education plans for their children.
- If you do this, get professional advice.
- Simplify and consolidate your financial affairs.
- Arrange joint tenancy of assets where appropriate. Get professional advice on this strategy.
- Create and update a list of what you own, where it is, and who your advisors are.
- Organize a list of the tax costs of your taxable financial assets.
- Confirm designated beneficiaries of your RRSPs, RRIFs, and TFSAs.
- Review your wills; assume these will be the very last wills you make.
- Select your executors wisely.
- Don't procrastinate!
- For a couple, ensure there is successful passing of the financial torch to the survivor.
- Transition your investment strategy for wealth decumulation? Or perhaps capital preservation?
- Grasp your transition to purely being a capitalist to support your lifestyle.
- Grasp the difference between total return and cash return in your portfolio.

If you recently retired, after a honeymoon period, you need to pursue your retirement dreams without delay. The unknowns of health hazards come out of nowhere, and quickly redirect the retirement agenda. If you are a traveller, be strategic about where and when you go. Do the exotic stuff abroad while you are physically able and also medically insurable. By this, I mean don't "waste" healthy travel years within your country. Fulfill your close-to-home bucket list when air travel is too taxing and/or you no longer can buy affordable travel insurance. As we age, dream travel can become overly wearisome—try two weeks of 6:00 a.m. starts to join a bus tour through Europe.

The social connections from work evaporate on retirement and replacement of connectedness is important. Hermits aside, people generally need to be connected with fellow human beings. We will return to this in the Section 4.4 Longevity, drawing from medicine and neuroscience.

Managing RRSP Conversion

You must convert your RRSP to a RRIF by December 31 of your seventy-first year. You then will start to receive mandatory annual payouts starting in the next calendar year. In completing your new RRIF account application, you must elect either your or your spouse's age to drive the annual payout calculation. It is generally wiser to use the younger person's age.

If you have multiple RRSPs spread around, this might be a good time to consolidate them into one.

If you still are carrying unused room, this will be the deadline to make your final RRSP contribution, unless your spouse is still under age 72, in which case you can continue to make contributions through your spouse until your spouse attains the seventy-first year.

You also need to understand that a contribution made does not have to be deducted immediately. (We shall call this an unused contribution.) You can deduct it in any year you choose, up to the year of death. In other words, tax-smart deducting might have you defer the year(s) over which you make the deduction claim…likely related to your future marginal tax rate(s).

Sketches in Personal Finance

We had a client in his late sixties who had $200,000 of unused RRSP room (because he never had the funds to contribute). His mother passed away, and we used some of his inheritance funds to make the entire $200,000 contribution in his seventy-first year, and deferred the large deduction spread over future years to offset his higher retirement income and maximize the marginal tax rate break.

If you are age seventy-one, have used up all your RRSP room, and are still generating new contribution room in the future (either from working or having rental income), you might embrace a one-off strategy in December of your seventy-first year: contribute the amount of the room you will create on January 1 of your seventy-second year (which is based on RRSP-earned income in your seventy-first year). Technically, this will incur a small penalty for being an "excess contribution" for the few days in December. But it will give you one more tax deduction that might be valuable at your marginal rate (and perhaps mitigate your future OAS clawback, as well, by lowering your net income).

Other Fourth Quarter Transitions

One of the most difficult issues is vacating the "old homestead."

Over the years we have shared with many elderly clients the advice: "You need to move **before** you need to move." This is painful, yet powerful advice. Maintaining the status quo is always more comfortable: the personal residence holds so many memories. Often, the over-whelming task of transporting all of one's possessions is too daunting. Our lesson in this practice is that those who grasp this difficult point, and do move on, invariably come out better in the long run. Those that don't often find themselves in a sticky situation, where they cannot or will not be able to transition to their next, and perhaps last, home. The change call here, for both seniors and their families, is carpe diem.

Sophocles opined: "One must await until the evening to appreciate the splendour of the day."

"Age-tality" likely will strike before mor-tality…as we experience losing competences.

So, how do we manage our ageing-self through our decline? And how do our loved ones help? Obviously, various formal estate-planning matters should be addressed including, in this example, a ready-to-go Power of Attorney document. But **deliberate** conversations are necessary, too. Ideally, it is the savvy elder who initiates these conversations. If, rather, it needs to be initiated by the younger generation, they need some "angle" to do so. This is likely one of those "lemons and lemonade" situations. Both parties should agree to identify the triggering moment when financial responsibility shifts, hopefully before crisis!

We go through all our lives from childhood with various "jobs" to be done. For adults, that includes home economics. The more aged we get, the more challenging it is to manage all of these "jobs." This difficult topic may be broached successfully by the following generation by using "proxy" questions. This is a style of asking difficult questions about someone's inner personal life by **objectifying** the topic to a different level or context, e.g., "Mom, what have you seen other people do, like your friends, in managing their finances at your age?" The younger generation may need to assume this "job" for the elder, and can position it as "gaining freedom," rather than "losing power" for the presiding generation.

This holds true for other jobs outside of financial responsibilities. At an appropriate time—before they cross a cognitive line—the presiding generation should call the family together to talk about the future. They may face resistance from their kids to have this conversation, but they must prevail. Having the conversation **before they need to** will pay back in spades when an unhappy day comes.

The family should discuss:

- What are the "jobs" that need doing in the parents' domestic lives?
- Who will step up for them and, if more than one, how will the jobs be allocated?
- What jobs are the parents going to retain?
- What are the trigger points that should initiate these calls to action?

The extra catch here can be that, when the day comes that the presiding generation has to give up something that they have always done (e.g., doing the monthly bill-paying), they dig in their heels. We discussed in an earlier chapter James Hughes' book and his concept of the "spirit of the gift." Here, we also need to be deliberate about the "spirit of control." Passing these jobs is not about the parents giving up control but, rather, about them gaining freedom. Once again, the inner battle within oneself! Does the presiding generation have the right attitude to embrace this new freedom? The other critical side of the coin is the family. The children who step up need to be well grounded for this to be successful.

Sketches in Personal Finance

"The bank is stealing my money…they are costing me $100/day in interest." So spoke my ninety-four-year-old client. Somewhat uncommon to her generation of women/mothers, she had had an active and responsible career in finance. At age ninety-four, she remained money-savvy (though now legally blind), but there was a little mix-up with regards to a tax payment she made through her bank. It was all sorted out fine, but she spent fifteen months, every day for hours, going through her bank statements because she believed the matter was still unresolved…against her favour. Every family visitor had to be her audience as she showed them reams and reams of bank statement printouts. We will pick her story up in the Longevity section.

It is also important to remember that couples seldom pass away simultaneously. If the Family financial officer is first-to-go, the survivor should not be burdened with acquiring the skillset at age eighty. Ideally, the couple should address this and plan for the knowledge transfer. If the non-financial spouse is resistant to this burden, have him/her talk with peers who do carry this skillset.

And finally, the last-to-die must play out the inevitable financial drama of whether enough money was accumulated during life to make it to the end, which may include expensive personal care. If an estate value does remain, then identify who you love and include those people in your estate plans. If you have difficulty deciding who is on that list, do not use this as an excuse to procrastinate. **Think about leaving some legacy upon this Earth**. We will return to this in the Legacy chapter.

4.3 Financial Plans

The Process for Making a Formal Financial Plan

I always have said that life's two biggest questions are: How long will I live? and Will I have enough?

To borrow from the old Amex commercial, the value of these answers is "priceless." The first answer is pretty hard to come by; the second is in your easy reach.

In its simplest form, the question in a retirement plan is: Will I have enough? However, many more very pertinent questions can be answered, too, like:

- Can I indeed retire early?
- What savings rate do I need through the remainder of our working lives?
- Is my investment risk profile too conservative for where I need to get to? Is it too aggressive and causing me to lose sleep?
- Can I afford to help my children and still have enough for later?
- What if I require expensive health care support in later years?
- Can I afford to support my charities as I would like?
- Can I keep my home?
- How much can I leave the children and still enjoy life?
- What is the role of "protection," i.e., insurance, in my financial health?
- Can I "live it up" in early retirement while I still have good health?

A formal plan starts with the collection of data about your financial affairs: incomes, expenses ("burn rate"), assets, and liabilities. The data is entered into one of many available, sophisticated planning software programs. The program then chugs out a collection of schedules that forecast your world going forward year-by-year for, typically, thirty to thirty-five years. Under the hood, the software carries various input assumptions about, for example, portfolio rate of return, investment risk strategy, saving rate, debt reduction, inflation rates, to name a few. The summary page—net worth—is a quick-and-dirty snapshot of how you are doing year-by-year and, in particular, as you get near the (projected) end of life. This raw, first cut is the Base Case V1.0. You and your planner would start by reviewing this version on-screen to get an initial sense of things. Invariably, **alternate scenarios** would be considered then, for instance:

- Retiring earlier
- Travelling more

- Helping the kids financially
- Selling assets

Any of these would result in an updated version of the Plan to V2.0, V3.0, etc. Ultimately, one final version will be selected. This would be **the plan** directing whatever action commitments are inherent in that version. That plan ought to be referenced back to in subsequent years in order to monitor progress. Alternately, circumstances may change in the future, necessitating some modification to that original version.

These are the inputs required to put your plan together:

- Recent brokerage and bank statements, house value, rental properties, vehicles, "other" assets
- List of debts, periodic repayment obligations, and prevailing interest rates
- Family incomes and data from recent tax filings
- Income expectations going forward…promotions, new jobs, full or part-time
- Future entitlements from pensions
- What's the routine family burn rate? Extraordinary costs: renos, schooling, travel, other family supports, fun costs, new vehicles?
- Annual saving
- Information on any known future windfalls
- Targeted retirement date(s)
- Change in lifestyle and burn rate post-working
- The detailed outputs, year-by-year for thirty-plus years
- Summary net worth
- Summary annual incomes from all sources and taxes due
- Summary of investment incomes by account
- Summary cash flow in and out

We have seen financial plans running eighty to ninety pages! This is the "encyclopedia" version. The "Coles Notes" version is a summary of key points in four to five pages.

A few years back, we surveyed our clients about financial planning. Amongst clients who had undertaken a full financial plan:

- 100% said the plan was good or excellent in clarifying a potential retirement date.
- 100% said the plan was good or excellent in defining an investment strategy for their portfolio.
- 85% said the plan was good or excellent in addressing the probability of running out of money.

Sometimes people have very specific questions to be answered…

Sketches in Personal Finance

Case A: "Can I retire?" The client desperately wanted to retire from an uninteresting job. The plan analyzed the financial math and found the long term a bit weak. A modified plan of working **one more year** made a material difference. Why? An extra year of working was one less year of life's consumption needing to be funded by the retirement pot of wealth. Also, as a net saver at that point, one more year of working meant one more year of adding to that retirement pot. So, the extra year of working served double-duty. **The Result**: 365 more ticks on the calendar lead to a more secure retirement.

Case B: "Can I become a snowbird?" The client was retired already with a plan. A vacation down south in the winter sun revealed the severely discounted real estate prices in the American sunbelt. "Can I afford to buy down there?" The existing plan was revisited with this purchase in mind. The financial math worked, with a few do-able adjustments. **The Result**: six-month stays in Palm Springs every winter…and cheaper living costs there that recoup some of the investment costs.

Case C: "How do I manage my inheritance?" The client received a significant inheritance that transferred over in kind as a portfolio exclusively of stocks. "Should I keep all of these stocks? They go up and down a lot!" The financial math concluded that the couple's lifestyle aspirations were reasonable and secure with a lower return/lower volatility portfolio, which would include some fixed income in place of stocks. The long-term estate value likely would be less as a result, but for the childless couple the ending estate value wasn't important. Being able to sleep with less volatility was more important. **The Result**: more sleep.

Case D: "How can we afford to fund three college degrees?" The couple had three sons, all fairly close in age, all advancing through their teens, and all university-bound. "While still paying down a mortgage, how can we pull this off"? The first part of the answer was to find $5,000 per year per child to contribute to a family RESP and receive $3,000 annually in government matching grants. The second part was to lay out a multi-year spreadsheet that started today and ended when the youngest son finished university. Each year, the students' tuition and living costs would be forecast, and each year the cash flow sources from RESP income, summer jobs, and scholarships would be estimated. To the extent there were shortfalls between the forecasted income and the outgoes over those years, this highlighted when and how much of a problem was developing, giving a heads-up to address additional sources. **The Result**: the youngest son graduated to become an accountant. (Bonus, huh!)

Case E: "How can I decide between me, my retirement years, and my kids?" Most of us are obliged to manage the balanced interplay of that triad: our today, our tomorrow, and our heirs. Once retirement commences, we leave behind the saving conundrum, because now we only need focus on living off our accumulated wealth. But peace of mind is still elusive because we have to trade-off that triad. Our experience, generally speaking, is that retirees should embrace whatever "bucket list" they have held for retirement and do it sooner rather than later. However, if that bucket list is expensive, the new conundrum is whether we are compromising our tomorrow and our heirs for our today. The financial math in a plan does an excellent job of addressing this. Living costs can be increased accordingly in the first retirement decade(s), and the impact of that can be seen for the subsequent retirement decades. The impact on estate values also will be apparent. **The Result**: if this forecast shows that "all three of you" can be satisfied, then all is good. If living it up is forecast to cause problems downstream, then trade-offs can be willingly addressed with prescience…and balance will be found.

Case F: "Can we each go it alone?" A couple had been clients of ours for many years, but they decided to separate. Naturally, each was concerned about what their financial future would be like when the family wealth was divided in two. While we had spent years serving the couple, at this point, we could not advise both through this process as a formal professional conflict of interest arises. However, as the party who knew much about their tax and financial affairs, we trod a middle line in terms of providing both party's advisers with information. This included preparing formal financial plans, showing what their worlds would be like in various asset settlement scenarios. **The Result**: both parties negotiated knowing how their own future worlds would play out. Sometime after the separation was completed, we returned to representing both parties as they got on with their lives.

Case G: "Can we take $160,000 from our portfolio now to give our daughter for a deposit on her first home?" The important point to grasp here is that the couple wasn't just giving up $160,000, but also all of the earnings on that capital for decades forward. This couple chose the prudent approach of **asking the question first**. We revisited their existing financial plan, withdrew that sum in the plan (15% of the portfolio value), and looked into their future. **The Result:** The answer was yes; their **long-term financial health could bear this**. In fact, the portfolio followed with a three-year annual compound return of 5.9%, which restored the borrowed capital.

Risk—That Four Letter Word

That won't happen to me.

Let's commence that "uncomfortable" conversation: the scare-mongering one about all the bad things that can happen to you (but never will, right?). They only happen to somebody else.

You might not be familiar with the term "**risk register.**" Governments in functioning countries have such documents for when (predictable) "bad things" happen, like an earthquake in Turkey. The document gives the people involved a heads up, a jumpstart on dealing with the situation. It is also a tool for business and project managers. It details identifiable risks, including description, category, potential actions, probability, negative impacts, and people involved.

Let's take this and zoom-in to you…your family. OK, this isn't going to be fun; just promise to spend one hour on this. Start by listing all the risks of bad things you can think of. Recall stories that have happened to people you know…or things you read or heard in the news. (A cyclist was killed by a truck near my home two days before I wrote this piece.)

Let's brainstorm together things that might happen in your world:

- Illness or injury temporarily impeding nuclear-family earned income
- Illness or injury in extended family
- Job loss
- Quick unexpected death, e.g., an accident
- Slower death from illness

Proactive responses include:

- Preventative—regular medical checkups, rainy-day financial silo
- Remedial—healthy lifestyle, organize financial affairs
- Restorative—initiatives to build and maintain healthy relationships and repair past failings
- Burden-sharing—insurance: life, disability, critical illness, home, car

A financial plan takes numbers (your income, your assets, your liabilities) and massages them to create other numbers (your affordable lifestyle, your financial legacy at death for your heirs) to answer that **second biggest question: Will I be OK financially?**

You may find that your financial plan doesn't tell you what you want to hear. The plan does not care about your quality of life. And it can become your taskmaster.

The impact of deferring retirement from labours has multiple impacts:

- Your burn rate is financed by your earned income through those extra working years.
- This leaves your savings capital untouched to compound some more for when you do retire.
- At the end of your earning career, your income potential may be at its peak, and your burn rate has reduced from the end of mortgage payments and raising a family; meaning that you are able to contribute **more** to your savings capital.
- Leaving your savings capital untouched for those extra working years means there will be fewer non-working years to fund.

Here is a dirty little secret about formal financial plans. Hiding between the sheets in this is a universal, fundamental point: **Every plan will always say that you will be better off financially by continuing to work…it's plain math!** So, if your goal is to die with your highest possible net worth or to live an amazing lifestyle, the answer is simple: Keep working until you die.

Are you ready to dive into the human value of working? If so, take this detour. (If you don't want to take this detour right now, jump ahead until you see the Circle/ easiest sign.)

The HFactor

*So, I propose a shift in the world of retirement planning by introducing a new concept called the **Human Value**, or "**HFactor**," which is the human value of continuing to work.*

This aspires to add a human element to the number-crunching process. What personal cost does one bear in going to work each day? We all view this differently, based upon our enjoyment of our work, commuting grief, toxic employer environments, etc. The HFactor identifies a number of these issues and ascribes a numeric score to each. The scoring system attaches larger numbers to the grief impact of staying at work. The sum of the scores is a number that becomes the discount rate to re-calculate. The larger the number, the larger the discount rate and, through the math of finance, the lower the value of continuing to work. The difference between the values produced by the HFactor discount rate and a conventional money discount rate is your **Cost of Freedom Index** for not continuing to work.

Want to test your HFactor for early retirement? Complete the following HFactor Score Chart and add up your score. (You can change the weightings above, or add new questions, that might relate better to your situation.)

HFactor SCORE CHART

1. My health is…	Good/OK/poor	0/1/3
2. Getting up to go to work is…	A pleasure/OK/a pain	0/1/3
3. My spouse no longer works, and my work commitments constrain our ability to enjoy life together.	No/a bit/yes	0/1/2
4. Most of our friends are retired, and I envy their freedom and lifestyle.	No/yes	0/1
5. The stress at my work-place is…	Not an issue/	0
	Manageable/	1
	Very difficult	3
6. Working restricts my time to enjoy travel, hobbies, activities.	Not at all	0
	Somewhat	1
	A lot	2
7. My work commitment prevents us from moving to our desired retirement location.	No/yes	0/2
8. It will be difficult to replace my social affiliations after my workplace.	Not at all	0
	Somewhat	1
	A lot	2
9. My commute to work is very difficult.	Not at all	0
	Somewhat	1
	A lot	2

Next answer these two questions:

- My anticipated annual income-after-tax if I continue working is $_____.
- I expect to work for _____ more years.

To calculate your **Freedom Index:**

1) Multiply the two figures that you filled in above to determine how much you will make before retirement.

2) Use your HFactor score as a discount rate and use a present-value calculator to determine your discounted **HFactor** amount.

3) Now use a conventional financial discount rate (typically, say, 4–8%) in a present value calculator to multiply the amount you will make before retirement.

4) Subtract the amount you got in step two from the amount you got in step 3 to determine your **Freedom Index**

Sketches in Personal Finance

Now let us consider Carl, who is thinking of working for **six** more years, during which he earns a salary of $100,000, which is approximately **$70,000** after tax. Carl filled out the nine questions on the H Factor chart and added them up. His "grief" score was **fifteen**, as he had a mix of "good" and "bad" scores. (Note that the maximum "bad" score is twenty.) This becomes his discount factor rate. He plugged these three variables into a present value calculator and he learned that, while his total extra earnings would be $420,000 (six years x $70,000), the discounted **HFactor** amount would be $264,915.

He revisited the present value calculator on the web and changed the interest rate input from 15% to 4% (the latter being a conventional financial discount rate that might be applied in a formal financial plan). This value was $366,950. The difference between these two values of $102,035 **is his Cost of Freedom Index** from six more years at the grindstone; the bigger the number, the bigger the value you ascribe to earlier retirement.

What does Carl do with this? First, he checks with his planner to see how important it is for his retirement forecast to keep working those six years…using the 4% discount rate. If he does not do so, does the overall picture look problematic? As noted above, the plan always will make working longer better for your net worth, probably meaning leaving more of an estate value for your heirs—but "what about me?" Second, Carl checks his HFactor. If the Plan says that his lifestyle will not be materially impaired by **quitting work now**, the **Freedom Index** says that not working for six more years is worth, say, approximately $17,000 per year (his Cost of Freedom Index divided by the number of years he still plans to work). Carl can apply the Human Value Factor to decide if all those fifteen grief points are worth $17,000 per year. Over to you, Carl!

A second shift in financial planning thought from the Human Value approach is that, like your conventional financial assets, **your career earning capacity** should be an **asset on your balance sheet** year-by-year…as it can be ascribed a value as much as your brokerage and bank accounts. The higher your annual income and the longer you work produces a higher capital value to your career. We introduced this concept in Section 2.4. Here, we can see it in application. The present capital value of Carl's $70,000 after-tax income at age forty was approximately $1.1 million, but with six years left before retirement, it is $366,950. Each year that he worked, this value decreases, and would reach zero should he retire at sixty-five.

So, if continuing to work takes a heavy toll on you—for whatever reasons—calculating your Freedom Index may offer you intellectual and psychological confidence to take the plunge.

But before you do, read Section 4.4 Longevity about what the futurists are saying…about the future!

*Welcome back to the **book's main pathway**.*

4.4 Longevity

Healthful Longevity

Let's start this with an Einstein thought experiment.

Assume you are perfectly healthy today. How much would you be willing to pay to ensure you will remain healthy for the next year…or two years…or five years? Stop and think about this! Having trouble with this one? Fair game—it's difficult! We are putting a price on life…perhaps like buying a futures contract on the stock market.

Before you get angry or frustrated with this question and turn the page, let's stay with this for a bit. **What is the price for quality of life**? For starters, its different for everyone: different with what they can afford, what their value systems are, how important leaving an estate for their heirs is, how much they are enjoying their lives today, and so on.

OK…fair's fair: I have to do this, too. So, I will give you my answer. But I don't want you to cheat and avoid the personal journey with this question. Thus, my answer will appear randomly somewhere in the rest of the book (and, no, this is not a trick to force you to read the entire book). Let's move on…

Retired…aged…geriatric…seniors… What are they to be called? *Geriatric* is an established term in medicine, introduced some forty years ago. But to use it in today's world is almost rude or condescending. Doing a definition search on "retired" or "retirement" most frequently refers to the **end** of something, cessation of paid occupation, rather than the **beginning** of something. I am of the opinion that we need a new term which is non-judgmental.

Longevity, defined as age at date of death, has extended significantly in a relatively short history of time, and is on a trajectory to increase even further. Yuval Harari cleverly focuses our thoughts to **bifurcate** the conversation about longevity. The default topic is really **Age Longevity**; the other one is **Healthful Longevity**, which encompasses mental and physical capabilities to continue to function in older age. The difference between the two is dramatically coloured by the statistics that 14% of Americans over age seventy-one and 32% over age eighty-five (25% in Canada) suffer from dementia/Alzheimer's.

Sketches in Personal Finance

"I am gonna keep working…. What would I do if I retired?" So spoke a very accomplished seventy-five-year-old client of mine. It is difficult to have an intelligent rejoinder to that statement. Daniel Levitin's book *Successful Aging* is an encyclopedia of wisdom on the fourth quarter. We can pick up where he ended in the book—his appendix of top-ten ideas. Number one was: "Don't retire. Don't stop being engaged with meaningful work."

My response to my client was this: "Today, at age seventy-five, you look at your world of choices and see a void of alternatives, leaving the status quo. But next year when you are seventy-six, it will be exactly the same. And when you are eighty in five years, it will be exactly the same, and again at eighty-five and so on. Only if you drop dead in your tracks will you be spared the regret of never staring down **change**. A half-way house to this problem is **incremental change;** try out **one** new thing, one new "hobby" and see how that fits. Then build from there."

We encountered Viktor Frankl in Section 2.5 Happiness and Meaning. He was a psychiatrist who coined the term "logotherapy" ("logos" being "meaning" in Greek). His premise was that the prime motivational force in people is to find "meaning." I will call it "purpose." While modern-day psychiatry has not embraced his belief in logotherapy, attaching "purpose" to life seems reasonable.

> *Nothing contributes so much to tranquilizing the mind as a steady purpose—a point on which the soul may fix its intellectual eye.*
> —Mary Shelley, writer

Author Joseph Coughlin has an interesting take on our changing, ageing society. He opines that there is an opportunity to impact the fourth quarter by offering seniors unexpected, unfamiliar routes to meaning. He then profoundly states that societies won't just be older, they will function differently. That said, today we are only in the early transition to such a new world because we haven't had enough time and experience with living longer, meaningful lives. So much of our traditional meaning derives from our work careers and raising our families. But these are "jobs" that ultimately get finished. Coughlin says that later life is devoid of landmarks (other than birthdays). Older people are not setting goals and pursuing them. "They focus less on new things and double down on the tried and true," he adds.

No one has been able to erect landmarks that signify success in ageing because no one even knows what later life achievements might look like. No one tells us what to aspire to in old age, leading to hard wiring that the elderly have no real aspirations. As a result, the remarkable duration of freedom we are granted is arriving with a sort of unsettling, unmoored sensation.

The withdrawal from the workplace, plus the decline of religious and civic institutions where generations comingled, have contributed to the dislocation of the elderly. Also, Western culture is less inclined to keep the elderly integrated and instead cloisters them in (expensive) seniors' residences. In the pre-media world, seniors had a larger footprint on the younger generations, contributing to the development of their burgeoning value systems. According to Coughlin, all of this leaves seniors with an extended stretch of life that is in dire need of "institutions"…**perhaps new ones that don't even exist yet.**

Futurist author Yuval Noah Harari augments this thought:

> *"Humankind in the twenty-first century needs to ask itself an unprecedented question: What are we going to do with ourselves? …People will have much longer careers, and will have to reinvent themselves again and again, even at the age of ninety."*

Presently in the twenty-first century, someone who has attained age sixty-five has an expected remaining lifespan of twenty to twenty-five years across most societies. Two generations back, that number was approximately ten years shorter. That's a lot fewer years to "fill in" with new purpose. (OECD Data)

I espouse a term I call **"80-x,"** where x is one's current age. Let's say that you are age sixty-five and thus, that number is fifteen for you. I am positing that you should consider that you have fifteen good years ahead of you to work on life's bucket list. This "80" number carries two caveats. First, some people are not that fortunate and are struck by death or significant illnesses long before age eighty. Second, some people will sail well into their nineties in good health. The point of "80-x" is to keep the foot on the gas pedal through those fifteen years. If you are blessed with more after age eighty—great…call it a bonus.

The term "bucket list" became fashionable thanks to the film with Jack Nicholson and Morgan Freeman. However, as that film fades into filmographic history, I hear the term being used less and less. And yet, it remains fundamentally a calling across time and generations. The change call here is to contemplate your bucket list…and embrace it.

The Boomer Generation is the largest cohort ever in history to file into this stage of life. And, as with all their earlier life stages, they are redefining ageing. Some of the cohort are passing through their senior years similar to generations before them…succumbing to the likes of cancer, heart attacks, and strokes. But many are moving through their senior years like the Energizer bunny. For those who retire from very busy and demanding careers, it seems there is no time for advance preparation. Figuring it out along the way seems to be the norm.

My metaphor is that it's like being placed in a retirement canoe and pushed off the shoreline with no map, no paddle, and no water current to carry you. As cartoonist Bill Watterson observed: "The truth is, most of us discover where we are headed when we arrive."

As Boomers advance through the fourth quarter, and later into overtime, they will be the generation who will be defining retirement purpose V2.0. This may prove difficult and frustrating at the cellular level, if not overtly. Like consumer products on the shelf, we all may have our "best before" date.

Ikigai is a Japanese term, which roughly means "the happiness of always being busy." That almost seems to be the opposite of what we Westerners think retirement is about: make my life less busy…less complicated! On the other hand, we working-stiffs frequently hear retired seniors say, "I am so busy now, I don't know how I found time for work before!"

Ikigai mirrors Western concepts we already have covered in the Invocation chapter: "Our health depends on that natural tension that comes from comparing what we've accomplished so far with what we'd like to achieve."

Wow…ikigai brings us back to Festinger's cognitive dissonance in Chapter 1.0 as a health cure.

"The happiest people are not the ones who achieve the most. They are the ones who spend more time than others in a state of flow."

Wow again…ikigai also brings us back to Mihaly Csikszentmihaly. His flow concept requires that we be in a distraction-free environment and have control over what we are doing at every moment.

> *The grand essentials to happiness in this life are something to do, something to love, and something to hope for.*
>
> *The people who live the longest have two dispositional traits in common: a positive attitude and a high degree of emotional awareness.*
> —Ikigai: The Japanese Secret to a Long and Happy Life

The main principles of ikigai are:

- Stay active; don't retire
- Take it slow
- Don't fill your stomach
- Surround yourself with good friends
- Get in shape for your next birthday
- Smile
- Reconnect with nature

- Give thanks
- Live in the moment
- Follow your ikigai—the passion inside you

What's in a NAME?

My recent reading on life in the fourth quarter has brought home some guiding principles to embrace, to which I give the acronym: NAME. This stands for nutrition, affiliation, mind, and exercise.

Eating healthily is a lifetime project, and there is so much more awareness today. I am not a nutritionist, but, personally, I think the bigger inner battle is about NOT eating bad stuff, more than it is eating good stuff.

For those who retired from careers, the workplace likely was a key source of affiliation…now removed. Coughlin believes that elder women are more likely to embrace a better old age; elder men are more inclined to remain in the current narrative of being old. Women seem more adept at building and maintaining relationships. Marcie Rogo created the website *Stitch* to facilitate social connectivity amongst the single, over-fifty set. She found resistance, however, because people found the idea somewhat forced.

Observations from the English Longitudinal Study of Ageing predict that loneliness will become an increasing phenomenon across English society in the decade ahead, as a growing cohort of elders live in social isolation. This has potential impact on health systems as this cohort may experience, because of their environment, poorer mental and physical health.

The importance of engaging one's **mind** became very apparent during Covid, when all of our worlds shrunk. Those whose bubble only included one spent a long time in their own company (that includes me). I came to the following realization: I very seldom learn something new listening to myself. We need to mix.

In my hometown, I started a group called "**Partners In Engaged Re-Living**"; these are my PIER Group. The "R" started out being for the word "retired"; however, I quickly learned that the "R" word "retired" is loathed by many, and that a new lexicon is called upon. Thus, I substituted the word: Re-living. My goal was to embrace retired and semi-retired guys to form affiliations and do things together. I host bi-weekly summer outdoor barbecues for eight to twelve attendees. I was the only one who knew each one of them. As their familiarity grew, common interests flushed out, which led to a hiking sub-group, another for guys interested in WWII, biking, photography, and other hobbies and intellectual overlaps. We aspire to a two-or-three-day retreat at a nearby resort. In the winter,

I host evenings with eight participants, called One-On-One. We break into two groups of four, and each foursome engages in three thirty-minute rotating chats one-on-one, talking about whatever they find in common.

> *My mind rebels at stagnation. Give me problems. Give me work. Give me the most abstruse cryptogram, the most intricate analysis, and I'm in my proper atmosphere. But I abhor the dull routine of existence. I crave mental exaltation...*
> —Sherlock Holmes in *A Scandal in Bohemia* by Arthur Conan Doyle

I love that one! (But note that Sherlock was "retired" three years before Conan Doyle passed away.)

Stagnation and boredom are lack of engagement. One of my dearest elderly clients is like Sherlock. In his mid-eighties, he self-published a book of his family history that he gave to all his offspring at Christmas. This took him over a year to complete. He was glad when it was done, but then he experienced the hollow void without it. Later, he told me he was trying to write short biographical stories but couldn't get motivated because there was no end purpose; they wouldn't become another book.

After my forty-seven-year career, and at age seventy, people occasionally ask me if I am going to retire. My response is: "Not yet! There are too many things that I haven't thought of yet. I **promise to retire** when I have thought of them all."

Neophiliacs is a modern term that describes people who desire novel experiences. Typically, we associate this with the evolving brains of young people...most notably young men. But researchers today are calling for seniors to embrace neophilia to extend longevity and happier, healthier lives, not to mention better memory and learning skills.

We are learning that an **exercise** regimen isn't just about the body from the neck down, but also about the brain: the exercise process flushes contaminants from the brain. We are learning how minor players in our overall life, like oral hygiene and restful sleep, may be clandestinely major players in our health narrative and linked to preventing cancer, Alzheimer's, stroke, and congestive heart failure. Balance on our feet can become an issue as we age. Historically, we viewed this as a **physical** danger. Falling often meant broken bones and hips, which can turn into the slippery slope to death. Today, we learn it is even more important because it also has a **brain health** aspect. Seniors should be doing balancing exercises, but not just to counter a potential fall. The physical firing of muscles also fires brain activity, contributing to a healthier brain. *Why We Sleep* by

Mathew Walker, PhD is a must-read, as is *Keep It Moving* written by renowned dance choreographer Twyla Tharp.

Yesterday's wisdom encouraged exercise for the body: heart, bone density, circulation, weight, etc. Today's neuroscience research also is expanding our understanding of the influence of exercise on cognition. Yesterday's wisdom identified that aerobic exercise three times a week boosts neuron regeneration in the hippocampus, and thus boosts memory capacity. Today, research (at UBC) is finding more specific effects related to different kinds of exercise; in particular, strength training (lifting weights). The research suggests that both are cognitively valuable in distinct ways: aerobic improves verbal memory whilst anerobic improves associative memory…and there is a gestalt effect from embracing both. "By combining aerobic exercise with strength training, you're getting a more potent neurobiological cocktail," says researcher Willem Bossers of the Netherlands. The anaerobic exercise triggers a growth hormone in the liver which promotes neuron growth and communication. The aerobic exercise boosts "BDNF," which protect neurons from oxidative DNA damage. The change call here is to challenge sedentary lifestyle and, for others, to broaden their exercise regimen.

Live Without Regrets
You may be familiar with the Terman Project, a longitudinal study through the lifetime of a cohort starting in the early 1920s. When surveyed in their mid-eighties, the members of the cohort were asked to reflect upon life and its regrets. Interestingly, the **regrets were mostly about things not done, not about things done to unhappy results**. The feeling was that life could have been even better if they had seized opportunities presented.

Twyla Tharp incants us: "With the time you've got, choose to make your life bigger. Opt for expression over observation, action instead of passivity, risk over safety, the unknown over the familiar."

As we get deeper into the fourth quarter and overtime, tackling Sherlock's abstruse cryptograms and intricate analysis may just become too much. Their relevance may fade, but our purpose need not. If you are a music lover, lock yourself up in your favourite space or crank on your favourite piece of music with ear buds, and tell me you can't find purpose. Music is the umbilical cord/chord to the soul!

- Go out and break bread with someone dear to you, spend time experiencing joy and affiliation, and tell me you can't find purpose.
- Read a book, whose author stimulates and teaches you, and tell me you can't find purpose.

- Strike up a conversation with a complete stranger…anywhere (maybe the grocery store line-up) and send that person off on their day feeling better about the community about them and tell me you can't find purpose.
- Go for a stroll in a beautiful place. (The Japanese call this *shinrin-yoku*, or "forest bathing.") Don't allow your brain to percolate on your problems of the day. Let your senses of sight, hearing, and smell control and focus your brain, and tell me you can't find purpose.
- Think of an old friend or relative you haven't touched base with for a long time, and get together. Talk about the past experiences you shared (and don't talk about your ailments) and rekindle that affiliation that never really died but was only starved for nourishment, and tell me you can't find purpose.

As you transition through the fourth quarter into overtime, you need to transition your purposes in response to your changing world state. This might start with what I call the "Helping Hand," which involves a sweep of your world to ask **how you can help**:

- Yourself today
- Yourself tomorrow
- Your spouse
- Your children
- Your grandchildren
- Your relatives
- Your friends
- The immediate world around you
- The broader world around you

Dennis Jaffe brilliantly inspires us to consider what your **persona** is when you reach out with your Helping Hand. He identifies:

- A sword to conquer/control
- A shield to defend
- An ornament
- Facilitator
- Manipulator

This is pretty heavy stuff, and very hard to self-assess. Most of these personae are not positive.

My great-nephew was spending three to four hours per day commuting between campus and his parents' home. I thought he could spend all those hours more productively engaging in campus affairs and making friends (which is what I did in my youth). I offered to pay for his residence fees. He chose to keep commuting three hours. When I shared this with his cousin, she asked me exactly what I had told him. Her response, effectively, was that I had fallen into Jaffe's paradigm.

Bottom line: if you are extending your Helping Hand, remember that, foremost, it is about them, not you. Deliberately and wisely script your offer.

Review your "assets"—both tangible and intangible—to see how they can contribute to your Helping Hand goals. Which are the **vectors** through which you achieve your Helping Hand goals? Personally, I have institutionalized a question I ask myself once every month: "Who in my world is hurting?" I regularly scour through my phone contact list (formerly called a Rolodex) and reach out to people I haven't exchanged communications with for a while. One of my personal Ten Principles is to "surprise and delight." What are the **vehicles** of your Helping Hand? I send a note to someone that I know is seriously ill or otherwise suffering. My connecting emails often close with: "Is there anything I can do for you?" I will randomly send a magazine subscription or a book to friends.

Consider also giving your time and attention to others. Are you a listener or a talker? In my opinion, the social media era has had a profound reverse effect on me-ness and empathy. I am not sure what will cause the pendulum to swing back on this one. Over the decades, I have encouraged people to contemplate this: "Are you interesting? Are you interested? Are you neither or are you both?" Wolfgang Goethe is famously quoted to say that he was born with eyes; therefore, it was his duty to see. However, I think a more powerful twist to that is: born with ears, it is my duty to listen.

I always recall a client fondly reflecting on his deceased father: "Dad always asked questions." Beautiful!

Are you a deep thinker who likes to contemplate the future unknown? If so, take this detour. (If you don't want to take this detour right now, jump ahead until you see the Circle/easiest sign.)

Longevity Tectonics

Let's take a Square lesson from geology and tectonic plates, which are massive slabs of solid rock that float and travel upon Earth's mantle. They move in response to the intense heat at Earth's core that causes mobility of molten rock within the mantle layer. This movement is, of course, slow: one to six inches per year (and the circumference of Earth at the equator is approximately 25,000 miles).

There are four different types of boundaries between plates:

- Divergent, where a new crust is created as the plates move apart
- Convergent, where some crust is destroyed as one plate drops under another
- Transformative, where two plates pass each other, and crust is damaged but not created or destroyed
- Boundary zones, where the plate interactions are unclear, because the boundaries are not well-defined, producing many possible, different movements

Harari, Coughlin, and many others are implicitly telling us that the long tail of longevity in humanity is in the **throes of tectonic shift**.

As with the Earth's geology, these things take a long time to happen. But when they happen…it's big…like an earthquake or tsunami. The difference between longevity and geology is this: it's about timelines and probability. Millions of people (including myself) geographically live along active fault lines, but we blindly rely upon the long tail of time and probability. The timelines for the impact of increased longevity are: a) much shorter and b) much higher probability. There is a third difference, too: we can't impact plate tectonics, but we can anticipate longevity tectonics and adjust our futures.

Using the plate tectonic types listed above, can we infer our future society? To do so, we need to substitute some terminologies and intuit the "equation." Read "society" for "crust," and read "the quarters" for "plates."

- Divergent: Society is re-written. Many fourth quarter people will continue their careers, though, perhaps on their own terms. They may continue to occupy the workspace to the detriment of second and third-quarter people.
- Convergent: Some fourth quarter people will be "destroyed." They will have been unable to provide adequately for their longevity, thus there will be significant have-nots, and second/third quarter people **will not be willing** to support and subsidize them, neither directly nor by taxation.
- Transformative: Some of society will be damaged. Again, the fourth quarter people will have been unable to provide adequately for their longevity; thus, there will be significant have-nots, and third quarter people **may be willing** to subsidize them but are not able to do so sufficiently to sustain their own lifestyle upon their own turn at fourth quarter.
- Boundary zones: Individuals will respond differently to their place as fourth quarter people (divergent, above), bifurcating that demographic. The have-not fourth quarter people will be fewer, thus with less profile and less political clout, and will be the ones to experience the destruction from convergence, above.

Will **one** of these options spell the future for humankind across the planet? Or will different societies/cultures around the world adopt **different** solutions? If so, what might that mean geopolitically? How might society harness the energy and wisdom of fourth-quarter/overtime people to make a better world and, at the same time, contribute to their meaningful lives.

Return to:

A Cultural Shift

It is trivial to say that the world is more global today than in ploughman times. But how much so at the granular level? Is it tourists, business-people, or freighters that make us global? Millions of Americans (including a past-president) have never set foot off their continent. The Japanese word *hikikomori* refers to pulling inwards. Seven of the top ten "Happy Countries" come from (mostly Northern) Europe, and the other three are Commonwealth countries. We Westerners can

acknowledge their wisdom, or ikigai above in Japan, but will the West be prepared to embrace those cross-cultural ideas and philosophies?

Many of you who raised children may have had the opportunity to send them on some sort of school exchange. The Rotarians have this as one of their fundamental programs. The distance travelled and the cultural difference may have been great or small. Perhaps it is time for similar international exchanges of third and fourth-quarter generations: a home-and-home exchange of **adults.**

Less energetically, the same could be achieved amongst cultures just across town. Years ago, I conjured the idea of four families of different cultural backgrounds rotating a home-and-home visit. I named it after the old Sidney Poitier/Katherine Hepburn film *Guess Who's Coming to Dinner*. Then there is Abraham Lincoln's quote: "I don't like that man. I must get to know him better"…it's time for lunch! We are reminded of Coughlin's **new institutions that don't exist yet**… maybe here's a start.

As society faces the call for elder reinvention, Harari opines that history is shaped by forward-looking innovators, rather than by those backward-looking. What a beautiful opportunity! How might society as a whole figure out how to harness the energy and wisdom of fourth-quarter people to contribute to their meaningful lives and to a better world for everyone?

In conclusion, I think that **discovery** is the primary reward to living longer. You get more years to find new things, meet new people, visit new places, and to think new thoughts you hadn't before. I encourage you to be deliberate with directing the longevity that plays out your future. Pursue intellectual growth and inspiration like a heat-seeking missile. Be an intellectual hunter/gatherer. Be like a bar mixologist: create your own new mind "cocktail" by being mentally nourished by new ideas that fold back into what you already have accumulated. Rock the boat by telling yourself something you don't what to hear.

4.5 Key Words and Concepts

Financial Planning:

48. Face Life's Second Biggest Question.
49. Face the peace of mind Rumsfeld quadrant.
50. Embrace the reward of stick-to-it-ness.
51. Understand the act of saving.
52. ESR vs. TSR
53. You + 40 years
54. S.I.T. review
55. The four quarters, and their to-do lists
56. Embrace life's transitions
57. When it's time to bring your calculator into the crystal ball
58. Will I have enough?
59. Formal financial plans: the encyclopedia
60. The HFactor: ME before my inheritors
61. The dangerous "R" word
62. 80-x
63. The ikigai solution
64. NAME
65. Purpose and neophilia
66. The evolving persona
67. What is longevity really about?
68. Plate tectonics and the fourth quarter

Chapter 5: Investing

Most people will become investors at some stage in their lives, whether caused by their own saving or by inheritance. Investing wisely and well is both important and difficult. The era of the internet has made patients into doctors and investors into portfolio managers…nowadays so-called DIYers. Both medicine and investing are complex subjects that "experts" dedicate lifetimes to. At the risk of sounding self-serving to my investment-management industry, investing DIYers are prime candidates for Rumsfeld's infamous: "We don't know what we don't know." If someone is thusly inclined, I think it is OK for the lay person to oversee a small part of their wealth under self-management. If the success of your portfolio is integral to the success of your remaining years, I encourage you to seek **competent** help. If you have zero interest in this field, hitch your wealth wagon with that trusted person and go enjoy life.

For the rest of you, and the rest of this section, I encourage investors to meet their trusted advisors part-way. Refer back to the Venn diagram relationship intersections in the Introduction. That also includes embracing my sea anemone metaphor and growing some finance-interest tentacles that allow you a reasonable knowledge base for dialogue with that advisor. Lastly, I return in this section to my skiing "degrees of difficulty" signposts. Some of these topics are complex and more directed at the keener. If you find yourself wandering onto one of these trails and becoming glassy-eyed, move on.

The section starts with building an investing philosophy, and then drills down to more detailed strategy. I encourage everyone to work their way through the first three sections. After that, we start moving into many Diamond subjects on equity markets, bond markets, inflation, foreign exchange, and the complexity of rates of return.

In school, you got "report cards" with grades to give feedback on how you were progressing. The **investing report card** should be an annual report that tells how you are doing…aka **rate of return**. The number seems so crisp and simple, that we ascribe great meaning and credibility to it. In fact, there are many rates of return statistics related to your portfolio that differ from each other and give you different perspectives. For instance, your recent one-year return doesn't mean much. What has been your five-year, average annual compound return? Your ten-year? Your twenty-year? Your lifetime return? What has been the return purely on your own invested capital? How has the market been doing? How have your friends been doing?

This is not a book on investing! The bookstore shelves are replete with books on that topic. I do not aspire that **my one section** in this book could compete with those. Also, many of those authors are way smarter than me. For sea anemone converts, I share in the Bibliography my recommendations of three excellent books on this topic.

Sections

5.1 Investing Philosophy

5.2 Investing Strategy

5.3 Safety

5.4 Rate of Return

5.5 Key Words and Concepts

5.1 Investing Philosophy

Philosophy versus Strategy

*I wish to dichotomize investing **philosophy** from investing **strategy**.*

The former is the big picture, which incorporates your **value systems and goals.** The philosophy defines **where** you are trying to get to and the strategy describes **how** you plan to get there. But first of all, **learn to love your portfolio.** Yup! You read that right. You are your portfolio, and your portfolio is you. Accordingly, you need to grow to love your portfolio, as you do other things and people in your life. Why? Because your portfolio is going to take care of you at a stage in your life. In the meantime, you need to take care of it so that it can, in turn, take care of you. How? Feed your portfolio as you would your child (that's called "saving").

Educate yourself on money management as you would on parenting. Expose your portfolio to reasonable risk, as you should your child, so that it/they can be better prepared for everything that life throws at them. Prepare your portfolio for crisis-management (a stock market collapse), as you should for your child's ups-and-downs in life. Don't let genomic toxicity (see Chapter 3) impair the success of your portfolio, or the raising of your child. Don't create a toxic, dysfunctional environment where your child is driven to drugs, or your portfolio is forced to pursue grand-slam home-run strategies to catch up by chasing bit coin, "Dutch tulips," and tech bubbles.

Think of investing as a journey.

Imagine your philosophy is loaded onboard a canoe, along with propulsion devices, including an outboard motor for fast movement, a paddle for slower movement, and a sail for when you wish to preserve your energy sources (gasoline for the engine and muscle power for the paddle). Lastly, there is the all-important "free" energy from the varying current in the water; this, of course, is the market itself.

Let's not forget the rudder and tiller on your vessel. These, too, are integral to having your strategy deliver you **where** you want to go. If you have done any kayaking or canoeing, you will recognize that there are environments in your journey where the wind and current are calm and steady, in which case you can set the tiller and leave it alone for a while, enjoy the scenery, and proceed in the direction you seek. When the currents change, or the wind comes up, you may need to be making adjustments to the rudder to maintain your heading in the desired direction. This is a metaphor for investing strategy.

Here is another travel metaphor.

As you enter the world of investing as a neophyte, the **metaphor of a train journey** is very instructive. Imagine, you want to get from Place A to Place B by train. Your trip on the train is only a part of the journey. It started somewhere before you got on, and it will continue somewhere after you get off. The train of course follows the tracks, and the tracks were laid according to geographic impediments—lakes, rivers, mountains. Unless you are travelling on the Prairies, the track pathway is unlikely to be a perfect straight line for your part of its journey. You will zig and zag, and maybe even backtrack a bit. You may pass through long, dark tunnels. You may have to ascend some mountains and descend others. The locomotive has powerful engines to propel you up and strong brakes for coming down. The dining car gives you the opportunity to enjoy along the journey. These elements are the **conditions precedent** of your own voyage.

The very day you saved some money and made your first investment, you hopped on that train at Place A, which already has travelled very far. Your portfolio has brakes to mitigate a steep descent. Your portfolio has powerful engines to meet the challenge of a steep ascent. You don't throw yourself off the train in a long, dark tunnel; you have the wisdom to hold 'em in a market "correction." You can extract some enjoyment along the ride…take some profit and cash flow to buy a new car or a holiday. The miles that pile up along your journey are the portfolio's compounding. Subject to a panic attack where you might choose to throw yourself off a moving train, you will stay on that train all the way to Place B (which for you is the day of your passing from this life). As a precis to the Legacy chapter, in fact that train journey did not end at Place B…it only ended there for you. Your beneficiaries are going to board that train, sit in your seat, and carry on even further.

The key point here for the novice investor is that it might happen that the very first part of the train journey might involve that long dark tunnel—a market crash. This might start you off with a bad mood. Gee! Train travel is no fun. And when you pass through that tunnel into the sun, your bad mood might take a while to dissipate (aka "gun-shy"). In the investing world, we call this a "bad start," and we will discuss this further in Section 5.4 Rate of Return.

Now imagine this scenario: you are spending the night in a wide-open desert.

The forecast is for a huge thunder-and-lightning storm, including torrential rain, a passing ice storm, clear skies, all followed by a 40°C heat wave. You have choices as to how you spend that twenty-four-hour period:

- Just stand there in the desert and bear it all
- Erect a pup tent

- Erect a rudimentary shelter with one room and walls and a roof, secured to the ground
- Build a small one floor house, with rooms and a window
- Build a modern house, with electricity and central heating and air conditioning, with vantage points of several windows

The more robustly you prepare yourself, the more likely you will endure all of these forces.

> *Investment management is not art, not science, it's engineering. We are in the business of managing and engineering financial investment risk.*
> —Charles Tschampion, director, General Motors Investment Management Corporation

When you build a new house, you start with design, drawings, and architecture. You don't just show up at the site with concrete, shingles, and two-by-fours. The planning phase is where your **philosophy** unveils. What **sort** of house suits you? A bungalow? A rancher? Multi-storey? A mansion? Wood siding? Stucco? Environmental? Open plan?

Now imagine you buy a lot in a nice neighbourhood and plan to build your dream house.

You hire an architect, develop the drawings for this beautiful home, hire a contractor, and then you and your spouse live out another dream...travelling around the world for a year. You excitedly return a year later and drive up to your newly built home. Your mind is flashing back to the image of the architect's drawing. But what you see is something completely different and horrific...

- The shingle roofing material has instead been applied to the siding on the front of the house.
- The roof is stucco.
- The front entrance door has been cut into the roof.
- The gutters are installed on the ground at the foot of the house.
- The front windows are installed crooked.

Your thoughts are: This isn't a house and How did this happen?

Both of these scenarios highlight Charles Tschampion's point that portfolio construction is about engineering. In the desert scenario, you metaphorically are experiencing what the financial markets will do to you over your many years as an investor, albeit here shrunk into twenty-four hours of weather. In this scenario, you are playing your cards to build a portfolio that perfectly suits the environment of any present moment, versus one that over-builds for any particular moment, not knowing what is coming next, but has the resilience to secure you through all of the scenarios. In the second, dream-house scenario, you see that, although you took the long view from the desert scenario and designed a sophisticated, all-weather structure, you failed to monitor it properly.

*So, investing **philosophy** needs to match up with investing **strategy**.*

Like a house, a sound, all-weather portfolio has a long list of design elements and "materials," along with solid construction. Also like a house, a portfolio needs maintenance and "seasonal" adjustments. For instance, well-constructed gutters will fail if they are not purged of leaves from time to time. A market runup, in say biotech stocks, may signal a strategy to reap some profit therein and re-balance. Hot water tanks and furnaces need to be replaced from time to time because they have been technologically superseded. New products and innovations create investment opportunities that didn't exist before and need to be reckoned into portfolio construction. In the spring, garden furniture gets moved outdoors and dusted off to enjoy on the back porch. The time adjustments of a portfolio are not on the same ninety-day cycle of our seasons; rather they are longer, looking to loosely defined market cycles. Different industrial sectors tend to lead in different parts of the economic cycle.

Financial Design

We normally associate the term "design" with, say, architecture, fashion, and industry.

I have researched design principles in these areas and attempted to draw parallels to personal finance. "Human centred design" is a **design philosophy**: it requires starting with a good understanding of people and the needs that they have. Great design requires communication of the purpose, structure, and operation of the object or service being received. Consumers need some way to understand the product or service they wish to use: what it does, how it works, and what alternative actions are possible. The degree of ease with which a user can find and understand the elements and features of a new system when they first encounter it is termed "discoverability." This requires:

- A conceptual model of the system (a financial plan…an asset allocation plan)
- Constraint mapping (to understand the upside and downside bounds of a plan)
- Feedback (an annual report)

- "Signifiers" to communicate when and where action should take place (internal portfolio management systems), and
- "Affordances" to communicate how your portfolio supports affordable lifestyle…or not.

Well-designed things (yes, even a portfolio) can induce pride and enjoyment, a feeling of being in control, pleasure, and possibly even attachment. From this research I have distilled financial design down to eight principles. It should:

1) Enable you to appreciate the design of your financial affairs, in order to instill the desire to contribute in your own way to its ultimate success.
2) Distill financial management down to its most fundamental properties and explain complex matters in an uncomplicated way.
3) Consider other stakeholders in the stewardship of wealth. It should inspire primary stakeholders to embrace future stakeholders in the dialogue about long-term, multi-generational wealth stewardship (Family Confab).
4) Enhance the experience of (what may be to many) the unpleasant task of prudent financial management, encompassing practicality and attention to detail.
5) Challenge the norms that prevail. It should stand out as confidently different, not following the herd.
6) Be timeless. It lingers. It evolves. It matures and becomes more confident.
7) Include the story of your life-lived, and your impact upon the world around you, both near and far.
8) Evoke meaningful stories that are intended to instruct and inspire you to draw from the life experiences of the many in your world.

Author Nick Murray distills the whole process:

- Goals dictate plans
- Plans dictate asset allocation strategy
- Asset allocation strategy dictates diversification
- Diversification dictates re-balancing back to the asset allocation strategy, and behaviour oversees the rest.

The investor needs to act out three critical behavioural principles:

1) Faith in the future over fear of the future
2) Patience to believe in your long-term asset allocation strategy
3) Discipline to hold your ground through trying markets

With that cryptic prescription, you need to:

1) Establish your goals
2) Lay out a plan to achieve them
3) Execute that plan
4) Monitor and modify to stay on track

Apologies if this sounds too **simple**. In reality, a lot of **complexity** lies under the hood to make all that happen. The goal-setting part is in your court. Converting that into a formal plan, building a diversified portfolio, and building a monitoring system that sets adjustment triggers can be passed on to, or shared with, a competent advisor.

Sketches in Personal Finance

"Stock XYZ lost 30% last year: why didn't you sell it before that happened?"

This was the first question from George when he came in to review his annual report. It wasn't a great investing year, to be sure, but the portfolio as a whole made 3%. Yet George couldn't let go of the loss on XYZ.

The philosophy lesson here is: "The portfolio's the thing, more than the individual things in it."

Let's go back to George's comment and to the world of investing. The global economy, and the stock market that follows it, is very complex. Individual securities don't go up and down in unison and in amplitude. That's a good thing. It would be beautiful and amazing if an investor could sell all things before they go down and buy all things before they go up.

Investing Over Time

History is a long period of time! How's that for profound?

Even those of us who pay respect to the lessons of history are torn between: **"History repeats itself"** and **"This time it is different."** My own experience is to run away as fast as you can from those who utter the latter. I think that what reconciles these two pieces of wisdom is the "translation" or "modernizing" of the "event." It is a classification issue. In the taxonomy of the biological world, all living things are classified by species, genus, family, order, class, phylum, kingdom, and domain. The Dutch Tulip Scandal of the 1600s saw rare tulip bulbs trading at six times the average person's annual salary. The British South Seas Bubble of 1720, which was involved in the slave trade, ruined thousands of investors. The Dot Com Bubble of 2000 saw its index rise by 400%, then fall by

78%. Yesterday, we could talk about marijuana stocks, and today we can talk about bitcoin. Tulip bulbs, slaves, and the internet have nothing in common along the lower taxonomy scale; ergo "they are different." But, at the higher level, they do. Chasing these shooting stars also ignores the wisdom that "the portfolio's the thing; more than the individual things in it." And, further, it belies the strategy of trying to "shoot out the lights" to compensate for a late start.

Early in the new millennium, an invaluable book was published, entitled *Triumph of the Optimists: 101 Years of Global Investment Returns* by Dimson, Marsh, and Staunton. It is an expensive, worthwhile book that should have a permanent place on your bedside table.

*Let's gain a **long perspective** of a hundred years of historical, **real** (after-inflation) returns in the **world equity** sector:*

Geometric real returns (%) by decade 1900-2000, for world equity markets

World	1910	1920	1930	1940	1950	1960	1970	1980	1990	2000
Equity	5.4	-3.7	13.0	1.7	1.0	17.1	5.5	0.9	13.5	5.4
Inflation*	1.9	6.8	-0.9	-1.8	4.5	2.4	2.6	7.6	6.2	2.2

*Canadian

Elroy Dimson, Paul Marsh, and Mike Staunton, *Triumph of the Optimists: 101 Years of Global Investment Returns*, Princeton University Press, 2002

The **nominal** equity return that we would be familiar with in the news is approximately the sum of the real return **plus** the corresponding period inflation rate. Note that North American **inflation data** were benign, compared to much of continental Europe in those World War decades.

Each decade has its own storylines in the history books, and the relative severity of each set of events may be debated. The low decade equity returns were of course the war decades of 1910–20 and 1930–50. Two of the big decade equity returns (1920–30 and 1950–60) were both post-war, as the world set about reconstructing the global economy previously destroyed by global conflict.

Ten-year investing periods may seem like a long time. If we were to present charts of the **annual returns in each year of all of those decades**, the data would appear more heart-stopping, with way more fluctuation than we see in the ten-decade points of data in the table. Remember: our mantra is to focus on long-term, **cumulative,** compound portfolio performance in this graph:

Cumulative decades compound geometric real returns, by decade 1900-2000										
World	1910	1920	1930	1940	1950	1960	1970	1980	1990	2000
Equity	5.4	0.8	4.7	3.9	3.3	5.5	5.5	4.9	5.8	5.8

Elroy Dimson, Paul Marsh, and Mike Staunton, *Triumph of the Optimists: 101 Years of Global Investment Returns*, Princeton University Press, 2002

Canada's hundred-year inflation rate was 3.2%. Thus, the hundred-year **nominal** return on world equities was approximately 9.0%.

Think about everything that goes on around the world…in a year…in a decade… in your entire lifetime.

It is interesting to note how the ups and downs of major economic events smooth out to a great extent for the patient, long-term investor, even within any decade. And each decade's storyline is different from the other. "**Patience**" is a state-of-mind, and "**long-term**" is a state-of-perspective. Properly managed, much wealth today truly will carry forward multiple generations into the future until the meteorite strikes.

As human beings, I think **we are pre-disposed to short-time horizons**. When I pose the question "What's the money for?," it is hard for:

- The forty-year-old to connect today's small pension savings with funding most of one's entire retirement life period, starting twenty-five years hence.
- The sixty-year-old to envisage that retirement pot being able to fund expensive long-term care, starting twenty-five years hence.
- The wealthy retiree to envisage that they will leave a substantial estate to their heirs, lasting long into the future.

In the last case, the wealthy retirees must get their head around how that next generation will handle the money. From an investment philosophy point of view, the investment timeline expands from their remaining lifetime to that of their inheritor(s). If the wealth pot is large enough, and the future inheritors are responsible, we must introduce the concept of being a "custodian," not owner, of that wealth. Then try thinking generations out to yet-unborn grandchildren!

Or embrace the millennium-old Iroquois Nation "Seventh Generation Principle." That's right…**seven** generations; whereas today in our world, CEOs are focused on the next quarter and politicians on their next re-election! As family CFO, we ought to be thinking 150 years ahead! But, in the context of the family financial genome, it may be more important for the family CFO to be cognizant of how bad fiscal management can become encoded in the gene pool and "expressed" long into the future.

Simplistically, there are **three steps** *to embrace in the long-term strategy of wealth building, and these three draw from a hippie author, a financial planner, and a bean counter.*

Step One: Don't be influenced by day-to-day events. Tom Robbins authored a book in the 1970s called *Another Roadside Attraction,* which was largely set in his home state of Washington. (You may remember his other book more readily, as it became a movie and had the catchy title: *Even Cowgirls Get the Blues*.) Throughout the storyline of the book, Robbins frequently re-quotes the following simple phrase: "And the world situation was desperate…as usual." Little did he realize he was saying something prophetic to the investing world. Nick Murray, who inspired us earlier, has his own similar term, which he calls the "apocalypse du jour."

I think both of these statements inspire Step One: ignore the daily news. The world news and the financial press will always provide something to worry about. I don't need to list examples—you can do that yourself. Some of these things are real and have some temporal impact on the planet; others never happen or have a meteoric fall from the front page. My advice is not to get caught up in this trap of being led around by the daily news. Consider it as **noise** in your long term. Investing is a long-term project, whether you are thirty or sixty or even older but building inter-generational wealth. It is important to not panic and sell at or near the bottom, and also to make sure that your over-all investment strategy (we call it "asset allocation") is sound.

Step Two: Ensure your investing is based on a plan. Nick Murray uses the term "planning-based investment management," which is, simply, that investment management ought to be "planning-based" and not "market-based." This leads us to the financial planner's role in this three-step process. A formal financial plan will have included in it an asset allocation strategy that will derive a proforma long-term rate of return from your investments, which should: a) deliver the lifestyle that you seek and b) deliver an ending estate value that you wish for your heirs. Based upon the numerous financial plans that we have prepared over the years, this proforma nominal long-term rate of return on a balanced portfolio is typically 5–6%. (Hold that number and move on to Step Three.)

Step Three: Monitor how you are doing. You can do this by calculating the actual historical rate of return on your portfolio. In fact, two numbers are required here, and one derives the other. The first is the series of annual **simple** rates of return earned year-by-year. This isn't the data to focus on because they likely will jump all over the place and not give you a clear picture of how you are doing long term. But these numbers can be used to derive a running, **long-term compound return**, and this is the one to compare to your Plan rate of return in Step Two.

If your long-term compound return in Step Three is at, near, or above your financial planning proforma return in Step Two, you know you will be on track to meeting your goals as dictated by the plan (as long as you also adhere to your budgeted spending plan). So, there, you're done!

Be Prepared for Hard Times

As with most market dips, the sentiment each time is that: "This time is different," and "The world will never be the same again." As a young man observing the past before my time (e.g., the Great Depression), I ignorantly concluded that each generational cohort on this planet needed to experience **one major financial cataclysm**, and that this experience would strengthen us in future such events. I was wrong: we typically **don't** successfully learn from these incidents. In fact, experiential memory in the investing world is quite short. I now believe that market experience is an annuity of unlike one-off events.

> *There are decades when nothing happens, and there are weeks when decades happen.*
> —Vladimir Lenin

This is how the market tends to react. Lenin might have coined that phrase as a Wall Street finance guru, not a champion of socialism.

I gave a keynote address entitled "Ten Commandments of a True Professional" at an accountants' conference in Niagara Falls.

The first commandment is known as **Nilson's First Rule**: "**Don't worry about problems you don't have**." This rule is universally applicable to life. It doesn't prescribe a Pollyanna or ostrich view towards life. We do need to have our eyes upon the horizon watching for potential things that might be coming at us. But the rule is most useful to the chronic-worrier types who see threats at every turn. This is a health-debilitating habit. The state of the stock market, and your financial well-being, provide a rich feeding ground for chronic worriers. One of my professional colleagues has been calling for a catastrophic market crash **every day for over twenty years**!

Imagine, for instance, the last twenty years of world stock markets.

That's roughly 5,000 trading days. In each one of those days, you implicitly made decisions about your investments, including **action** (buy/sell) and **inaction** (hold 'em). Hold 'em means you take the ride of the ups-and-downs and maintain your position. "Buying" means adding something that you hope is cheap and going up, and selling means unloading something you think is going down and sitting on the sidelines. What if you were wrong and did the opposite?

Let's imagine you have a proclivity to jumping off and let's imagine further you sat out .002 of those 5,000 days (ten days) that happened to be the **ten best days in the twenty years**. Guess what those ten missed days would do to your twenty-year return. According to J.P. Morgan Asset Management, did you know that indiscretion to miss the best .002 of 5,000 days of the S&P 500 index, for instance, would reduce your twenty-year return by more than half? And what if you missed the best thirty days in 5,000 days? Your twenty-year return would be negative. Worse still…seven of those best days showed up within weeks of the worst twenty days. **It is important to stay in the game.**

Let's revisit Larry's portfolio trajectory again from Section 4.1, except this time with a different vantage point.

This graph shows the monthly values of his portfolio over twenty-eight years. In one month of every year, the portfolio grew by his annual contribution, but all the other months simply reflect market movement. Think about all the news that happened over that span of time. The larger dips that happened seemed significant in the moment, and none of the upticks seem particularly notable in the graph. Even the two noticeable dips in 2008 and 2020 bounced back fairly quickly and continued growing. When you string it all together, $34,000 starting in early 1995 became $1.14M at the end of 2023.

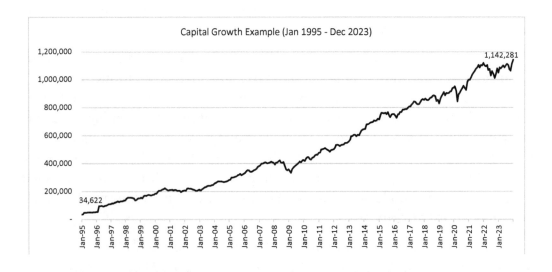

5.2 Investing Strategy

Planning at the Investment Level

We started with **Money Philosophy** in Section 2.1, which spoke to the financial aspects of your life: your job, your spending habits, your dependents, your legacies, etc. Then we advanced to Chapter 4, where we embraced having a big-picture **financial plan**. Then we advanced to **Investing Philosophy** in Section 5.1, where we drew from your value systems to apply a set of principles to guide making your money grow. This **Investing Strategy** section grabs the baton from these philosophies to steward the day-to-day and year-to-year management of your investing wealth.

The dictionary defines "strategy" as a plan of action designed to achieve a goal or aim. So, for starters, we need to know what our goal is. "Making a ton of money on the stock market" is not a useful goal.

I am reminded of Lily Tomlin's famous quote: "All my life, I really wanted to **be** someone; now I realize I should have been more specific!"

*After Chapter 4, we need a set of more specific micro-plans at the **investing level**.*

Strategic asset allocation is an investing strategy that sets percentage targets for the major asset classes, defined as cash, fixed income, and equities. At any point in time, your actual portfolio can be tallied at current market values on these same percentage parameters and compared to plan, thus giving guidance for future action. If, for instance, equities rise whilst fixed income remains flat, your equity percentage will become greater than its plan percentage. This is a "sell signal" that implicitly responds to that old axiom: "buy low; sell high."

The asset allocation strategy needs to dig deeper into a set of sub-strategies for each of the major asset classes. Let's start with equities where we drill deeper into Canadian markets, global markets, and industrial sectors.

Domestic vs Foreign Markets: Across world economies, investors tend to have a "home bias." One reason, of course, is familiarity. The companies and stocks produce the products in your environment, which you are familiar with. A second reason is foreign exchange. Once you start investing in foreign markets, you will also be investing in the currency swings between that country and your own. Currency movements can be significant. They can amplify or modify the success of the two respective economies. Ultimately, you call upon your portfolio to provide cash flow for your spending habits, and these tend, of course, to be in your domestic currency. The investing world gives investors the opportunity to "hedge" out the currency aspect of foreign investing. A reason for venturing abroad might be the thinness of your own domestic stock market. For instance, Canada is not the home for significant health, technology, and consumer companies.

Global Economic Centres: The largest economies in the world, by far, are the US and China, with, of course, only the former having a sophisticated capital market system. Falling next and far behind are: Japan, Germany, the UK, France, India, Italy, Brazil, and Canada. Investing strategy typically allocates targets regionally, rather than by country. Like Canada, some regions have both strong and weak industrial sector presence.

Industrial Sectors: "GICS" is the Global Industry Classification System that, since 2001, attempts to standardize the classification of the activities of companies across the globe to allow greater comparability for global investors. In economic theory, different industrial sectors lead the way through the economic cycle from early boom to late boom to recession, and back again to the next early boom. Thus, investing theory says that if you can accurately label where the economy is at a point in time along that cycle, you know what sectors to buy and what to sell. This has been termed a sector-rotator style. The trick, of course, is identifying the cycle. And, if everyone were able to call this accurately, the advantage would be removed anyway as everyone would be a seller or buyer.

Monitoring and Calls to Action

With targets set for asset allocation, global diversification, and industrial sector diversification, there are **three sub-strategies** to monitor and manage. A statistic for each one of these identifies the degree of variances from Plan, termed "Call-to-Action" indices. They provide a very quick "report card" on the state of the portfolio—and the markets. They are the "First Responder" to taking action.

The three Call-to-Action Indices are:

- The **Asset Allocation** Call-to-Action statistic might bring to attention that **equity** markets may be out-performing **bond** markets at points in time…inviting to "sell high."
- The **Global** Call-to-Action statistic might bring to attention that one **region** may be out-performing others at points in time, and again inviting to "sell high."
- The **Industrial** Call-to-Action statistic might bring to attention that one **industrial sector** may be out-performing others at points in time. Once more, inviting to "sell high."

*When a Call-to-Action index suggests selling to take profits in either an industry or a global region, you then must decide **what** to sell.*

You need to scroll through your holdings to see what security can achieve that sell call. The securities you hold will be some combination of direct stocks (shares in a bank or Apple, for instance) and "funds." The latter might include mutual funds and exchange-traded funds, which are baskets of many companies. Stocks tend to belong in a particular sector (again, a bank or tech stock), although some companies are "conglomerates" with many subsidiaries in many different sectors. Funds tend to be "conglomerates," although they are not termed so. The basket of companies tends to include holdings across all industrial sectors, albeit disproportionately. I term these as "shotguns"—one fund investment is shooting at many different sectors. If the call-to-action is to take some profit in the tech sector, for instance, it does not work to sell a shotgun basket, which might only hold, say, 10% in tech. You also would be selling down all the other sectors, too, which you don't want! However, some funds are single sector focussed, e.g., every company in the basket is a tech company. That is a rifle that you can use to achieve your purpose.

The same principle holds with global investing securities. Some are region specific, e.g., the US only, and thus are a rifle. Some hold a basket of companies from around the world, and thus are a shotgun. Practically, it is difficult to build rifles into a small equity portfolio. There are not enough dollars, and therefore not room for enough positions to have the freedom of holding rifles.

If you are seeking **two** strategic calls-to-action, e.g., take profit geographically in the US **and** take profit industrially in tech, then you would be looking to sell a security that holds only **US** tech companies, as opposed to holding a basket of **global** tech companies.

However, remember that transaction costs on buying or selling can have too big an impact on small trades. In an extreme case, those fees can eradicate the market profit you thought you were enjoying.

Other Thoughts on Strategy

As you raise the bar of your portfolio management, there are numerous other strategies and angles to think about.

Your job as an asset class (cross-correlated risk)

During your worker/capitalist era, you may face the opportunity to participate in a company stock purchase plan. The plan might have an extra kicker whereby the company contributes (effectively more) compensation to the stock purchase.

We have seen these to be a mixed blessing. Here's why: in a stock portfolio of many holdings, one of the goals is diversification, and one of the issues is how correlated these holdings are to each other. The more correlated, the less diversification you have actually built. Back to the company stock option: you now have created a correlation between your employment income and your capitalist income. If the stock is a star, you are happy. But if the company hits bad times, the stock price can fall through the floor, and you may even be laid off or forced to take a significant wage cut.

A related but different angle on this is what I call "legal insider info." Covid created a complex economy: many businesses flailed or died and others exploded with success. One of the former was the cruise ship industry. As usual, two schools of thought existed: one that the industry would return to normal when Covid passed; the other that the industry would never be the same. Through Covid, the travel agency business died! If you were an agent, your income probably went to zero, and you were in fact working for free helping to retrieve pre-Covid deposit refunds for all your clients. With pent-up travel demand and extrapolated hope for relief from Covid, travellers eventually started to book cruises. The agents were on the front end of this. Their industry connection gave them the (legal) insight that cruise ship stock prices might jump. So, agents started phoning their investment advisors. Everybody likes a hot stock tip! But for the agent, back to that cross-correlated risk: if they are right, their earned income is going to go up…likely substantially…perhaps tens of thousands. If they bought $5,000 of cruise ship stock and it doubled, they would make $5,000. If the runup was less than double, the cash win would be less than that. Given the very large risk (and multiple risks) on their worker earnings, does it make sense to double-down with their capitalist earnings? Remember: there is no guarantee that the stock is going up. Even if it did, it might only be ephemeral if Covid takes another nasty turn in the news.

Starting late/playing catch up

If life's circumstances have caused you to come late to the savings game, re-read the baseball analogy in Chapter 4. The strategy of baseball coaches isn't to hit a grand-slam homer in the bottom of the ninth. Rather, it is to get players on base, advance the runners, and get "home." The late-comer investor may take the position that they need to execute a riskier profile (i.e., higher equity component) to make up for lost time and get a grand slam homer. Here's the truth: Mr. Market doesn't know you and doesn't care about you. Mr. Market is not going on a tear to accommodate your come-lately needs. Recall the train-ride metaphor at the start of this chapter. You need to employ a sensible risk profile.

Get old...get conservative?

Historically, the school of asset allocation suggested that the stock market proportion be ramped down as we age, and bonds increased. The logical argument here was that as we grow older, we run out of runway to have the market recover after a crash; notably so, if we face expensive long-term care in our final years. This outlook flourished in what the modern era refers to as the "golden era of bonds." The wisdom of this strategy is also situation-specific. If the forecast is that your wealth will out-live you, then the value of your estate will pass on to your younger beneficiaries. This could morph your asset allocation strategy to the counter-intuitive logic that that wealth should be deployed according to the younger, inheriting generation—even though it is still your money. Some seniors get this; some say, not my problem.

A different take on asset allocation

It is generally accepted that the stock market out-performs the bond market over the long run. Despite that, bonds are held to: a) provide cash flow from interest payments for any cash calls and b) act as value insurance in market crashes. (However, if you are in **accumulation** mode, then a) doesn't matter.) The Nick Murray wisdom on asset allocation is to grow the portfolio with 100% stock market exposure. When the crashes occur, the story goes that the market will come back, so b) doesn't matter. His strategy includes holding pure cash to cover one to two years of cash calls, so that no call in that period would force an equity sale at distress prices. This strategy doesn't cover for unscheduled cash calls.

Shifting gears—accumulator vs. decumulator vs. maintainer

Most of us work in an occupation in our **accumulating** years, hope to earn more than we spend (i.e., save), and have those savings grow. When we start our first job as a young person, we are 100% worker and 0% capitalist (measured by the relative proportions of our income from work versus investments). Slowly over our career, our savings grow and the capitalist proportion begins. Then we begin to see the power of capitalist compounding—that beautiful thing that awed Einstein. While we do not associate compounding with our worker earnings, for many of us that effectively happens, too, as our experience and value grow and are valued in the workplace with promotions and higher wages.

Eventually, that retirement date comes for most of us, when those two proportions precisely flip: our worker earnings are 0% and our capitalist earnings are 100%.

At that time, we may shift into the **decumulating** years. Our investment portfolio needs a "heads-up" on this retirement moment **because now its job has changed**: the portfolio now is paying for your lifestyle, thus, there are significant monthly cash calls to pay the bills. Ideally, the portfolio is already engineered for this day.

However, health issues or job loss could precipitate the day. This might require some re-engineering. The point is that the portfolio ought to be able to **meet the monthly cash calls** with no, or very little, market risk. That day of a 30% market drop does not come pre-announced, nor does its recovery date. Remember Nick Murray's approach about keeping two years of (scheduled) calls in cash.

We see the same re-engineering in a smaller and briefer situation: education portfolios.

Prudent parents start socking away annual saving for their children from birth to high-school graduation. Those include the same accumulation years as for a retiree, so there may be competition for scarce saving. But then, from age eighteen onwards, the education account goes into decumulation years (much briefer than the retirement years—or at least Mom and Dad hope so). The account might be drawn to zero in four university years. If the market serves up its 30% decline in that period, it may not recover in time, and a lot of the eighteen years of earnings went down the drain. Thus, the investment strategy needs to be reengineered away from the risk of the market. In fact, being in cash/bonds for the last few years might be the wisest decision.

Some of you may pass through a third portfolio mode of **maintainer**. This occurs when, for instance, you move into semi-retirement mode and still have some earned income, or if you retired with a separate stash of cash that you can draw down before you access your portfolio. In these scenarios, your portfolio neither receives cash nor cash calls, and simply grows by its rate-of-return.

It's not necessarily all or nothing with RRSPs and RRIFs

RRSPs must be converted to RRIFs by the end of the calendar year of your seventy-first birthday. You are permitted to do so earlier. A childhood friend of mine saw her investment advisor do the conversion in her sixty-fifth year. The next year she was obliged to a large taxable withdrawal of approximately $70,000. This significantly drove up her tax rate, and she didn't need all the cash flow! The rules allow that conversion to a RRIF can be reversed and restituted to her RRSP. Now, she could withdraw a smaller taxable sum to meet any cash flow needs and manage her tax rate.

Funding cash needs in your sixties and thinking outside the box with RRSPs and RRIFs

A common strategy is to defer the RRIF conversion until age seventy-one. If you need some cash during your sixties, just deregister what you need from your RRSP, but remember to think about taxes. If you have a spouse with a lower tax rate than you, you would be better off to transfer some of that deregistration over—but you are not allowed to do so. Instead, look at your RRIF as a "conduit." Transfer the funds you need from your RRSP to your (otherwise empty/dormant) RRIF and then deregister from there. By changing the source of the payout, you have the option of splitting this taxable income with your spouse's tax return.

Sketches in Personal Finance

Dividing the pie: We had a new client come in with $1 million to invest from the recent sale of a rental property. She also had a twenty-year $1 million portfolio extant with another advisor. I suggested that the two portfolios needed to be combined in order to make a coherent overall strategy. (Think about the metaphor of building a house with two different builders.) After some thought, she opted to keep them separate. I asked her back, at which time I said that we respected her right to execute her own wishes, but that we didn't believe this was in her best interest in the long run, and we would decline the engagement as we would be "partners" in a thing that was destined not to succeed. Here's why…

Have you ever given your kids a jigsaw puzzle to work on? Think about a rainy vacation day at your summer camp. The kids are stuck inside, and bored. You pull out a jigsaw puzzle box and pour the pieces onto the kitchen table. The picture on the box is of a dog and a cat. The two kids start to squabble, so you separate them and give roughly half the pieces to each. Neither of them gets the box with the picture. You tell your son to make a dog and your daughter to make a cat.

What's going to happen here? Failure! Each child will have pieces that belong to the other, but that won't be known until the end. Neither can effectively figure out how to take all those random pieces and make a dog and a cat. Should they come together later at the kitchen table, the half-built picture that each brings to the table probably will not meet in the middle to complete the proper image.

Two investment advisors are not likely to coordinate the construction of two portfolios to make a coherent whole. They are not going to consult with each other on buying and selling. If you charge one of them with the "growth" portfolio and the other with the "safe" portfolio, the benchmarking of returns against each other will never be "a fair horse race."

The importance of a monitoring system

Running out of money is, of course, the biggest scare for any of us. For starters, any financial plan should give a very early heads-up that problems may develop in the future, e.g., an insufficient saving program—too high a burn rate. Accordingly, strategies should exist from the get-go to avoid this. But creating a plan is just the start. What happens from then forward creates the reality. Keep the perspective that people don't tend to run out of money overnight; rather, they are travelling along some shortening runway. They need an early warning system, like a pilot landing a plane.

Sketches in Personal Finance

I had an elderly client headed down this path, which led to the creation of the following graphs as early warning devices. The first graph shows a) the declining portfolio size (the bars), b) the accumulating draws (top line) and c) the accumulating portfolio income (bottom line). The client has had the **same** monthly draw since inception, hence the straight diagonal line. You can easily see that she has drawn more than the portfolio could make every year **since the start**. You can also see that the gap between the two lines is widening. Coincidentally, the total draws over those years were almost exactly what the starting portfolio value was: $800,000. Thus, the value in 2021—$480,000—was the amount of investment income earned over the fifteen years. This represented a compound, annual return through the period of 5% on a portfolio with a conservative 70% fixed income allocation.

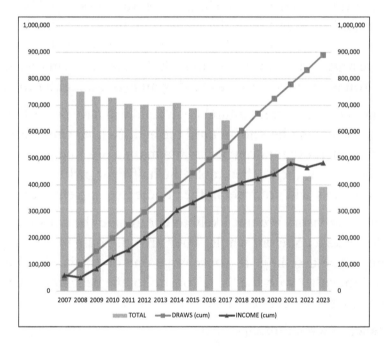

The second graph below speaks to the same issue with a different representation. The large bars are exactly the same as on the previous graph—the tracking of portfolio value. The smaller bars are the cumulative shortfall of draws over income. The inference from this graph is the rapid rate at which the shortfall is catching up to the value of the portfolio; other words, the portfolio is running out of money. Since she is age eighty at the time of writing, the present situation would fund her for another thirteen years.

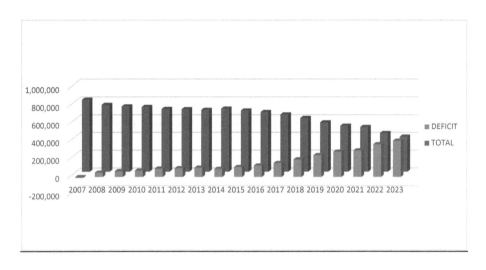

Get to work!

This can happen when new money is deployed into the market which shortly thereafter falls 15–30% (think September 2008). That market fall recovered quite quickly then (six months) compared to previous meltdowns, but nonetheless the three-year annual compound return from start approached zero. And those three years of zero return hurt the running compound return for the next decade or more. The flip side of that was the Covid market fall of March 2020. If cash was deployed into the market at that time, the one-year returns were 20–40% on the **new** investment, giving instead a "good start" to the future long-term compound return.

Sketches in Personal Finance

A client kept her investment funds with another advisor; her husband kept them with us. When he passed away, she decided to leave his funds with us, thus splitting her advisors. She later sold a property and deposited the funds with us. Given the high state of the markets at the time, we decided to hold the funds in cash for a while. One day, she called and enquired why we had not deployed the funds, and she commented that her other advisor would have done so by now. "He really **works** it…."

> *The lesson here is that sometimes a portfolio needs to appear indolent; doing "nothing" may actually be doing "something." An advisor's worst nightmare is a "bad start," when new money is deployed into the market, which soon after falls significantly.*

Strategy and inflation

In the adult lifetimes of many people living today, the 1970s and 1980s were back-to-back decades of high inflation. In 1991, the Canadian government and the Bank of Canada agreed on targets for inflation reduction with the aim of keeping inflation at 2%, which still remains the target today. So, we have had thirty years of managed low inflation, which does not cross our radar screen very much.

But with the global economic impact of Covid, Central Banks pumped up the money supply in response, causing inflationary concerns. In August 2020, the US Federal Reserve (the Fed) announced a new inflation policy called Average Inflation Targeting (AIT). Following periods when inflation has been running persistently below 2%, their monetary policy now will aim to allow inflation moderately above 2% for some period of time, such that the average 2% target is attained over an averaging period. So, the US Central Bank is giving itself permission to support interim periods of higher inflation.

The impact of a country's inflation management has many vectors. Bond investors anticipating higher inflation seek higher interest rates to invest. Meanwhile, the higher rates punish the market prices of their existing bond-holdings.

Higher domestic rates attract incoming investment funds from abroad. Those incoming funds raise that country's foreign exchange rate. The strengthened domestic currency encourages imports and discourages exports, the latter of which would be bad for the domestic productive economy...and this all circles back to you.

We each experience the impacts of inflation wearing many different hats: as employees, consumers, investors, taxpayers, and perhaps as businesspeople. The incidence of inflation, a term in economics, aspires to identify who actually bears the brunt of inflation. When a business experiences inflation in its production inputs, does it merely pass this on to consumers by way of higher prices? Does it share that cost increase by moderating employee wages, or do the business shareholders (investors) bear it? Or is the increase somehow apportioned amongst all of those?

As an investor, inflation acts to reduce the purchasing power of your capital. At approximately 2% per year, this is not a lot, but it is a "death by a thousand cuts"! Thirty years of 2% inflation since the early 1990s means the purchasing power of your capital today has dropped by almost half.

An inflation hedge is any strategy that protects against decreased purchasing power due to rising prices. For investors, classic inflation hedges include gold, materials, energy, other commodities, real estate and, arguably, equities in general.

At the big picture level, absorb this data from the *101 Years of Global Investment Returns* in the Canadian stock market and globally. The first chart below shows the spread between nominal (N) and real (after inflation—R) Canadian stock market returns by decade. There were three decades of notable disparity, and two of those were twenty years back-to-back 1970–90.

Non-cumulative Real and Normal Returns on Canadian Equity, by Decade (%)										
For:	1910	1920	1930	1940	1950	1960	1970	1980	1990	2000
R	6.4	0.4	15.5	2.9	4.2	12.5	7.1	2.4	5.5	7.8
N	8.3	7.2	14.6	1.1	8.7	14.9	9.7	10.0	11.7	10.0

Elroy Dimson, Paul Marsh, and Mike Staunton, *Triumph of the Optimists: 101 Years of Global Investment Returns*, Princeton University Press, 2002

The second chart below compares those same **Canadian** REAL returns to the **global** scene. The 100-year average inflation rates in both Canada and the US were approximately 3%.

Non-cumulative Real Returns on Canadian Equity and Global Equity, by Decade (%)										
For:	1910	1920	1930	1940	1950	1960	1970	1980	1990	2000
Canadian Equity	6.4	0.4	15.5	2.9	4.2	12.5	7.1	2.4	5.5	7.8
Global Equity	5.9	-3.2	12.9	1.5	1.9	16.9	5.4	0.7	12.4	6.2

Elroy Dimson, Paul Marsh, and Mike Staunton, *Triumph of the Optimists: 101 Years of Global Investment Returns*, Princeton University Press, 2002

Sketches in Personal Finance

"I've never had money before! How do I deal with this?" Carole asked when she came to me in the late-1980s. She was in her mid-fifties when her father died and left her a fairly large investment account. She sought our help to build a pathway to a more enriched, but responsible life. Here's what we did: we started an annual tracking of her portfolio results. This is routine now in the financial services industry, but it wasn't back then.

Let's say that in Year One, the $1 million account earned 5%, or $50,000, of which $20,000 was cash income and $30,000 was unrealized gains. Inflation then was, say, 2%, but had been 10%+ a decade earlier. Armed with this recent experience, Carole was determined to maintain her "purchasing power" by leaving some income on the table. This meant that 2% of the 5% return was inflation-protection. On the opening $1 million, this was $20,000, reducing her spendable income from $50,000 to $30,000 that first year. If inflation was 2% again in Year Two, her adjusted capital now needed to be $1,040,400. She didn't necessarily need to spend the available income in any particular year, but when she wanted to, her discipline was to be able to spend whatever the portfolio was worth above the annually adjusted capital amount. Very responsible.

*Here is an **optional detour** for those who are ready to head into some more advanced concepts about tax-smart investing. (If you don't want to take this detour right now, jump ahead until you see the Circle/easiest sign.)*

Tax-Smart Investing

Adding tax-smart investing principles to your investment strategy is both wise and productive. This strategy is necessarily executed as a sub-strategy applied within and across accounts. For individuals, essentially there are **two kinds of "tax" accounts**: sheltered and non-sheltered (trading). The sheltered accounts have two branches: deferred (RRSP/RRIFs) and tax-free (TFSAs). Next, we need to understand the **kinds of taxable income** created by our investments: interest, dividends (Canadian and foreign), trust income, and capital gains. The table shows how/if each kind is taxable and also the timing of taxation.

Tax treatment/ Timing	Interest	Canadian dividends	Foreign dividends	Trust income	Capital gains (realized)
Trading	Fully/annual	Annual, with dividend tax credits/annual	Annual, with foreign tax credits	Annual, with some tax-free return of capital	Annual, half-taxable
RRSP/RRIF	Fully/deferred	Deferred, dividend tax credit foregone	Deferred, no foreign tax	Fully/deferred/ Some tax-free return of capital	Fully/ deferred
TFSA	Tax-free	Tax-free but dividend tax credit foregone	Tax-free but foreign tax applies	Tax-free	Tax-free

The table conveys that there can be a lot of complexity to applying tax-smart investing to your long-term wealth accumulation. I say "can be" because that is only if you have more than one of these types of accounts. When you are just starting out as an investor, you may only have one kind of account, e.g., an RRSP or a TFSA. In that case, ignore this section and move on until the future. For everyone else, use the table by income-type.

In economic history, eighteenth-century David Ricardo inspired international trade by introducing his concept of **comparative advantage**. He said that, even when one trading nation was absolutely more efficient than another trading nation in producing every single good, it was still advantageous for the inferior nation to produce something, and for the two nations to trade. The more efficient nation ought to focus on the goods for which it had the highest relative, or "comparative," advantage and leave the other goods to the inferior nation.

And so, David Ricardo offers that legacy today for the world of **tax-smart investing in the TFSA era.** As all forms of investment income are tax-free in a TFSA (except foreign dividends), it obviously has an absolute tax advantage over RRSP/RRIFs and trading accounts. However, TFSAs have relatively more tax advantage with some types of income than others.

In the spring of 2009, I presented a research paper at a financial conference, which spoke to Ricardo's comparative advantage principle in order to provide guidance on which kinds of income are the most tax-smart in a TFSA. TFSAs had just been introduced that year by the federal government, and most financial institutions were filling those original TFSA contributions with fixed income instruments, i.e., bonds, GICs, and term deposits. I undertook longitudinal modelling with various different mix strategies for the three different kinds of accounts.

The conclusion was that TFSAs were best suited to capital gains holdings. If the gains were derived from stocks, then non-dividend-paying stocks would be better, particularly for Canadian stocks. Simpler still, foreign stocks enjoy tax-free appreciation and their (foreign) taxation of dividends is neutral.

In summary, prudent tax-smart investing practices include:

- Emphasizing interest-paying investments in pension sheltered accounts and equity investments in non-sheltered accounts.
- Controlling the timing of realizing taxable capital gains in non-sheltered accounts by holding more direct investments and exchange-traded funds.
- Altering the mix of interest-paying and equity investments between a couple, bearing in mind their relative tax situations.
- Bearing in mind one's tax rate today versus expected future rates.

- Holding compounding-interest-bearing investments, like strip bonds, in sheltered accounts instead of non-sheltered accounts, to simplify annual tax preparation and match cash inflows to tax outflows.
- Holding investments with cash inflow from tax-free return of capital in non-sheltered accounts. This includes many income trust units that can distribute their capital cost allowance as tax-free return of capital. Upon sale, this potentially converts taxation from interest income tax rates to more favourable capital gains tax rates.

Tax-smart investing runs into practical constraints in the real world. Two of the three kinds of investment accounts that you can have are subject to contribution constraints (TFSAs and RRSPs), thus impacting the size of those accounts. These two accounts may be too small to house all of the kind(s) of income that is optimal in them (e.g., fixed income in an RRSP); thus, you are likely forced to invest sub-optimally tax-wise in order to achieve your overall investment strategy.

I am not aware that any researcher has modelled tax-smart investing to determine its value to after-tax portfolio returns. I am presently working on modelling a tax-smart portfolio index.

*Welcome back to the **book's main pathway**.*

5.3 Safety

Risk: Danger or Opportunity?

When you hear the word "safety," what associations fire in your brain? Spend a couple of minutes interviewing yourself on that and write down your reactions.

In the dictionary, safety is the condition of being protected from harm or other non-desirable outcomes. Safety can also refer to the control of recognized hazards to achieve an acceptable level of risk.

In one sense, going through life is a giant inner game of "knowing oneself." Once again, *gnothi seauton*, as the Greeks say. This has an all-important knock-on effect to financial fitness.

The strategy around investing is, to some extent, about fear and responding to fear. In the Oxford dictionary, "fear" is defined variously as:

- Painful emotion caused by impending danger
- Anxiety for safety
- Having uneasy expectations

All of these definitions resound with each of us. Let's revisit neuro-scientist and author Dr. Gregory Berns from Section 2.6 on decision-making.

The amygdala is the part of the brain that processes fear and emotional responses. It has a long memory and thus stores past bad experiences. Berns suggests that fear comes in three types: fear of failure, fear of the unknown, and fear of looking stupid. There are ways to manage the amygdala's processing of fear. The answer is, first, to reframe the situation to a non-emotional context, and second, to reframe the fear into assessment of risk. This moves the brain's processing away from the emotional amygdala. The third step is to reframe the assessment of risk into ambiguity and statistical uncertainty, the latter of which can be measured by mathematical probabilities. This process moves us from emotional reaction to logical action.

Think of a football offence facing a big "fourth and one" to potentially win the Super Bowl in the last minute. It faces the repercussions of failure to pull it off, the fear of looking stupid by calling a bad play, and the fear of the unknown as to what the defence is going to do. In modern football, the coach's play call is now influenced by "the analytics"—computer-generated stats on such previous circumstances and the probability of success of various play-calls. The analytics can't guarantee the play but convert from emotional (the coach called that same play successfully four years ago) to statistical uncertainty.

In the world of investing, there are countless "analytics" that we can augur productively to graduate from base fear to risk assessment.

Sketches in Personal Finance

An elderly client has invested $8 million with us for seventeen years. He grew up in Europe at the tail end of the Great Depression and WWII. In our periodic meetings, he occasionally asks what he is going to do when the Market crashes and all that money is gone. To be fair, that generation, at the tail end of their lives, have experienced events that most of us can't begin to fathom. So, his fear comes from somewhere real.

British author Dylan Evans suggests that people have differing degrees of **risk intelligence**.

He defines the term as the ability to estimate probabilities accurately. He posits that most people simply associate the term "risk" with "danger," whereas those who study risk professionally also associate the word with "opportunity." A high level of risk intelligence is not attainable without a high tolerance for ambiguity. "Catastrophizing" sees the glass as always half-empty and focuses on all the things that can go wrong. The statistical concept of "expected value," identified by Pascal and Fermat in the Seventeenth Century, mathematically combines probability with outcome in order to give greater perspective to the uncertain event. Chronic worriers tend to measure only outcome, thus ignoring probability and expected value, which leads to "worse-case thinking substitutes:

- Imagination for thinking
- Speculation for risk analysis
- Fear for reason

Evans outlines a four-step approach to shift from an outcome-based decision style to one of expected value. Addressing probability to embrace expected value requires fact-gathering. This process can be faulty, though, as we filter out facts that are inconsistent with our a priori inclinations. The wise approach is to deliberately seek out a diversity of opinions, especially those contrary to your own, and to incorporate them into your probability assessments.

Evans likens risk assessment to a parabola, where the top of the left side represents complete certainty of the outcome ("**I fully believe this will happen**"); the top of the right side also represents complete certainty ("**I fully believe this will not happen**"); and the bottom represents complete uncertainty—i.e., 50/50 ("**I haven't a clue what will happen**"). Risk intelligence hangs out on either slope of the parabola…a more likely world, where an outcome is somewhere between "certain knowledge and complete ignorance."

People quickly associate the words "risk" and 'risky" when they start thinking about investing. By nature, no one likes risk. When queried, we tend to describe our investing attitude by a short phrase, like "I am conservative." That translates to say: I don't like risk. Some respond by making their investing strategy "risk-free," which may mean they park it under the pillow or they buy term deposits and GICs. At the opposite end of risk, some spend their investing lives chasing the "Last Chance Mining" big strike. Books on investing address risk and usually cover a conventional list. We aspire here to identify a **broader and deeper list of risks.**

Investor Risks

Let's review various investor risks under the banner of **safety**.

Inflation risk and purchasing power

The GIC lovers fail to understand that, in buying GICs, they have preserved their capital from the vagaries of the stock market—but only in nominal terms, not in real terms. The difference between those two is inflation. European grandparents and South Americans have experienced hyper-inflation in their lives, so they appreciate the risk of ignoring inflation. North Americans have experienced double-digit inflation in their lives, as well. But, for recent decades, Western economies have been managing inflation. In Canada and other Western economies, the inflation rate hovered around 2–3% for almost thirty years, but recently got a jolt from Covid economies. That's a small number, so we tend to ignore it. Mathematicians refer to the Law of Large Numbers. There is no Law of Small Numbers, but if there was, it would refer to 2% inflation over many years. If you are age fifty, for instance, and your cost of living today is, say, $75,000, that same basket of goods will double to $150,000 by the time you turn age eighty-six. While you are working, your earned income tends to increase (i.e., you get a pay raise) to stay abreast of inflation. When you retire, the return on your capital may be paying the bills. If your nominal capital is not keeping abreast of inflation, then your real capital (purchasing power) is declining. **The risk here is that if your investing strategy does not address inflation, your real income from GICs will not keep up.**

This problem exacerbates if that low GIC interest is earned in a taxable account. The combination of inflation plus taxes applied to a low-interest return actually can mean a negative real return. Now you really are falling behind.

The famous balanced portfolio

Your portfolio asset allocation strategy between fixed income and equities largely defines your exposure to stock market collapses. The conundrum is that investors are loath to sign up for 1.5% returns on their fixed income. **The risk here is that an economic tsunami will severely punish a highly equity-based portfolio,** likely both at the moment of the collapse and also in the time interval to recovery. Today, this requires a shift in mindset as to the purpose of fixed income. For the portfolio as a whole, you need to be concerned about long-term return on capital—that's the long-term compound rate of return.

Everyone understands diversification, but it's another matter to execute it in a portfolio. There are so many layers to proper diversification. The first layer is the asset allocation strategy between fixed income and equities. But that's only the bare start. The second layer is deployment of equity capital around the world. On the equity side, we see many outside portfolios that invest solely in the Canadian stock market. As Canada counts for roughly 4% of the world's economic activity, this leaves the other 96% off the table. The third layer is deployment of equity capital across businesses engaged in diverse pursuits... we refer to these as "sectors." The fourth layer is spreading your equity capital across many holdings. We recently saw a portfolio that the investor described as "conservative," which violated all of these. It held only Canadian equities and the entire equity portfolio pinned its hopes on a total of nine Canadian stocks: 47% of that was entrusted in three of Canada's banks, 15% in one telecommunication company, 24% in real estate, and 14% in one utility.

Foreign currency risk
If you have addressed the second layer above by placing your investing funds out around the globe, then you do add another risk component: foreign exchange. Your return on holding a foreign security has two parts: the domestic return on the security +/- the movement of the Canadian dollar against that currency. In any given short run (like 2015), foreign exchange can have a huge impact on foreign investing returns. For instance, the annual return to July 31, 2015 for the *USD TIPS* ETF was 17.98% with the exchange gain and –1.44% without.

If the long term is the focus, then exchange movements tend to minimize. That said, "bad start" is another phenomenon to be wary of; buying US dollars today at seventy cents may promise an "ouch" in the future if the Canadian dollar recovers significantly. If the investor response to that is to "stay in Canada" portfolio-wise in order to avoid the exchange risk, then the risk shifts to Canadian geography and sectoral weightings (discussed earlier).

Another aspect of exchange *risk* happens when we take **ourselves** out of the country. Exporting our vacations out of Canada also gets more expensive, particularly if those trips are six-month snowbird winters where your living expenses are paid in US dollars. If your portfolio holds foreign investments, and ergo implicitly foreign currencies, then you are winning back some of that hurt by way of US currency gains when buying US goods and vacations. If you steadfastly remain a Canada-only investor, you are not.

The risk of unrealized gains
We have seen mature portfolios that have observed the buy-and-hold strategy across the years. The portfolio may be blessed that certain holdings have significantly increased in value in a taxable account. We might call this "The Law of Large Gains." **The risk here is that the investor is reluctant to sell down the holding and expose the tax liability, instead exposing the holding to losing some of its gain.** "Don't let the tax tail wag the investing dog" may be the appropriate response. If the holdings are in **tax-sheltered** accounts, TFSAs and RRSP/RRIFs, then an immediate tax problem is non-existent.

The example above has other aspects to it as well. The appreciation in an equity portfolio is in **two** categories—realized and unrealized. The latter simply means that the security has been held throughout the period and has gone up…on paper. Buy-and-hold is a mantra we read in investment publications. But what does this mean? We tend to interpret that it means, for instance, buying Apple stock and never selling it. But this strategy needs to be re-interpreted to mean holding the overall equity position, not the specific stock holding. The management of a) periodically rebalancing to the overall asset allocation plan and b) responding to movements in the industry sector proportions addresses this risk.

The risk of realized gains
A client once told us: "You never lose money taking profits!" Well…sort of. **The risk here is reinvestment risk: the risk that the profit you just gained could be given away with a loss on the next thing you buy.** Your hero status in selling a winner can change into being a goat because that next purchase is a loser. One key here is to focus on the mantra: *The portfolio is the thing, more than the individual things in it.* Accordingly, the metric that counts the most is the long-term compound return of the portfolio, not what you just made on selling Apple shares.

The risk of market timing
This subject inevitably segues into the matter of **market timing** if your profit-taking was **market-focused**, rather than **individual stock-focused**, because you believed that the market was going to collapse. There is endless research on this topic, supporting whichever side of the coin one chooses to believe. For sure, it must be recognized that **market timing requires getting it right TWICE**—once getting out and then later getting back in. Longitudinal data on timing shows, for instance, that being "out" for the five biggest market days in the twenty years

from 1994 to 2014 would have meant that an initial investment of $100,000 would have grown to approximately $280,000, vs. approximately $420,000 if the investor had simply stayed in.

The risk of cash calls
If you are at a stage where you require regular draws from your portfolio to fund life, then you must manage the **risk of bad timing** in converting investments into cash to fund those calls. The stock market can get cranky quickly and fall 30% in a very short time. You don't want to be cornered into selling beaten-down stocks to buy this month's groceries. There are several strategies to insulate this. One is to keep six to twelve months of your cash calls IN CASH. Another is to fund cash calls by pre-mature selling of bonds, which typically don't get beat up when the stock market does. Another is to manage your one to two years of cash calls with a periodic series of maturing bonds.

Managing future cash calls has another time dimension, too: the longer term. The day after you receive your final paycheque, your investments take over as the prime breadwinner. If you were not looking out in advance to that day, your portfolio may not be suitably constructed to send your future pension paycheques. In other words, you still may have a heavy growth orientation with stocks. **The risk here is that your stock portfolio may get pounded right when you need to liquidate part of it.** You need to prepare for this well in advance—not just one or two years—by shifting investment holdings to be able to produce that monthly paycheque without exposure to stock market vagaries. Quantify at least the first five years in the future when you will be calling on your portfolio. This also is relevant for RESP liquidations.

The risk of ignorance
Sound portfolio management is complex: there are so many layers to it. Let's revisit Donald Rumsfeld's famous quote: "There are also unknown unknowns— the ones we don't know we don't know." This applies to managing money, and it applies to all of us. **The risk here, of course, is making our investing decisions in a vacuum of unknown unknowns**. The aspirant solution is relentless pursuit of knowledge to shrink those "unknowns."

These previous three sections were about understanding who you are as an investor, how that translates into a model of investing and how that drills down to the mechanics and monitoring of your portfolio. It may be a long time ago that you went to school and got a report card. The next section is about the report card on your (and your advisor's) stewardship of your wealth. It turns out that there are several interesting metrics for this, each with a different insight.

5.4 Rate of Return

Lies, Damn Lies, and Statistics

Whether you are numerate or innumerate, numbers have this tantalizing cachet of simple perfection, as they distill something down to convey information to us.

A number, like "10," is so pristinely clean, but what does it mean? If it were the assessment of Bo Derek's beauty in the old movie of the same name, it would imply perfection. If it were your score on an exam out of 100, it would be a disaster. And how is the number itself arrived at? How is beauty assigned to 10? How are your answers (e.g., in an essay question) assigned a 10?

At first glance, it is difficult to argue with rate of return as the report card of success in the world of investing. But we do need to dig deeper. For starters, it is very important to appreciate that the rate of return will be **correlated with the degree of risk assumption** by the investor. This relationship is asymmetric; increasing your (potential) rate of return requires increasing your risk. In other words, higher returns are not rewarded "for free." But the opposite is **not** a given: taking on higher risk does not guarantee higher return. The shorter the investing period, the truer that statement. So, if you have your heart set on some rate of return, you will need to embrace: a) your investing time horizon and b) your appetite for risk. Another important point is that your rate of return isn't comparable with your cousin at the family dinner table because her risk profile may not be the same as yours—and her time horizon might be different, too.

A second, important point is to refocus your report card from investing success to wealth accumulation success. This requires looking in a different direction: to your goals, not your cousin's portfolio. The formal financial plan we discussed in Section 4.3 should encompass those goals and would include a table of your forecasted wealth accumulation year-by-year for thirty to forty years out.

Here's the next important point: your lifetime success at wealth accumulation is the product of three factors:

1) Your contribution of capital to your investments ("**saving**")
2) Your "burn rate" (**"spending"**) and
3) Your *long-term rate of return* ("**investing**")

So, your rate of return in the previous paragraph is only one of three on the score card of wealth accumulation.

Imagine that at age forty you are bestowed with, say, $100,000, and you use that to raise your bar of personal financial management.

So, you get a formal financial plan prepared. It presumes to invest that $100,000 to earn an estimated rate of return for the rest of your life. You commit to a certain lifestyle (burn rate), and you plan to save $10,000 a year for the rest of your working life. The plan you prepared at age forty would tell you what your wealth should be at, say, age sixty-five. Now, let's fast forward to your retired years. Let's imagine further that over those years your investment portfolio hit it out of the park and earned a rate of return much higher than the plan. Based on that, your report card would read: "great job!" But you lived a more extravagant lifestyle and never managed to put aside that annual $10,000 of saving. As a result of all of that, your net worth at age sixty-five is way less than the plan said at age forty: not a "great job." So, the simple—and important—point here is that **rate of return is contributory to your wealth accumulation, but it does not make your future.** Therefore, it is not your report card.

The final point here is that most people don't create a formal financial plan at age forty, as in the above example, so they don't have that quick reference chart to monitor and assess their report card target of wealth accumulation. That leads to the old line that it is easy to attain goals when you don't have any. So your behaviour change for WealthNess ought to include some financial targets.

Next, let's go under the hood of rate-of-return to achieve two objectives: first, to understand what goes on behind the rate of return numbers and, second, to offer you some alternative ways of studying portfolio success.

Studying Portfolio Success

"Does the income in my portfolio include my contribution of savings?" my client Doug asked.

The quick answer is, "No." That would be a clever formula for making **great** returns—contribute lots of money! In fact, of course, the amount he contributes to his portfolio during the year does impact his rate-of-return, but in the **denominator** (invested capital), not the **numerator** (portfolio income).

As human beings, we have been mindful of "rate of return" for thousands of years. Despite our long history with it, we don't necessarily understand it, even today. Simply said, it is:

$$\frac{\text{Income}}{\text{Amount invested}}$$

This leads us to a further necessary refining element in the denominator.

If he contributed a sum of money on the **last** day of his reporting period, this would add to the denominator, but there was no time to invest those funds to earn income and to increase the numerator. Otherwise, his advisor might say, "Please, can you wait and invest those funds tomorrow, on the first day of the new reporting period, so it doesn't hurt this year's return?" Of course, it does not make sense to allow investors to contribute only on day one of the year; so instead, the denominator of invested capital needs to be **time-weighted for contributions** within that reporting period. But we aren't finished; there are further complications. If this was the very first year that Doug started investing, then what we just explained is good. However, imagine this is Doug's second year of investing, or fifth year, or twenty-fifth year. Here we need to introduce another element.

Let's imagine Doug starts by investing $100.

Let's say he earned interest income in that first year of $10. Thus, his first-year return was 10%, and the portfolio starts its second year with a value of $110. If the income in the second year is once again $10, this time his return is only 10/110 = 9.09%. Doug may be disappointed with his advisor that he earned a lower return in his second year, even though both were $10. Obviously, this happened because the denominator in the second year increased to $110, by the $10 earned and reinvested in the first year. This is how the financial services industry calculates annual returns. The financial math principle here is that when Doug earned $10 in year one, and decided to leave it in the portfolio, that $10 of income "capitalizes" into principle (the "amount invested") for year two. In other words, year one income (the numerator) adds to year two's capital (the denominator). It is as if Doug is sent the $10 of income in year one, and he decides to send it back to reinvest. Let's call this the **Invested Capital Return (ICR)**.

Of course, this is what compounding is all about—reinvesting your earnings—which Albert Einstein famously described as the most powerful force in the universe, the "Eighth Wonder of the World."

Next, let's understand the numerator, which is the "income" that the portfolio makes. It, too, needs a deeper understanding. The income from your portfolio includes some or all of the following:

- Interest from fixed income instruments, e.g., bonds, GICs, term deposits
- Dividends from companies (foreign and domestic)
- Payments from trust units, like a Real Estate Investment Trust (REIT)
- Appreciation or depreciation in the values of everything you own

- Appreciation or depreciation in the foreign exchange movement between your domestic currency and the country currencies you invest in

The last two items, unlike the other three, can be positive or negative. Further, these gains or losses are of two sorts: **unrealized** (meaning that you still own the things whose value went up or down on paper in the period) and **realized** (meaning that you sold things during the period whose values went up or down). We refer to unrealized losses as "paper losses."

For rate-of-return calculations, we apply a similar principle to the gain/loss determination as discussed above for the denominator. What does that mean? Let's imagine that Doug invested $100 in Year One and all of that was invested in one stock. At the end of Year One, let's say that stock was worth $110. Doug's unrealized gain is $10, and his first-year return is 10%. Now, imagine that the stock fell to $105 at the end of Year Two, creating in that year an unrealized loss of $5, and his return that year is -4.5% (-5/110). Like the interest income above, note how the "gain" (albeit unrealized) in the prior year capitalizes into next year's amount invested. He is still up $5 over the two-year holding period. Let's go forward one more year, and assume that the stock recovered to $107, at which time Doug sold the stock. For Year Three, he has a realized gain in the year of $2, and his Year Three return is 1.9% (2/105). Over the whole three-year holding period, his gain was $7 ($107–$100).

Simple returns are the history of portfolio returns year by year. Doug's simple returns were 10% in year one, -4.5% return in year two, and 1.9% in year three. **Compound returns** are the cumulative, running average return per year across multiple time periods, e.g., three-year, five-year, ten-year, and since inception. Using the wizardry of a financial calculator, we can determine that Doug's three-year average annual compound return is 2.30%, that being somewhere between those three simple returns.

Compound returns are at the core of assessing the success of your portfolio in the long term.

How to Make Easy Money in a Bar

The Rule of 72: Even a mathophobic can appear to be a finance genius in a bar or at a cocktail party, knowing the "Rule of 72." The number "72" is a "magic number" for mathophobes derived in present value calculations by math wizards. It is a two-second way to determine either: a) the number of years it takes for money to double, given an annual rate of return, or b) the average return needed to have money double in a given number of years.

So, for example: a) if your money doubled in twelve years, your return would have been 6%. (72/12) or b) earning a 7.2% return would have your money double in ten years (72/7.2). Note that this calculation excludes any further contributions of capital during that time period but assumes compounding the income.

Are you ready to deep dive into a different and insightful rate-of-return statistic? If so, take this detour. (If you don't want to take this detour right now, jump ahead until you see the Circle/easiest sign.)

Sketches in Personal Finance

Let's leave Doug now and revisit Larry yet again, from Section 4.1 and 5.1.

The graph below tracks both his annual simple returns (the erratic line) and the running compound returns (the more stable line) for his portfolio. The longer the investing period, the more insightful the compound return is. Ideally, every investor would have this running statistic tracked over their entire investing life. Note the relative stability of his compound returns since 2002, despite the gyrations in the simple returns.

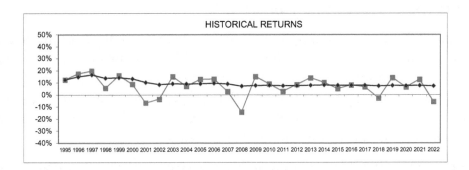

Let's continue with Larry to introduce a **third rate-of-return**, which doesn't get much, if any, press. If you have young adult children, be sure they get this!

Larry's graph in Section 5.1 showed the relevant proportions of his contributions and portfolio growth over the twenty-eight years. The portfolio totaled $1.05 million at the end of 2022. His contribution was 21% of that value, and the average, annual compound return was 7.26%; ergo, he was on a pathway of having his wealth double every ten years. One final note, the Rule of 72 only works with non-taxed or deferred tax portfolios, e.g., pension accounts, tax-free accounts. Remember that the **value** of a portfolio at the end of a year becomes the **invested capital**—the denominator—for the **start of next year**. This is the rate-of-return statistic conventionally reported in the financial services industry. As indicated earlier, I call this "conventional" return the **Invested Capital Return (ICR)**. (Note this is my terminology, and not one used at large.)

Now I wish to introduce a different rate-of-return, which I will call the **Contributed Capital Return (CCR)**. Its calculation is different from the Invested Capital Return in the denominator. Here, the investment is **only the capital contributed by the investor from saving**. In other words, **it does not annually capitalize each year's earnings into the next year's capital**. Here are the same graph lines of simple and compound return—but for Contributed Capital Return, not ICR.

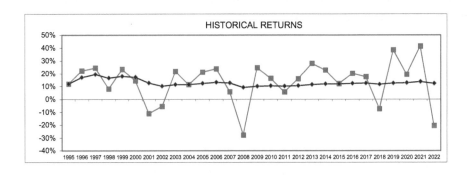

Lawrence's compound CCR was 12.32%, while his compound ICR was 7.26%. The difference between the two is a hard-math snapshot of the value of Einstein's compounding. When Einstein extolled the beauty of financial compounding, he was implicitly assuming that the investment income was always deployed back into the portfolio. In other words, if you, the investor, **drew out** all of the earnings annually for lifestyle, then there would be no compounding.

Authors Dimson, March, and Staunton concur that reinvested dividends are a crucial contributor to long-term wealth. At first this sounds insightful; however, when we realize that the simpler term for "reinvested dividends" is simply "saving," we all appreciate that saving, by ploughing back the earnings, makes our portfolio grow.

In summary here, perhaps even Einstein was a bit overcome with compounding.

The money isn't mysteriously doing all the work to make you rich under the guise of "compounding"; you too are doing part of the work by reinvesting/saving the investment earnings. If you started by investing $1,000 and smoothly earned 6% every year but spent that on groceries, twelve years later you still would have $1,000 invested—no compounding. And now the purchasing power of your original $1,000 would be crippled by twelve years of even modest inflation. So, understand that compounding is not a free lunch.

I refer to the industry ICR as an **Investor's return** and the CCR as a **Saver's return**. The Invested Capital Return is a marker on **how your investing is doing** out there in the market. The Contributed Capital Return is a marker on **how your saving and investing** is doing.

So, which one is right ICR or CCR?

The answer is…BOTH, because they each serve different purposes. There is an inherent logic in valuing the Contributed Capital Return: if you didn't invest your savings in the first place, you wouldn't have the capital in the market earning income to be "capitalized" and reinvested—the compounding. So, the disciplined act of saving over the twenty-eight years rewarded this investor's Contributed Capital with 12.32% per annum. The Invested Capital Return statistic needs to remain as the industry-standard for comparability. But the Contributed Capital Return is an excellent financial planning tool as personal motivator. (For Diamond and Square folks, you might be curious to roll up your sleeves and actually do this alternate return calculation to learn your Contributed Capital Return. For Circle folks dabbling here, you have a simple, major take-away: what Contributed Capital Return tells you about the reward for saving.)

Moving on, in order to gain a deeper understanding of the **components** of rate of return, for the last ten years I have been tracking four income sources on a quarterly basis in another real portfolio.

1) Cash income (being interest and dividends received)
2) Price change
3) Foreign exchange change
4) Other (essentially the tax value of dividend tax credits on Canadian stocks in taxable investment accounts).

Price and foreign exchange each have two sub-components: realized and unrealized. "Realized" means that transactions have been executed to lock in the currency or price gains. "Unrealized" means that the currency or price gains are "on paper" only as you still hold the investment, and thus the gain at any moment in time can change with future market developments.

Any time analysis of markets can only offer "qualified" observations. Market cycles are long, and any intra-period data analysis only speaks to the period in question (in this case, ten years) and is not necessarily inferential but is at least interesting.

The cash income component is quite stable across time. A ballpark number today would be 2%, and indeed this portfolio consistently returned in a range from 2.21%–2.75% per annum across the ten years. The amount has been dropping consistently over the decade because bond coupon rates have been falling.

Dividend tax credits are very consistent over time and are a very small component.

The two wild cards are foreign exchange and price movement. Across the forty quarters of the decade, foreign exchange contributed a quarterly high of 4.46% and a low of –4.9% but averaged out at only .16 of 1% per quarter. Price movement similarly contributed a quarterly high of 6.22% and a low of –7.51% and averaged out at .52 of 1% per quarter. (Notably, those two outliers were only nine months apart.)

The proportions between realized and unrealized returns may be influenced somewhat by the kind of account(s) involved. In trading accounts (which are non-sheltered), realizations cause tax liabilities. In RRSPs, RRIFs, and TFSAs (all tax-sheltered accounts), tax considerations are not required in the "sell" decision. The account in this data is a trading account; therefore, taxes are an issue, and the realized components in the table above are minimized.

Below is the actual graph for this portfolio, in which one can gain perspective on the relative contributions of price/exchange movement and cash income over this ten-year time period:

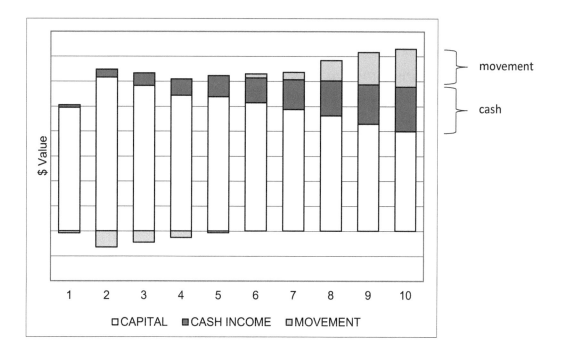

The capital portion is declining across the years because the client has a monthly draw to fund his burn rate. Despite the drop in the capital, the overall portfolio is increasing…because the investment return is greater than his draw.

Clients who are retired, and perhaps in decumulation mode and thus seeking cash flow from the portfolio to fund life, need to grasp insight from this information. The average cash income component was 2.7% per annum while the average total portfolio return is 5.6% per annum. The table shows that roughly half of the return comes from cash income and the remainder is largely from unrealized sources. Mandatory RRIF withdrawal rates are, for example, in the range of 4–8% through the early years of retirement, post age seventy-one. Thus, the extra cash flow needed beyond cash income (2.7%) to top up required withdrawal rates (4–8%) must come from capital in the short run, or conversion of unrealized price movement to realized price movement in the short to long run.

*Welcome back to the **book's main pathway**.*

The Effects of Down and Up Markets

People with a retail background will jump on this next point in a flash: product mark-ups versus gross margin. When the stock market falls 20%, a $100 portfolio is now only worth $80. For the market to recover that $20 requires an uptick of 25% ($20 made on $80), not 20%. A down market of 20% followed by an upmarket of 20% still leaves you down by 4%, or $4. Somehow −20 = +25!

The formula to determine what return in year two offsets the loss return in year one (R1) is: $1/((1/R1+1))$.

Another lesson here is the **impact of off-setting net-zero years on the long-term compound return.** Two years that offset each other bring you back to where you were, but that means having two years that didn't get you anywhere. If your required long-term rate-of-return is 5%, then you expect $1,000 to become $1,102.50 2 years later (that equals two years of returns plus compounding). If, instead, you experienced a calamity year and were then fortunate enough to achieve a net-zero recovery of that in the following year, you only got back to $1,000 and didn't add the extra $102.50. So, you have fallen behind your goal.

"My broker got me 26% this year," so my neighbour gleefully proclaimed recently. That's a great return! But we must remember the influence of the times: "It was the best of times; it was the worst of times…"

Such was the famous opening line of Charles Dickens' *A Tale of Two Cities* in 1859. He carried on with more powerful prose:

> *It was the age of wisdom, it was the age of foolishness,*
> *it was the epoch of belief, it was the epoch of incredulity,*
> *it was the season of light, it was the season of darkness,*
> *it was the spring of hope, it was the winter of despair.*

His book was set at the time of the French Revolution and in the cities of London and Paris. But he could be a **stock market analyst** in today's world, speaking about people's investing behaviours. Note that he didn't become famous for saying, "It was average times." And so, we must draw upon but diverge from his famous insight as we tackle a related topic in modern-day investing—rates of return.

We humans have been counting and ac-counting since we climbed out of the primordial mud.

Our numeracy has its comfort-zone. BIG numbers overwhelm us and small numbers fail to impress. Perhaps we are the Three Bears of Numbers! In the financial world, a market recovery of 25% after a "crash" of 20% in the previous year, is a two-year result of 0%. For transparency, that 25% ought to be classified as a **"recovery" rate of return**—getting back what you just lost—to give the investor proper perspective. In the real world, such two-year results won't tidily square to zero. The second year may not fully recover, or it might fully recover PLUS make some more. (This latter, we call "productive" return.) To be equitable, we should also apply this logic in the opposite direction: when we have a great year followed by a losing year, we should call that a "correction" return.

The financial services industry reports "compound" returns but on three-year and five-year rolling periods—not the two-year period above. Compound returns come in two flavours: cumulative and average. The latter is the reported industry norm. A two-year compound return, either average or cumulative, would provide the same perspective as "recovery" and "productive" returns.

Fortunately, the annual market returns (particularly for balanced portfolios) do not gyrate so significantly that we need to build "recovery" returns and "productive" returns into ongoing financial accountability. But when those "black swan" times come, it is insightful to dust off this valuable perspective.

Are you ready for a deeper into Recovery Returns? If so, take this detour. (If you don't want to take this detour right now, jump ahead until you see the Circle/ easiest sign.)

*A further lesson is that the punishment of bad years on your long-term compound return varies with the **duration** of your lifetime investing history.*

The longer that history, the smaller will be the long-term impact of bad years; and the shorter that history, the greater will be the long-term impact. The investing year of 2008 dealt a horrible blow to portfolio values, inspiring the financial press to Chicken Little scenarios, sending some retirees back to work and causing many people to cast aspersions on equity investing. As it happened, starting in

March 2009, the markets roared back, appeasing investors after a fairly short six months of angst. The following table walks you through this phenomenon for the period 2008–9–10 for select client portfolios: (see following commentary)

# of investing years	Annual simple returns			Required return	Long term compound returns	
	2008	2009	2010	2010	2008	2010
16 years	-2.1%	-17.6%	+21.2%	42%	8.0%	7.0%
16 years	-1.5%	-15.2%	+18.5%	42%	9.6%	8.4%
10 years	+0.3%	-13.9%	+18.9%	33%	6.9%	5.7%
7 years	-0.2%	-11.9%	+12.1%	37%	9.8%	6.7%
7 years	-5.6%	-27.1%	+27.5%	60%	8.1%	4.6%
6 years	+1.7%	-16.8%	+17.5%	40%	8.1%	4.9%
6 years	+2.7%	-12.5%	+13.9%	35%	8.6%	5.6%

The first column shows the number of investing years of the portfolio. The next three columns show the simple returns in the years 2008–10. The two compound columns on the far right show the portfolio's long-term returns before the 2008/9 calamity, and then after the 2010 recovery. In each example, you see that the long-term return has taken a drop. For long-held portfolios, the drop was approximately 1%, but for shorter portfolios, the impact typically was in excess of 3%; in other words, fewer averaging years were available to fall back on. The shaded column in the middle makes a notional calculation of what recovery rate was required in 2010 to: a) recover the 2008–9 loss and b) keep the same pre-2008 long term compound return through 2010. You will see that those notional returns for 2010 typically needed to be in the 40% range, whereas in fact they were only in the 20% range; thus, losing ground on the long-term compound returns over three difficult years.

These kinds of calculations and observations are subject to start-and-end bias; in other words, what range of investing years are counted in your compound return. If you start tracking your compound return through a bull market, your compound return will start high, and subsequent calamity years will cause a large drawback.

Total rate of return can be tracked longitudinally, both in simple and compound returns, by individual security, account type, and total portfolio.

Welcome back to the **book's main pathway**.

Individual security returns

There is a saying in the industry: "The portfolio's the thing, more than the individual things in it." Thus, **total portfolio** compound return is the most important investing return statistic for the investor. However, the **individual** security returns may be of interest to monitor how particular stockholdings have fared over time, and vis-à-vis other holdings.

The components of rate of return on the whole **portfolio** are the same as those for an **individual** holding, e.g., a stock. Your Invested Capital Return on one hundred shares of a stock is the dividend income plus/minus the change in market price, divided by the opening market price at the beginning of the period. The Contributed Capital Return substitutes your cost price for the opening market price. The alternative perspective of **portfolio** return on **compound versus contributed** capital also can be applied to an **individual** stock. For instance, the Bank of Nova Scotia (BNS) was trading at $7.90 in the mid-'90s. The bank had an excellent balance sheet, a history of unbroken annual dividends dating back to the 1830s and a very long history of **consistently growing** its dividend. Back further, the BNS annual dividend at the time of writing is $4.24 per share, which yields an impressive annual Return on **Contributed** Capital of 54% on the original purchase price of $7.90—and that's not counting price appreciation. This is an excellent example of how long-term growth in corporate earnings, resulting in growth in dividends, powers the overall portfolio's Return on Contributed Capital.

Returns by Account Type

Tracking simple and compound returns by investment account (i.e., RRSP/RRIF, TFSA, trading accounts) should not be dwelled upon; each account pulls its weight according to its relative size, its purpose, and its role in tax-smart investing. For instance, tax-smart investing suggests loading TFSAs with appreciation/foreign equity and loading RRSP/RRIFs with fixed income; the former will have way more volatility and the latter will have way lower returns. Think: "The sum of the parts equals the whole," or better still with tax-smart investing—gestalt, where the whole is more than the sum of the parts. In summary, you ought to be interested solely in the return of the portfolio as a whole.

Long-term compound return: Geometric vs arithmetic

Geometric takes into account the compounding that occurs between a start-period and an end-period. It ignores all the action that happens **between** those two dates. Arithmetic takes the annual returns over "n" periods of time and divides that sum by n to get the average.

Geometric return has a fault in its execution. By simply using starting and ending values, it assumes the only "growth" comes from compounding income over the n periods. In other words, it can't handle capital contributions being added along the way.

Rate of Return and Asset Allocation

The asset allocation plan largely drives the portfolio's long-term success and volatility. The key aspect of that plan is the **allocation between fixed income and equity**. It is insightful to view this allocation as a partnership between those two asset classes, as they proportionately share the load in building your financial future. The success or failure of each over any period of time is the product of the complexities of the world's events and commerce.

For the wise investor, **long-term compound return** is the most important. Ideally, it can be referenced back to a formal financial plan that you had prepared, which included in its long-term forecast an average long-term compound return that drives the prediction of your financial future. The target and actual returns can be compared periodically as a marker towards achieving your financial goal.

Historically, the "fixed income" partner has born the lion's share of responsibility to produce **cash flow** into the portfolio. Equity's responsibility was more to produce appreciation than cash flow. But with bond coupon rates dropping from 18% in the early 1980s to less than 1–2%, the fixed income partner is not carrying that responsibility. On the other hand, companies are paying healthy dividends, which come with valuable dividend tax credits in non-sheltered accounts.

Some extra programming of portfolio rate-of-return can dissect the rates of return of these two partners (here in a real, sample portfolio):

	Interest	Dividends	Cash Return %	Gain	Gain Return %	Total	Total Return %
Fixed Income	$8,846	n/a	2.24%	$1,501	0.38%	$10,347	2.62%
Equity	n/a	$22,054	3.09%	$11,855	1.66%	$33,909	4.75%

The **denominator** in each partner's return calculation is the capital invested respectively in fixed income vs. equity holdings. We see that the cash return of dividend income on equity (3.09%) exceeded that of interest income on fixed income (2.24%). And for the period, the equity market rose, adding a further 1.66%. The overall portfolio return, weighted by the asset allocation between fixed income (40%) and equity (60%), was 3.98%.

Benchmarks

Benchmarks long have been an industry approach to evaluate portfolio success, by comparing it to something else. Again, this process is so pristinely simple that we are attracted to it. Your number is "7%" and the other number is "11%," or say "4%." You respond accordingly with disappointment or elation. In a perfect and fair world, benchmarks are brilliant. But under the hood…not so. To be compared, they must be comparable. If 7% is your return this year on a balanced portfolio, and 11% is this year's return on the S&P 500 (itself, a benchmark for the US financial market), they are not comparable. So, you would need to concoct some collection of weighted benchmarks of various sorts that reflect the character of a balanced portfolio.

Next, that 11% S&P return is the geometric return over some period. We learned above that geometric return is a price appreciation; it is only return on the same amount of capital. That means NO infusions or withdrawals of capital during the period. So, if you added or removed capital from your portfolio over the period, right away your comparability is shot. Also, it doesn't include the cash income return from dividends (that statistic was called "total" return). Finally, the benchmark return assumes being fully invested in the S&P 500 for every day of the whole period. Your own portfolio may have spent some time holding cash prior to deployment.

Next, if that compared return amount isn't a **single period**, but is some **long-term** compound return number, your asset allocation strategy may have changed over the period. Thus, your concocted weighted average benchmark above would need corresponding adjustment.

While I, too, am attracted to the pristineness of numerical comparison as an assessment tool, my conclusion is that, under the hood, financial return benchmarks are too dirty. Where does that leave us? One executable alternative is a goals-oriented approach. At the big picture level, this can work in either or both of two ways—both requiring and referencing a formal financial plan. If you have one, it will include two useful pieces of data for benchmarking. First, implicit in that plan is a lifetime average rate of return. This was an important number when you undertook the plan, because implicitly you determined and accepted that that rate of return satisfactorily contributed to the financial goals you have set till your death. So, you can use that number as the benchmark to your actual current, compound return. If your actual return is greater than or equal to this plan benchmark, you are OK. You can say that your portfolio, and perhaps therefore your portfolio manager, is delivering.

There is a catch, though (sorry): the second piece of benchmark data in the plan. This involves comparing what your portfolio is worth (in dollars) to where your plan would have you be at that same time. The **plan return** might be attained, but the **plan dollars** were not. This shortfall is a reflection upon you. Your lifelong plan is the flow of money-in and money-out. The money-in is your own earned income, saving and portfolio income. The money-out is your burn rate. So, if the dollars are short, you may have saved less than planned or spent more than planned. Bottom line: monitor your progress to your long-term financial goals.

5.5 Key Words and Concepts

Investing:

69. Love your portfolio
70. Investment management is part engineering, part design.
71. Define your philosophy, then develop your strategy
72. Strategy is partly about timelines for cash calls: What's the money for?
73. Strategies and sub-strategies: the sum of the parts equals the whole
74. Investing perspective is important: one hundred years
75. Beware the apocalypse du jour
76. Getting on the market train, and poor starts
77. Using rifles and shotguns
78. Watch creeping inflation over your shoulder
79. Understand and execute tax-smart investing principles
80. Spend the right amount of time with your portfolio
81. Diversification and discipline
82. Dichotomizing risk and fear
83. Embracing risk intelligence
84. A "safety" check-up
85. What's in rate-of-return?
86. Different rates of return for different purposes
87. The inspiration of contributed capital return
88. Monitor your progress to your long-term financial goals

Chapter 6: Legacy

Multi-Generational Wealth Transfer

And then he did something he had never done before...he died.

Let's start with a downer...and build from there:

> *I am absolutely convinced that wealth can and does destroy any family, no matter what the level of wealth involved.*
> —Philip Marcovici, lawyer, author on wealth management

Have you considered that your wealth can destroy your family? Human beings have been dying since we first walked on this planet. So, we have lots of experience with it. In the Investing chapter, I said to be wary of the expression "This time it's different." Here in the Legacy chapter, I say, "This time it's different." Here is why....

For starters, historically, multi-generational wealth transfer was only an issue for the "rich," the most minute percentage of the population.

The vast middle class wrote their wills and that constituted estate planning. There was little deliberate schooling of the next generation to prepare them to manage that wealth transfer, because the sums were not significantly large. Today's middle-class cohort has enjoyed the largest, broadest distribution of wealth in the history of the planet. So, everyday people today have insufficient historical frame of reference for how to deal with multigenerational wealth stewardship. And that is sad. Today, the broad populace needs to be more attentive and deliberate with their legacy strategy.

Furthermore, people on average are living longer...around the planet. However, once again we must be wary of the "damn lies and statistics" saying; it varies with which statistic you choose to use. Commonly, the published stat is "life expectancy from birth." This stat has grown enormously, but on its own, it does not mean we all are living vastly longer. That stat has improved due to our massive modern-day success at curbing infant mortality. If the average lifespan in the Garden of Eden was to be, say, sixty, and Eve died at birth, then Adam would be expected to live to 120. In other words, adding a lot of humans dying at a young age has a significant impact on the lifespan statistic.

The more relevant life expectancy statistic is this one: having successfully achieved age sixty, what is the average life expectancy? According to global data from WHO, a Canadian can expect to live approximately twenty-six years longer.

That ranks #3 out of approximately seventy-five nations. Even the last-ranked (UAE) make it to age eighty.

The increasing longevity has, of course, multiple impacts for estate matters. For starters, it means that retirement wealth and income sources have to be sufficient to fund more years of life. The last of those years may include expensive years in assisted-living. The new longevity, of course, has impact at the societal level, and therefore on government expenditures for health care and assisted-living subsidization.

Second, longevity has impact upon the inheriting generation.

Increased longevity is increasing the average age of beneficiaries. In other words, the "children" are getting their inheritance at an older age; thus, fewer years of enhanced living, and fewer years of being "experienced" with handling wealth. This is particularly impactful when these recipients are struck by ill health during their seventies. "All the money in the world and no opportunity to enjoy it" is what I have seen in these situations. Is there any lesson here?

Third, might the new longevity lead to more inter vivos gifting to the following generation, in order to help them when it really matters?

Indeed, this is what is happening and has been for a generation of time; a time period that correlates significantly with the explosion in real estate values and a time period that correlates significantly with the ascent of significant wealth in the Asian economies. The gifting generation "writes the cheque" with the background uncertainty of their longevity and financial needs. The wise ones are having a formal financial plan done (yes, even at an advanced age) or updating their previous one to gain some insight into their risk.

Fourth, might the long-term impact of increased longevity cause a sea change in how we look at will-making?

Might future wills **skip a generation** to the grandchildren, who might be forty to fifty-five years old and more able than their parents to enjoy the better lifestyle afforded by an inheritance? What would happen to the generation left out in this seismic shift of estate strategy? That "lost" generation might have to fund their entire retirement through their own means. They might feel some entitlement as they sacrificed their early retirement to parent care.

Fifth, couples do not tend to pass away together.

In Canada and the US, the average age of becoming a widow is in the late-fifties. The average duration of widowhood in the US was found to be fourteen years. Yuval Harari spoke earlier about how extending the life cycle will likely intensify serial marriages; the average "marriages-per lifetime" will increase, creating more step-relationships. Healthy retirees may find a second life with a new partner, and that new partner may be significantly younger. This is when things can get uncomfortable at the merged-family Christmas dinner table. The "flow of financial energy," i.e., inheritance, may change. This can be particularly troublesome when the two new partners come together with significantly different wealth. The new, younger partner may be almost the same age as the widower's offspring. If nothing else, the inheritance impact for the offspring may be significantly delayed until the passing of the step-partner. Or the widower's new will may attempt to divert some or all of the willed wealth to the new partner.

Estate of Mind

Inertia is the enemy of inter-generational wealth transfer. Survey statistics report that half the population does not have a will, and I think the half of those who do, don't have a will that reflects their current wishes. The change call here is to get proper counsel in organizing your affairs. Remember the all-important point in matters of estate planning: a will is only one (potentially very small) part of your plan.

Most people assume that: estate plan = will. Not true. The "Last Will and Testament" is a document that dates back to ancient Greece and Rome and early Britain. Various historical cultures have used other processes to outline inheritance law. Even today, we have statute law that backstops those who pass away without a will. In the modern Western world, "estate plan" is the appropriate term, and it has a new "equation": Estate Plan = will plus Designations plus Legacy.

The will itself is simply an algorithm...a formula...in words. It says:

"Gather my assets, pay my debts, give certain things to certain people, and give what's left over to some other person(s)." That last person(s) is the residue beneficiary of the result of the algorithm.

Harari posits: "Algorithm is arguably the single most important concept in our world. An algorithm isn't a particular calculation, but the **method** followed when making the calculation."

The Persian mathematician Muhammad ibn Musa al-Khwarizmi is credited historically as the father of algebra and "algorithms" (roughly derived from his name), which use **symbols** in place of words. In reality, wills are all about words. I created an "algorithm" called Will Mapping...a pictorial representation of "who gets what." I have found that building a mind map: a) creates some simplicity for the trustee and b) occasionally flushes out misconstrued intentions.

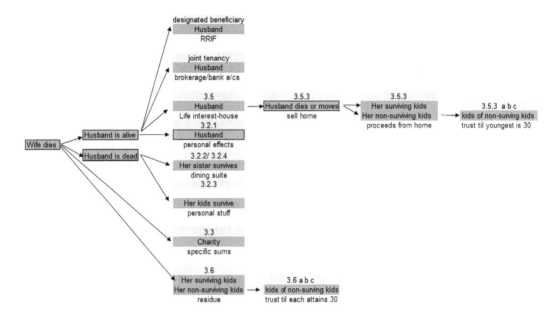

An estate plan has a form, a substance, and a spirit. It is the ultimate summation of one's life, and thus ought to be a beautiful thing.

Many people do not spend time contemplating their passion legacy, believing that is the sole territory of "the rich." I think it is insightful to consult a dictionary definition of "legacy." One that I like says legacy is about: "Translating and extending your values or accomplishments in ways that help others to find future success."

*The **form** is the actions taken within the legal financial system.*

There is a lot of misunderstanding around the form. Many people believe that simply refers to having a will. For most people, it is more than that. Our financial system has procedures, like trusts, "designated beneficiary" elections, and joint tenancy arrangements that supersede directives in a will. Designated beneficiary elections can apply to life insurance policies, RRSPs, RRIFs, and TFSAs. "Joint tenancy" can apply to bank accounts, brokerage trading accounts, and real estate. The person or persons you name therein receive that wealth outside of the will provisioning. A benefit of distributing your wealth in this fashion, versus a will, is that the particular account can be transferred to the inheritor much more quickly than through a will, as it only requires presenting a death certificate. Also, a will must be "probated" through a government process that costs money…essentially a "wealth tax." The extra complexity often causes the will executor to engage expensive professional legal assistance, thus increasing estate costs even more.

CHAPTER 6: LEGACY 221

Be aware, however, that your friend can become your foe. A designated beneficiary election that you made in order to save time and money can blow up if you don't give it a place of mind. The reason is changing circumstances. Your designated one may die, be superseded by someone new in your life, or fall out of your life. Examples include:

- A widow changes her designation from her deceased spouse to her sister, but then she remarries, and forgets to name her new spouse.
- A woman named her spouse, who pre-deceased her, and she forgot to amend the designation. When she died, that asset now had to pass through the will and probate, costing money.
- A widow named her sister, but they had a falling-out. When the widow died, the sister got the funds.

These situations, unfortunately, are often only exposed upon a passing. There can be a third sting involving death taxes. Normally, the designated beneficiary receives the funds "free of tax." If there is a death tax (e.g., an RRSP or RRIF), that tax must be borne within the estate, thus being paid by those beneficiaries, who may be different than the designated beneficiary. That said, there are circumstances where the death tax can fall upon the designated beneficiary: when the estate isn't sufficiently liquid to pay that tax.

The **substance** is who gets what, as per the will and the designations. Aspire to not make your estate plan unduly complicated—think of your poor executor. For the wealthy, this may not be practicable. However, I think it needs to be said that ofttimes when a complex estate plan is necessary, it is because all the proper things in this book were not heeded when it mattered. We put way too much emphasis on tax and other legal structures, and too little on the real impacts upon the recipients.

It might be a good time to revisit the section on Root Purposes and the questions: Who do you love? What do you love?

We protect who we love, but we also need to protect what we love. The spirit is what underlies your choices of who gets what. Your philosophy about money, in that earlier section, should be colouring your estate algorithm. You might want to go back to that chapter to re-familiarize yourself with yourself, and re-address your estate plan. Which lives touched you, and did you touch in return? What causes touched you? Make your estate plan the equivalent of the last, great hug you give to them.

The great, late Belgian singer/songwriter Jacques Brel paid tribute to his French counterpart Charles Trenet in saying: "Without him, we would all be accountants."

Let us not all be estate lawyers in crafting our legacy.

Let's also revisit Robert McGarvey's quote in the Root Purposes section: "Assets are institutional vessels that capture and store human energy."

So, your will is about **your spirit** and the future flow of your energy as your inheritors take those assets forward into their lives…and beyond.

We spoke of entropy in Section 2.2 Root Attitudes: the gradual decline (of a system) into disorder. Entropy bears upon multi-generation families and their stewardship of WealthNess. Does that family have enough character, values, and virtue to avoid entropy? If you are both the Presiding and Leading generation in the family, you must be mindful of the risk that the family bears after your passing.

Bombogenesis *is a term in meteorology, attributed to McGill professor John Gyakum.*

It refers to the process of a rapid fall of barometric pressure in the centre of a low-pressure system, signalling a pending powerful storm. That could be **you**. If you have tightly retained control of the family WealthNess, the centre may not be able to hold in your absence, and some degree of chaos may ensue. It is challenging enough to manage your own world of wealth and happiness, much less that of influencing your succeeding generations, but so you ought to, nay, must! The family might define a "motto," as existed in heraldic history, which encapsulates and inspires its members to fend off financial entropy—"discrete wealth" for instance.

Let's remember here what John Bogle asserted earlier in the Financial Planning chapter…that: "The heart of a family is not its power or material things but its values."

*Let's do some **time-travelling** together.*

Imagine it is the future…and you have just passed away. There are two moments I ask you to think about: your Celebration of Life event and the reading of your will.Imagine you are the one there to read out your wishes to your family of beneficiaries. Think about what you would want to say, and how you would say it….seriously…spend some time on this and write things down because next there will be a test! Now, go get your will and read it. Next, compare the notes you just made with the will. Are they similar…or way different? I suspect, the latter. We have become victims of a legal meme as to the language we portray to our families upon our passing. It is like we are guilty of **alexithymia**—lacking the words to express our emotions and feelings. If we have not "taken care of business" whilst alive in preparing our family for their inheritances, then the will lets us off the hook with its legalistic exit language.

Our biggest job estate-wise is not creating some clever, tax-avoidant, and bullet-proof will.

Our biggest job began years before that when our beneficiaries were born and raised. The legacy of how to live with degrees of wealth far exceeds the extent of the wealth itself. Here, many of us fail! Section 2.3 Kids and Money spoke about how early on children start forming their attitudes towards money. So if you overlooked that moment, maybe by decades, how do you recover and make up for the missed moment? To be sure, it may be too late. If you really, truly care, you need to have a deliberate plan to ameliorate the past. This no doubt will take you out of your comfort zone.

Strengthening Your Legacy's Spirit

Your biggest legacy is not the net worth you pass on to the next generation, but rather the attitudes, financial and otherwise, that you impart. Understand the difference between your area of direct impact versus indirect influence.

> *There are two ways of spreading light: to be the candle or the mirror that reflects it.*
> —Edith Wharton, twentieth-century author

Here is a four-part program to strengthen the spirit of your legacy.

First, spend time with yourself (and your spouse) to reflect on all those years past. Think about the family finances:

- What challenges there were, what failures?
- What was the family lifestyle like?
- Did the kids have jobs?
- What presents did they routinely get on occasions?
- Did the parents volunteer? Make donations? Did the kids do so?
- What cross-section of families did they associate with?
- What was their periodic allowance?
- How much travelling did they do?
- What kind of car did they drive (if they had one)?

Speculate how **they** would finish these sentences:

- Our family finances are…
- Our family values are…

Can you succinctly summarize your beneficiaries' attitudes towards money today?

If you do this with your spouse, be sure to do it separately, and then compare notes. Now look across the landscape of these answers and ask yourself whether your beneficiaries have a healthy attitude towards money. But…before you do that, go back to the Invocation chapter and reread the section on Festinger's cognitive dissonance. Make sure your conclusion is not guilty of confirmation bias.

Second, take the insights you gained above and have a conversation with your inheritors. This event may become **epic** in the family history. While you need to be chairperson, it needs to be a dialogue, a **charette,** which means "a meeting in which all stakeholders attempt to resolve conflicts and map solutions." You need to be pre-scripted for this meeting. You need to give disclosure and ask for disclosure.

Third, don't expect that everything will be sorted out in that one meeting… retreat, reflect, and return in a follow-up meeting.

Fourth, as valuable as this process may be, you may feel overwhelmed to undertake it. Consider seeking professional assistance from someone in your orbit of advisors.

"Apres moi, le deluge." This was Louis XV's famous quote, conveying indifference to whatever happened after he was gone.
Is this your real intent in not preparing your successors? Or a default result from procrastination? As beneficiaries get older, the more important it is that they are brought into the process inter vivos to know what they can expect. Get them **used** to the idea of WealthNess: doing so means they are more likely to succeed with new wealth. You may bequeath some wealth inter vivos to give them practice or, alternately, "shadow" practice…

Sketches in Personal Finance

A wealthy, widowed, childless client came into my office to talk about his estate legacy. He had only one close, genetic heir on the planet, his nephew, who was a fifty-year-old bus driver in a family of four. The nephew owned no real estate and had no assets other than a small company pension and government pensions.

We talked at length about the nephew, his financial situation, and his general make-up. It was incumbent upon me to mention the concept of a trust upon death, which would give the nephew indirect benefit, but leave some trustee as his overseer. This structure would cost some money, and also require sussing out the appropriate trustee, which might need to be institutional. It also begged the question of what would happen to the trust funds upon the nephew's passing.

In the end, I suggested my client have a private talk with his nephew and ask the question: "How would you handle receiving $500,000?"

His answer was "buy a home."

This wise response was comforting to the uncle.

Recognize that will preparation is not one-stop-shopping. Accept that you likely will create several iterations of your will over your lifetime…simply because of changing life circumstances. In fact, it is important to ensure that those changing circumstances are recognized and acknowledged by you as a call-to-action. Your ensuing wills might:

- Name guardians for your minor children
- Create trusts for your children through their early adulthood, in order to protect them from themselves
- Remove those trusts as your children age and mature
- Include grandchildren
- Remove an ex or deceased spouse
- Include a second/third spouse, all the while protecting your own heirs
- Give that new, late-in-life spouse a life interest in your home, but protect that value for your heirs
- Include legacy donations, as you become less concerned about your heirs' financial circumstances

Last-Minute Estate Planning Issues

An elderly couple needs to be wary of a potential trap. They may write mirror "crossed" wills and designate each other and agree that the survivor will amend the estate plan upon the passing of the first. Remember, of course, that a testator must be of sound mind. If the surviving spouse crosses that line before the other spouse passes, it is too late to craft one more final will. It also is too late to make or amend the designations related to **RRSPs, RRIFs, and TFSAs** and to joint tenancies. That means that the previous crossed-wills and designations of the couple might have to stand at the end.

A deathbed is never a happy place to address last-minute financial and estate planning issues. Sometimes, there is no choice. With forethought, some of these matters can be put in place, such that your advisors can deal with these things while you are full-on with care.

An example is unused TFSA contribution room for the ill party. If the deceased has a surviving spouse, the TFSA transfers over to the survivor's TFSA and retains the lifelong tax-free status. Capital compounding in a tax-free account over the life of the survivor is way better than in a taxable account. Ideally, there is some way for the funds to be found by the advisor (in cash or kind) to top up any unused room while the family is taking care. If no funds can be found, then this strategy is a non-starter. In the scenario where the ill spouse does not even have a TFSA, a "phantom" (not the technical term) account should be set up in advance and left latent.

Note that this strategy merits consideration in the narrower situation where the ill spouse is an American joint tax filer (and the spouse is only Canadian). Again, a "phantom" TFSA could be fully populated near death bed with the entire lifetime contribution limit that went unused due to the US tax-filing issues. (Note that simple FBAR filing would be required during the phantom years.)

Are you ready to explore other kinds and aspects of your legacy? If so, take this detour. (If you don't want to take this detour right now, jump ahead until you see the Circle/easiest sign.)

Other Callings

Your longevity and legacy could overlap in a "retirement project": your autobiography! Stay with me on this one…I think it is one of the most important contributions you could make to the future. Here's why…

I encourage you to read journalist Richard Fisher's book The Long View about time.

The past, present, and future are extremely inter-linked, but we are not choosing to see that. Today's Western world is very mired in the present…and Me. I recently met and dined with the student president of a hundred-year-old university with a population of 70,000 students. She was just completing her one-year term as leader. She shared her own wise observation, as a twenty-one-year-old, that issues today had probably cycled through the campus years ago, but **there is no**

treasure chest of the past to draw from. And so for a family. Some (we would call "primitive") cultures had no written word, but their history was passed down "around the fire." Gutenberg's printing press changed society, but it didn't change the family. How many families have written documents of their history? Imagine, in extremis, that they all do. Like a family operating manual. So, my exhortation to you is to be a leading light. Write that book in the free time of your fourth quarter. All my life I have declared that every single soul on this planet has one book in them. In the Longevity section, we agreed that one of the most important things in the fourth quarter is finding purpose.

You can acquire some guidance on topics and format by googling this. Material in this section, as well as the Family Confab section, will provide some topic guidance. It is easy nowadays to self-publish enough copies for the family. In fact, you will discover that there are internet businesses that will help you write it.

Moving on, in his impactful book *Enough,* investor/philanthropist John Bogle invokes: "Each of us who prospers in this life...[has] a solemn obligation to recognize their good fortune by giving something back." And, "These are not acts of charity but payments forward to express thanks for the opportunities afforded in a lifetime."

In his 1889 article titled "Wealth," Andrew Carnegie said that a person of wealth has three choices: wealth can be left to the family after death, bequeathed for "public purposes" after death, or administered during one's lifetime for the same purposes. On the conventional estate bequeathing to family heirs, he said:

> *Why should great fortunes be left to children? If this is done from affection, is it not misguided affection? Observation teaches that, generally speaking, it is not well for the children that they should be so burdened. Neither is it well for the state. Beyond providing sources of income, and very moderate indeed, men may well hesitate, for it is no longer questionable that great sums bequeathed oftener work more for the injury than for the good of the recipients. Wise men will soon conclude that, for the best interests of the members of their families and of the state, such bequests are an improper use of their means.*

Carnegie was not a fan of "control from the grave." He said: "A powerful man dead is no longer powerful. The fortune he has bequeathed is out of his control and subject to the will of others."

And so he chose "Plan C"—massive distribution to the public good while he was alive: "… the surplus wealth of the few will become…the property of the many…

and this wealth, passing through the hands of the few, can be made a much more potent force for the elevation of our race than if it had been distributed in small sums to the people themselves."

In so saying, Carnegie was a fan of inheritance taxes and not a fan of direct charity, per se. His views, while personal, were not new. The ancient Greeks believed that the wealthy in fact were **bestowed their wealth only as custodians on behalf of all society**. When large public projects needed to be created and funded, it was expected that the wealthy would "answer the call" accordingly.

We are now three generations into the most broad-based wealth accumulation in the history of the planet.

With each successive generation, the level of "comfort entitlement" rises. Today's young generation is often living at home until age thirty while their great-grandparents' generation found themselves in the trenches in WWI even younger than that. The world's rate of wealth accumulation likely will continue to create massive new middle and wealthy classes in the next generations. Western society has an urgent call to reinvent itself in the coming new world order if it seeks to maintain its place in the wealth chain. Failing this, the upcoming generations may be in for a surprise vis-a-vis the living standards they have grown accustomed to.

This has something to do with how the "out-going" generation chooses to cast their estate plans for their successors. The US estimate is that $41 trillion dollars will pass from the Boomer generation. Need it go to the direct natural heirs, in spite of Carnegie and the ancient Greeks, as an "insurance plan" in case the West fails to reinvent itself? Or does the Boomer generation impact civilization by adjusting the contrast between the palace of the millionaire and the cottage of the labourer?

It could be as simple as adding one extra residual beneficiary, designated in some fashion as the public good, which I call the **"n+1" strategy**. In other words, for instance, one's three children would receive three-quarters of the estate and the other quarter would go to "society." While the hyper-wealthy often do this, e.g., endowing universities with vast sums, I believe that the middle class could do so as well.

An estate donation strategy is particularly productive when the deceased leaves a large RRSP/RRIF, which is otherwise wholly taxed at death (assuming no surviving spouse or dependent child).

Sketches in Personal Finance

A case study is a recent example in our practice. The deceased father left an estate to his three surviving children with a principal residence of $1.2 million and a RRIF of $800,000. The former is tax-free and the latter is fully taxable. The death tax on the RRIF depends upon some other real facts but might approximate $400,000. So, the after-tax estate to the family would be approximately $1,600,000, or $533,000 per child.

If the **"n+1" strategy** was used in the will, there could be a charitable donation of $500,000, which would generate a large tax break to mitigate the tax on the $800,000 RRIF. The after-tax estate decreases by the $500,000 gift but increases by the tax saving of $250,000. The net result is an after-tax estate of approximately $1,350,000, or $450,000 per child. In the end, the $500,000 donation cost each heir approximately $83,000.

Another aspect to this is the law related to making **charitable donations in-kind**, rather than in cash, e.g., donating a security. In summary, the law creates an incentive to do this and relieves the capital gain from tax that you would have had, had you sold the security first and then donated the cash proceeds.

Let's consider this in the previous case study. Imagine that the deceased also had an investment portfolio of, say, $200,000, of which half had become unrealized gains over the years. The entire estate in this case is now $2.2 million. The extra death tax on the investment portfolio would be approximately $50,000. So, the after-tax estate to the family would be approximately $1,750,000, or $583,000 per child.

But now, let's return to the "n+1" strategy with an extra twist. The executor directs that the charity, which receives $500,000, will receive the investment portfolio in-kind worth $200,000 plus $300,000 in cash. So, the after-tax estate to the family would be approximately $1,800,000, or $600,000 per child. The cost to the heirs of the $500,000 donation is only $200,000, less than half the endowment, and only $67,000 each.

My apologies for all the number-crunching here! But I hope there is an insight here. This **"n+1" estate planning strategy leaves a double legacy**, one to the public good of charitable giving and one to your young heirs, for whom an example is set of melding private gain and public good. In costing heirs $67,000 each, you were able to leave half-a-million dollars legacy to something you love.

*Welcome back to the **book's main pathway**.*

The Joy of Caring

Author/science journalist Marta Zaraska cites research that generosity and caring, in the form of monetary donations, contributes significantly to good health and the sense of happiness and satisfaction. She notes: "The gains can be as varied as better sleep, better hearing, stronger muscles, and lower blood pressure."

The research also suggests that you need to believe in the cause of your charitable directive; let you and I call that "passion." The stronger the passion, the greater the "fix," and the more direct the line of cause-and-effect.

My experience over five decades is that potential donors' gifting intentions are coloured to some extent by the view that too much of a donation is applied to administration and, in particular, to executive compensation. Many people feel this way, whether it is true or not. Cynically, it may provide a "convenient out" from being charitable.

Sketches in Personal Finance

Over the years, I have tried to focus our clients on finding specific donation outcomes that are near and dear to them. Recently, one client donated $25,000 to a very small, low-profile local charity that provides accommodation to family members who must travel to accompany their loved ones who are undergoing major treatments. For that charity, this was a huge endowment.

Fifty years ago, as an undergraduate student at my alma mater, I had the opportunity to create within the Business School Faculty an award program that recognized teaching excellence. The "prize" was purely recognition. That program carries on to the present day. Recently, in my estate planning, I was able to endow a future large capital sum that **now** attaches a significant cash prize with this award. I am not obliged to part with my capital, lest I need it, until I pass. However, the award kicked in 2022. My obligation until death is to fund the annual award payout, which itself qualifies for donation tax-relief. This is like that old proverb of having your cake and eating it, too. Each year until I pass away, I have the joy of attending the award ceremony and seeing an excellent teaching professor being lauded.

Recent (2022) research at Harvard has shed some interesting light on charitable giving. Harvard professor Ashley Whillans et al reported that charities were more likely to encourage higher giving by appealing to wealthy people's **sense of power** rather than to their **community spirit**. At first, one might interpret the concept of "power" negatively; rather, I think it is about power to seek direct cause-and-effect. I think it is about **empowerment,** not **power.** My advice is to find your passion, and then find a way to enhance whatever that is. If you structure it as I have, you get to see the result from the ground up, not heaven down.

Charitable thoughts are (hopefully) about doing good things…giving back… responding to your passions.

Charitable actions—let's face it—are partly about "tax breaks." **Welcome to your promotion…to be Finance Minister for a day.** The tax reduction on a donation can run from 50–70%, meaning for instance, that the cost of a $100,000 donation is only $30–50,000. The rest of that $100,000 that you directed to a charity that speaks to your passion has, effectively, been contributed by the federal purse. In other words, your own actions prioritized $50–70,000 of the government's funds from their purposes to yours. That is powerful. Congratulations, Finance Minister.

> *This is why taxes as a form of pro-social spending are likely not as good for (your) health as are (your) voluntary donations.*
> —Marta Zaraska, author

Now extrapolate this out to amounts larger than $100,000 and also across millions of citizens, and you can see the power to the people. Each **micro** charitable act accumulates at the **macro** level and makes huge statements about where society-in-aggregate seeks to do good…trumping elected politicians and bureaucrats along the way. In summary, as you reflect upon your charitable inclinations, remember that your donation has a much grander implication: you are a tiny-but-important voice in how our society is shaped.

Other Considerations

Childless couples face a different task in establishing their estate plans.

I call them "free agents." They start with a tabula rasa of inheritors. There are both upsides and downsides to this. On the downside, they don't have the "no-brainer" default of simply naming their offspring. Another possible downside is the potential expectations from further circles out: siblings, nieces, nephews. On the upside, they may have degrees of freedom to do great things for the world at large. Another possible upside is that they may not have to struggle with attaching strings to troubled inheritors.

Sketches in Personal Finance

My own childless uncle died on the farm he had settled as a young man sixty-five years prior. He chose the niece-and-nephew route, splitting his estate equally amongst ten inheritors. His spirit was to change a lot of people's lives in a small way.

Another widowed client of mine passed away with $8 million of assets. She went the other route—small gifting to nieces and nephews—and large bequeaths to high-profile charities, with targeted purposes.

If you are a free agent, I encourage you to do the hard work of finding the locus of your life's passions, and then create the means to carry them out.

Almost all families have some form of legacy assets, even as simple as Great-Grandma's wedding ring. I believe it is important that the personal effects section of the will speaks to the distribution of these items that are emotional and/or valuable. It is not fair to pass this job on to your trustee. That person may be a family member and is part of the family politics or is at arm's length and will get mired in those family politics. Either way, it gets unduly messy.

More substantially, family cottages or family businesses are frequently a legacy asset. Such assets have both **emotional and financial value**. Often, they are not easily divisible in their form, to share between multiple beneficiaries. Even if they are, the practicalities of sharing may not exist. Think of "time-sharing" a family cottage, where one sibling lives near the cottage and the other lives 3,000 miles away. Also, the local sibling may want the cottage but cannot afford to "buy out" the other sibling's half. Lastly, inevitably, the long-held family cottage will have a large estate capital gains tax, which requires funding.

My forty-five years in professional practice has not found a cookie-cutter solution to this problem. Each problem finds its own solution. Most of the time, regrettably, one party is unhappy with the outcome. The best advice is for the presiding generation to take the lead and tease out this difficult conversation whilst they are alive and functioning.

Author Joshua Foer said of the world memory champion Ed Cooke: "He lived life as though it were an art." Beautiful—what a legacy upon which to sail off. My personal rendition as the ultimate compliment is: "You have interesting friends."

A professional football player plays seventeen games a year, each an hour long…that's seventeen hours. Assuming his team's offence and defence spend equal time on the field, that means he spends a maximum eight hours a year earning his living, where he is performing his craft for others to see. Eight hours is his **performance** time…in a whole year! The time most of us spend in a single workday. His **preparation** time for those eight hours includes training camp, weekly training sessions during the season, and much of the year maintaining fitness. I couldn't begin to estimate those hours, but the ratio of performance to preparation is staggeringly small.

The rest of us "**perform**" every day out there for the world doing whatever it is we do. How much time do we build into **preparing** for what we do? And what is that **ratio** compared to the footballer? Life's sub-title, called your "legacy," is the equivalent to the footballer. Your **performance** time is the reading of your will—tiny; your **preparation** time is everything you do throughout your life to touch all you leave behind—huge!

6.1 Key Words and Concepts

Legacy:

89. The five impacts of increasing longevity
90. Drafting the unwilful will
91. The form (legalese) and the substance (spirit)
92. Preparing your inheritors: apres moi, le deluge!
93. N+1
94. Targeted donations and passions
95. Finance Minister for a day
96. Mind Mapping

Chapter 7: Coda

Thanks to Gutenberg and Tim Berners Lee, in our modern world there is an explosion of advice and wisdom available to us in the world of personal finance. That's the good news…and the bad news. There is a world of information, but we must have the inclination and time to wade through this endless resource and separate the wheat from the chaff.

I am grateful for all the beautiful and wise words and thoughts created by my fellow human beings throughout our history. Can any of us imagine how proud Socrates, Sophocles, and Aristotle must feel from their graves to still be quoted regularly thousands of years after their passing? Amidst the various crises in our modern world that we ought not to be proud of, I feel very privileged to live in this time with the eight billion people on the planet, which includes many very prolific and brilliant people.

Here in this book, I wish to acknowledge and pay tribute to modern-day thinkers from a plethora of disciplines, which I have aspired to morph into the world of "home economics."

The phrase "Standing on the shoulders of giants" goes as far back as the twelfth century and is attributed to Bernard of Chartres. More famously and recently, it has been associated with Isaac Newton's genius in the seventeenth century and more recently with Einstein and Hawking. Not being of the stature of Newton, Einstein, or Hawking, I cannot presume to have stood on the shoulders of those who have inspired me; rather, I humbly aspired, at best, to stand on the tippy toes of my own giants of intellectual financial thoughts.

I wish to thank the many authors who, unknowingly, through their written words have touched my mind and my soul with their beautiful, wise, poignant thoughts on life. I was blessed to experience your brilliance in print; it would have been even greater to break bread with you. I can't even say, "You know who you are," because you don't. I honour you through my "Anemone" blogsite at www.donnilson.com. Thank you all for being the next millennium's Socrates, Sophocles, and Aristotle.

I owe much gratitude to my business partner, Gary George, who had a larger duty to "mind the shoppe" while I spent a quarter of the last three years in writer's isolation. I also owe appreciation to our associate, Michael George, for allowing himself to be tricked into the role of my research assistant.

I also say thanks to the crew of the *Seabourn Odyssey,* where I sequestered for ten days to re-read the entire final manuscript whilst sailing along the Alaska/BC coastline.

With closure from the Introduction, I thank the thousands of clients who have allowed me to contribute in some small way to their lives. Forty-five years later, I still represent 175 multi-generational families, who have blessed me with the opportunity to live, love, and learn with them.

I hope that the many learned quotes will inspire and sustain you in your path to multi-generational WealthNess.

> *No problem can be solved from the same consciousness that created it.*
> —Einstein

> *Scientific revolutions tend to emerge not from a sudden discovery but by asking better questions.*
> —Lisa Feldman Barrett, author/psychology professor

Hence, in your reflective moments, always ask yourself: What's next? What's broken? What have I taken as a given?

It is for future historians to gaze back upon us and assess what we have done. Past historians have done this previously and ascribed labels to various past epochs of humanity: the Industrial Revolution, the Age of Enlightenment, the Medieval Ages, the Agrarian Revolution, and so on. I think the era after WWII will be tagged the Age of Materialism. Each era spends out its time, as proclaimed by those future historians. They will determine after the fact when this Age of Materialism ended and a new one, not yet labelled, began.

Ray Dalio's *The Changing World Order* is a must-read. He brilliantly and painstakingly looks at humankind's track record over millennia. We presently are in a "big shift in relative wealth and power and the world order that will affect everyone in all countries in profound ways." He speaks of three important cycles that have written and re-written the rise and fall of world powers for time immemorial. He includes hundreds of charts that identify overlapping long-tail historical trends to offer up insights.

One trend of emerging-power societies that lies in the graphical weeds, I think, refers back to the Dutch-clogs phenomenon over three generations. In Section 2.1 Money Philosophy, we studied parvenu, nouveau riche, and noblesse oblige. As a new nation takes its turn at power in the global order, that first generation generates and experiences unprecedented wealth. There is an exhilaration of the new experience of what wealth can buy. We also use the term conspicuous consumption. Fortunes are spent on expensive cars, real estate, Prada, etc. Their children grow up in this environment of privilege and so it spills on to the generation after that.

In the present world environment, massive wealth accumulation has been built and spread across a small proportion, albeit large in absolute numbers, of middle and upper-middle class, who are living in that conspicuous consumption phase.

In Chapter 6: Legacy, we learned of the ancient Greek belief that the rich were bestowed their wealth only as custodians on behalf of all society and would answer to the call when public needs arose. This likely didn't just happen out of the blue, but evolved thanks to the maturity of having wealth.

Now, let's overlay this with the twenty-first century, eight billion people, and the state of Mother Earth (to whatever extent your belief system believes). There perhaps has never been such a clarion call to borrow from the ancient Greeks. Managing wealth well takes experience…long tail experience! The present cohort of rookie Wealthies hasn't had the evolutionary time to do this. Money and purpose urgently need to align in the cross-hairs to convert New Wealth Problems to Mature Wealth Solutions. The evolutionary journey to WealthNess… on steroids!

Ray Dalio's coda is written to you and me:

> *Know all the possibilities, think about worse-case scenarios, find ways to eliminate the intolerable ones and create "insurance plans" (my words) to survive the tolerable ones.*
>
> *Diversify well*
>
> *Put deferred gratification ahead of immediate gratification, to ensure your long-term future (my words)*
>
> *Hang out with the smartest people*

If the Age of Materialism has overstressed Mother Earth and wreaked havoc with climate change, it also has impacted the organism called family. Thus, I add to this the importance of imbuing all of the above to **future** generations.

Let's reflect on the front cover, starting with one last nod to the Ploughman and to the Astronaut, resurrecting that old, fun question: Which would you choose to have lunch with? Are you a historian? Or a futurist?

And "The Evolutionary Journey to WealthNess"…

Were you able to undertake a personal journey through these pages? Was the pathway intellectual? Fact-driven? Spiritual? Reflective? Did you challenge any of your givens?

Did your views on personal finance and other aspects of life evolve? Perhaps "evolution" is too airy-fairy…let's bring it down to earth:

Did you reshape goals?

Did you see your role change for the following generations?

Did you find more common financial ground with your partner?

Did you grow new tentacles of interests?

And lastly…WealthNess…the destination of this journey:

"A state of abundance of health and material possessions to achieve a life well lived."

WealthNess does not need to be the destination of Your Journey! My "WealthNess" was perhaps really only a temporary marker drawn by me for you…until you, as the saying goes, "did the work" and can now intellectually and spiritually define your own Journey.

Full disclosure: I graduated from kindergarten summa cum laude…and it was all downhill from there. If you embrace everything that we have shared here… and act, you will be far better at steering your family financial genome on the ground than me.

Let's give forgotten mathematician George Birkhoff in the Money Philosophy section one last nod too, where he defined beauty as order reduced by complexity. We all can distill his mind-blowing formula with one simple take-home to our personal finance and life in general:

To increase the beauty in our life, we must either:

- Increase the order, or
- Decrease the complexity, or
- Some combination of both

My partner would say that only an accountant could find beauty in personal finance. Bear with me…remember where we likened building a portfolio to building a house. That involved architecture, design, and execution. And of course, houses can be beautiful. And so, I believe the management of our personal finances, too, can reflect beauty. And correspondingly can be "butt ugly." As you close these last pages on our journey together, think about Harvard mathematician George Birkhoff. Think about his algorithm and how your personal finances can be made better through increasing its order and decreasing its complexity. That, we all can understand and embrace.

Let's go back to the beginning in the Introduction, where I told the story about the fly stuck in the window at the golf club…and the metaphor of being lost in seeking WealthNess. I hope that you found here what you were looking for; but in truth, like the fly, perhaps you didn't **know** what you were looking for when you first set out…as Columbus didn't arrive at the place he thought he was seeking.

I hope that you now can complete these phrases:

- My (Our family) financial goals are…
- I (We) will achieve these by…
- My (Our family's) other goals are…
- I (We) will achieve these by…

When the Y2K millennium came around, there was a listing of the top one hundred pieces of literature of all time. It included Cervantes' *Don Quixote* (at #22). He was portrayed in film in the 1970s by the brilliant actor Peter O'Toole. (You can find his full-length jailhouse soliloquy on YouTube.)

> *When life itself seems lunatic, who knows where madness lies?*
> *Perhaps to be too practical may be madness,*
> *To surrender dreams—this may be madness,*
> *To seek treasure where this is only trash,*
> *Too much sanity may be madness,*
> *And maddest of all, to see life as it is, not as it should be.*

Cervantes' quote has directed my entire adult life. There is so much that I have wished to share with you from my life's experiences and from a lifetime of reading the words of authors far wiser than me. Thanks for sharing this journey with me. Do not feel daunted by all of this. Remember: Love your portfolio, love your personal finances, love all the people whose lives you touch. It is within your reach to achieve WealthNess and to contribute to a better world. Society, not politicians, defines the pathway of each epoch. And society is the aggregation of you and me and everybody around us.

Lastly, psychologist James Handel said of Sigmund Freud: "He was wrong about many things; but he was wrong in such interesting ways."

I have offered various ideas and thoughts to you. If you are unsatisfactorily persuaded by them, I hope that they have at least inspired you to think and to challenge your own thoughts.

Reading a good book by a good author is like spending time fireside with that person. You become friends. Everything shared is potent…provocative…notable. Turning the last page and closing the cover is like losing a friend. Recall my implicit contract between a reader and an author: "Take me to places that I have never been and introduce me to thoughts I have never had."

I hope I have met my end of that contract.

> *Science is a process, not a conclusion.*
> —Tom Nichols, author/professor

Similarly, learning by reading is a process, not a conclusion. It begins, not ends, with the turn of the final page. The author's work ends on that page, and the reader's begins. I hope that you have seen different things and seen things differently. As those little sea anemone creatures on the ocean seabed bid to each other: "May your tentacles grow," and as you turn this last page, I hope that you might conclude, "I feel like I just earned a PhD in personal finance." Thanks for joining me.

Don

7.0 Key Words and Concepts

Coda

97. Stand on the tippy toes of giants.
98. Consider every learned person I have quoted to you as your personal friend.
99. Create an awesome multi-generational family.
100. Lastly…get that fly out the window at the golf club!

Afterthought

I opened Section 4.4 with the thought experiment question about five years guaranteed with good health and promised my participation.

We could invoke author Gary Klein's trick on decision-making in Section 2.6 to flip the question around to gain insight: What would you be willing to pay to know when you will **not** be healthy and die. Weird? Not really…many of you have done just that; it's called life insurance. I opened Section 4.1 stating that life's **second biggest question** was: "Will I have enough?" But we dodged **life's biggest question:** "When will I die?" If you know that you will die in, say, a year (and the insurance company doesn't), buying life insurance would be a good investment…albeit for your heirs. The payout on your passing will vastly exceed one year of premiums. We really should rename that "no-life" insurance!

But somehow, this is a different question…because its outcome is about THEM; my question is about YOU. **And the response isn't a money question**…what would I pay in dollars? At that point, it would morph back to being a THEM question, because you would be taking from your estate value to buy the deal. Therefore, it must be something else. That's where it gets confusing.

I personally struggled with this a lot and intended to delete it from the manuscript. But I kept staring at it.

For me, the question was not "What would I pay?" or "What would I give up?" So, I took the question to ask, "What would it be worth to me?" The question is asking me: what do I get out of the deal, and what am I giving back? To me, it means that all my faculties, mental and physical, would remain available to me and that ensures a quality of life for those five years. To borrow from the old Amex ad, that is priceless. What the deal is worth to me is **gratefulness**, and what I give back would be the act of gratefulness to the world around me.

But that's me. For you, maybe this takes you back to Section 2.5 on happiness. What is your own Happiness Index? What is your joy and love of being alive? Of being with the people you love? Doing the things that you love? Places that you love? What is five years guaranteed of these worth to you? All of which define the essence of your life.

In final closing…I already have picked out my tombstone. It will read:

"Always ask questions."

Ohh! And one more…

"Imagine."

Bibliography

Introduction

Nakazawa, Donna Jackson, *The Angel and the Assassin: The Tiny Brain Cell that Changed the Course of Medicine.* New York: Ballantine Press, 2020.

"Individuals who could endure flights." *National Geographic* magazine, October 2020.

Robson, David. *The Expectation Effect.* New York: Henry Holt and Company, 2023.

Tharp, Twyla. *The Creative Habit: Learn It and Use It for Life.* New York: Simon & Schuster, 2003.

Chapter 1: Invocation

Ball, Philip. *Curiosity: How Science Became Interested in Everything.* Chicago: University of Chicago Press, 2013.

Barker, Eric. *Barking up the Wrong Tree.* New York: HarperOne, 2017.

Beinhocker, Eric. *The Origin of Wealth: Evolution, Complexity, and the Radical Remaking of Economics.* Boston: Harvard Business School Press, 2006.

Brown, Brene. *Atlas of the Heart: Mapping Meaningful Connection and the Language of Human Experience.* New York: Random House, 2021.

Clear, James. *Atomic Habits.* Penguin Publishing Group, 2018.

Fink, Anne-Marie. *The Money Makers: How Extraordinary Managers Win in a World Turned Upside Down.* New York: Crown Business, 2009.

Godfrey-Smith, Peter. *Metazoa: Animal Life and the Birth of the Mind.* New York: Crown Business, 2021.

Harari, Yuval Noah. *Home Deus: A Brief History of Tomorrow.* McClelland & Stewart, 2015.

Housel, Morgan. *The Psychology of Money.* Petersfield, Great Britain: Harriman House, 2020.

Leslie, Ian. *Curious: The Desire to Know and Why Your Future Depends on It.* London: Quercus, 2014.

Livio, Mario. *Why? What Makes Us Curious.* New York: Simon & Schuster, 2017.

Pascale, Richard, Jerry Sternin and Monique Sternin. *The Power of Positive Deviance: How Unlikely Innovators Solve the World's Toughest Problems.* Boston: Harvard Business Press, 2010.

Penrose, Edith. *The Theory of the Growth of the Firm.* Oxford University Press, 1959.

Seelig, Tina. *In Genius: A Crash Course on Creativity.* Harper Collins, 2012.

"So how do we fix things?" *New Scientist Magazine.* January 16, 2021, p.39.

Chapter 2: Chrematistics

Morris, Tom. *If Aristotle Ran General Motors.* New York: Henry Holt and Company, 1997.

2.1 Money Philosophy

Barker, Eric. *Barking up the Wrong Tree.* New York: HarperOne, 2017.

Bejan, Adrian. *The Constructal Law of Design and Evolution in Nature.* London: The Royal Society Publishing, 2010.

Birkhoff, George. *Aesthetic Measure.* Cambridge, Mass: Harvard University Press, 1933.

Case Schiller and Quigley, *Comparing Wealth Effects: The Stock Market vs. the Housing Market.* New Haven: Yale University, 2006. http://cowles.econ.yale.edu/

Eagleman, David. *InCognito: The Secret Lives of the Brain.* Toronto: Penguin Group, 2011.

The soul "is the bearer of moral qualities," www.plato.stanford.edu

2.2 Root Attitudes

Honchos, Coset and Wernli. "Culture, money attitudes and economic outcomes." *Swiss Journal of Economics and Statistics,* 2019, 155:2.

Jantsch, Erich. *The Self-Organizing Universe: Scientific and Human Implications of the Emerging Paradigm of Evolution.* Pergamon, 1980.

Johnson, Steven Berlin. *The Invention of Air: A story of Science, Faith, Revolution, and the Birth of America.* New York: Riverhead Books, 2008.

Laundre, John. "The Landscape of Fear: Ecological Implications of Being Afraid." *The Open Ecology Journal,* 2010, 3: 1-7.

McLuhan, Marshall. *Understanding Media: The Extensions of Man.* Signet Books, 1964.

"The modern world of science is shedding light…" *Discover Magazine*, June 2021.

Paine, Robert, *Journal of Animal Ecology,* 1980, Vol. 49, No. 3.

Stanley and Danko. *The Millionaire Next Door.* Gallery Books, 1996.

2.3 Root Purposes

Goldbart, Stephen. *Affluence Intelligence: Earn More, Worry Less, and Live a Happy and Balanced Life.* Cambridge: Da Capo Press, 2011.

Hughes, James. *The Cycle of the Gift.* Hoboken: John Wiley & Sons, 2013.

Murray, Nick. *The Excellent Investment Advisor.* Nick Murray Co. Inc., 1996.

2.4 Root Purposes

Barker, Eric. *Barking up the Wrong Tree.* New York: HarperOne, 2017.

Bejan, Adrian. *The Constructal Law of Design and Evolution in Nature.* London: The Royal Society Publishing, 2010.

Fisher, Richard. *The Long View: Why We Need to Transform How the World Sees Time.* London: Headline Publishing Group, 2023.

Jaffe, Dennis. "Six Dimensions of Wealth." *Journal of Financial Planning*, 2003.

Lusardi, Annamaria. *Household Saving Behaviour.* Cambridge, Mass: National Bureau of Economic Research, Feb. 2008, WP13824.

McGarvey, Robert. *Futuromics: A Guide to Thriving in Capitalism's Third Wave.* Ovidus Publishing, 2016.

Thaler, Richard and Benartzi, Shlomo. *Using Behavioural Economics to Increase Employee Saving.* University of Chicago, 2004.

2.5 Happiness and Meaning

Anielski, Mark. *Wellbeing Manifesto.* London: New Economics Foundation, 2006.

Anielski, Mark. *The Economics of Happiness: Building Genuine Wealth.* Gabriola Island: New Society Publishers, 2007.

Ashton, Kevin. *How to Fly a Horse: The Secret History of Creation, Invention and Discovery.* New York: Doubleday, 2015.

BAV Group. Best Countries: Annual Ranking. University of Pennsylvania.

Blanchflower, Dr. David. *Is Happiness U-Shaped Everywhere.* National Bureau of Economic Research, 2020.

Brown, Brené. *Atlas of the Heart: Mapping Meaningful Connection and the Language of Human Experience.* New York: Random House, 2021.

Csikszentmihalyi, Mihaly. *Flow: The Psychology of Optimal Experience.* New York: Harper Collins, 1990.

Cusano, Pasquale. *NUVO magazine.* Vancouver: Publishers.

Frankl, Victor. *Man's Search for Meaning.* Boston: Beacon Press, 1959.

Green, Stephen. *The Human Odyssey: East, West and the Search for Universal Values.* London: Society for Promoting Christian Knowledge, 2019.

GINI Coefficient. www.//data.worldbank.org

Harari, Yuval Noah. *Home Deus: A Brief History of Tomorrow.* McClelland & Stewart, 2015.

Helliwell, John, Richard Layard and Jeffrey Sachs. *World Happiness Report.* Sustainable Development Solutions Network.

Lickerman, Alex, MD. "The set point theory of happiness." *Psychology Today* magazine, April 21, 2013.

Morris, Tom. *If Aristotle Ran General Motors.* New York: Henry Holt and Company, 1997.

Random Acts of Kindness, http://randomactsofkindness.org

Schiffer and Roberts. "Another take on happiness is that…" *American Psychologist* magazine, July 12, 2018.

Sheldon, Ken, PhD. American Psychological Association, April 2001.

Singer, Tania and Matthieu Ricard, quoting Shantideva. *Caring Economics: Conversations on Altruism and Compassion, Between Scientists, Economists, and the Dalai Lama.* New York: Picador, 2015.

2.6 Good Decision-Making

Bahcall, Safi. *Loonshots: How to Nurture the Crazy Ideas that Win Wars, Cure Diseases, and Transform Industries.* New York: St Martin's Publishing Group, 2019.

Berns, Dr. Gregory. *The Iconoclast: A Neuroscientist Reveals How to Think Differently.* Boston, Harvard Business Review Press, 2010.

Crick, Francis, Nobel Prize winner, 1962.

Dalio, Ray. *Principles for Dealing with the Changing World Order.* New York: Avid Reader Press, 2021.

Dudek, Evan. *Strategic Renaissance: New Thinking and Innovative Tools to Create Great Corporate Strategies.* New York: Amacom, 2000.

Grant, Adam. *Think Again: The Power of Knowing What You Don't Know.* New York: Penguin Random House, 2021.

Klein, Gary. *Seeing What Others Don't: The Remarkable Ways We Gain Insights.* New York: Public Affairs, 2013.

Loewenstein, George. *The Empathy Gap, Explained.* The Decision Lab, 2005. http://thedecisionlab.com

O'Brien, Michael and Alexander Bentley and William Brock. *The Importance of Small Decisions.* MIT, 2019.

Chapter 3: Families and Finance

3.1 Couples and Money

Dalio, Ray. *Principles for Dealing with the Changing World Order.* New York: Avid Reader Press, 2021.

Papp, Lauren, Director of the Couples Lab at the University of Wisconsin, Madison. http://news.wisc.edu

3.2 Kids and Money

Beinhocker, Eric. *The Origin of Wealth: Evolution, Complexity, and the Radical Remaking of Economics.* Boston: Harvard Business School Press, 2006.

Brooks, Arthur C. *From Strength to Strength: Finding Success, Happiness, and Deep Purpose in the Second Half of Life.* New York: Penguin, 2022.

Christensen, Clayton and James Allworth and Karen Dillon. *How Will You Measure Your Life?* New York: Harper Collins, 2012.

Family Narratives Lab, Emory University. scholarblogs.emory.edu

Grant, Adam. *Think Again: The Power of Knowing What You Don't Know.* New York: Penguin Random House, 2021.

Hughes, James. *The Cycle of the Gift.* Hoboken: John Wiley & Sons, 2013.

Hughes, James. *The Voice of the Rising Generation.* Hoboken: John Wiley & Sons, 2014.

Owen, David. *The First National Bank of Dad: The Best Way to Teach Kids About Money.* New York: Simon & Schuster, 2003.

Penn State Freshmen. www:/http.dearpennfresh.com.

Petrini, Carlo. Founder Slow Food Movement in 150 countries.

Watson, Lyall. *Gifts of Unknown Things.* London: Hodder and Stoughton Limited, 1976.

3.3 Family Confab

Anielski, Mark *Wellbeing Manifesto.* London: New Economics Foundation, 2006.

Jaffe, Dennis. "Six Dimensions of Wealth." *Journal of Financial Planning*, 2003.

Wheatley, Margaret. *Who Do We Choose to Be.* Oakland: Bennett Koehler Publishing, 2017.

Chapter 4: Financial Planning

4.1 Preparing for the Future

Bogle, John. *Enough: True Measures of Money, Business and Life.* Hoboken: John Wiley & Sons, 2009.

Fulghum, Robert. *All I Really Need to Know, I Learned in Kindergarten.* New York: The Random House Publishing Corp., 1986.

Housel, Morgan. *The Psychology of Money.* Petersfield, Great Britain: Harriman House, 2020.

Klein, Gary. *Seeing What Others Don't: The Remarkable Ways We Gain Insights.* New York: Public Affairs, 2013.

4.2 Planning for Ages and Stages

Feiler, Bruce. *Life Is in the Transitions.* New York: Penguin Random House, 2020.

4.3 Financial Plans

HFactor discount math. https://financialmentor.com/calculator/present-value-of-annuity-calculator

4.4 Longevity

Bossers, Willem. *Physical Exercise and Dementia.* University of Groningen, 2014.

Coughlin, Joseph. *The Longevity Economy: Unlocking the World's Fastest Growing, Most Misunderstood Market.* New York: Perseus Books, 2017.

Csikszentmihalyi, Mihaly. *Flow: The Psychology of Optimal Experience.* New York: Harper Perennial, 1990.

English Longitudinal Study of Ageing. http://www.elsa-project.ac.uk

Frankl, Victor. *Man's Search for Meaning.* Boston: Beacon Press, 1959.

Friedman, Howard and Leslie Martin. *The Longevity Project.* Hudson Street Press, 2011.

Garcia, Hector and Francesc Miralles. *Ikigai: The Japanese Secret to a Long and Happy Life.* New York: Penguin Random House, 2016.

Harari, Yuval Noah. *Home Deus: A Brief History of Tomorrow.* McClelland & Stewart, 2015.

Jaffe, Dennis. "Six Dimensions of Wealth." *Journal of Financial Planning*, 2003.

Levitin, Daniel. *Successful Aging: A Neuroscientist Explores the Power and Potential of Our Lives.* Penguin Canada, 2020.

Morris, Tom. *If Aristotle Ran General Motors.* New York: Henry Holt and Company, 1997.

Rogo, Marcie. www.stitch.net

Shelley, Mary, nineteenth-century author of *Frankenstein*

Tharp, Twyla. *Keep It Moving: Lessons for the Rest of Your Life.* New York: Simon & Schuster, 2019.

University of British Columbia, Archives of Internal Medicine. *Strength Training for Seniors Provides Sustained Cognitive Function.* January 2010.

Walker, Dr. Mathew. *Why We Sleep: Unlocking the Power of Sleep and Dreams.* New York: Scribner, 2017.

Watterson, Bill, Cartoonist, Calvin and Hobbes

Chapter 5: Investing

Crosby, Daniel. *The Laws of Wealth: Psychology and the Secret to Investing Success.* Petersfield, UK: Harriman House Ltd, 2016.

Housel, Morgan. *The Psychology of Money: Timeless Lessons on Wealth, Greed and Happiness.* Petersfield, UK: Harriman House Ltd, 2020.

Murray, Nick. *Simple Wealth, Inevitable Wealth.* The Nick Murray Company, Inc., 2008.

5.1 Investing Philosophy

Dimson, Marsh and Staunton. *Triumph of Optimists: 101 Years of Global Investment Returns.* Princeton: Princeton University Press, 2002.

Housel, Morgan. *The Psychology of Money: Timeless Lessons on Wealth, Greed and Happiness.* Petersfield, UK: Harriman House Ltd., 2020.

Murray, Nick. *The Excellent Investment Advisor.* Nick Murray Co. Inc., 1996.

Robbins, Tom. *Another Roadside Attraction.* Ballantine Books, 1977.

Tschampion, Charles, former Head of General Motors Pension Fund

5.3 Safety

Berns, Dr. Gregory. *The Iconoclast: A Neuroscientist Reveals How to Think Differently.* Boston, Harvard Business Review Press, 2010.

Evans, Dylan. *Risk Intelligence: How to Live with Uncertainty.* New York: Simon & Schuster, Inc., 2012.

5.4 Rate of Return

Dimson, Marsh and Staunton. *Credit Suisse Global Investment Returns,* Yearbook 2023 Returns. Credit Suisse Research Institute, 2023.

Chapter 6: Legacy

Bogle, John. *Enough: True Measures of Money, Business and Life.* Hoboken: John Wiley & Sons, 2009.

Fisher, Richard. *The Long View: Why We Need to Transform How the World Sees Time.* London: Headline Publishing Group, 2023.

Foer, Joshua. *Moonwalking with Einstein: The Art and Science of Remembering Everything.* New York: Penguin Books, 2011.

Harari, Yuval Noah. *Home Deus: A Brief History of Tomorrow.* McClelland & Stewart, 2015.

Marcovici, Philip. *The Destructive Power of Family Wealth: A Guide to Succession Planning.* Chichester: John Wiley & Sons, 2016.

Whillans, Ashley and Elizabeth Dunn and Lara Aknin. "The Emotional Rewards of Prosocial Spending Are Robust." *Sage Journals,* Nov. 9, 2022.

World Health Organization, The Global Health Observatory. www.who.int

Zaraska, Marta. *Growing Young: How Friendship, Kindness, and Optimism Can Help You Live to 100.* Toronto: Random House, 2020.

7.0 Coda

Barrett, Lisa Feldman. *How Emotions Are Made: The Secret Life of the Brain.* Boston: Houghton Mifflin Harcourt, 2017.

Birkhoff, George. *Aesthetic Measure.* Cambridge, Mass: Harvard University Press, 1933.

Dalio, Ray. *Principles for Dealing with the Changing World Order.* New York: Avid Reader Press, 2021.

Nichols, Tom. *The Death of Expertise: The Campaign Against Established Knowledge and Why It Matters.* New York: Oxford University Press, 2017.

Printed in Canada